THE CHARTERED INSTITUTE OF MARKETING

Professional Diploma in Marketing

STUDY TEXT

Delivering Customer Value through Marketing

Valid for assessments up to September 2013

The Chartered
Institute of Marketing

BPP
LEARNING MEDIA

First edition July 2012

ISBN 9781 4453 9146 5

e-ISBN 9781 4453 7619 6

British Library Cataloguing-in-Publication Data
A catalogue record for this book
is available from the British Library

Published by

BPP Learning Media Ltd
Aldine House, Aldine Place
142-144 Uxbridge Road
London W12 8AA

www.bpp.com/learningmedia

Printed in the United Kingdom by Polestar Wheatons

Hennock Road
Marsh Barton Industrial Estate
Exeter, Devon
EX2 8RP

Your learning materials, published by BPP Learning
Media Ltd, are printed on paper obtained from
traceable sustainable sources.

We are grateful to The Chartered Institute of Marketing for
permission to reproduce in this text the unit syllabus.

Lead Author: Colin Linton

Contents

		Page
Introduction		
Studying for The Chartered Institute of Marketing (CIM) qualifications ▪ The Professional Diploma Syllabus ▪ Assessment ▪ The Magic Formula ▪ A guide to the features of the Study Text ▪ Additional resources ▪ Your personal study plan		v
Chapters		
Section 1: Product proposition and brand management		1
1	New product development and positioning	3
2	Managing and developing an organisation's product portfolio	23
3	The role of branding and branding strategies	37
4	Pricing, pricing concepts and price setting	49
Section 1: Senior Examiner's comments		65
Section 2: Channel management		67
5	Channel management, distribution strategies and control	69
6	Channel intermediaries and stakeholders	97
7	Contractual requirements and service level agreements (SLAs)	117
Section 2: Senior Examiner's comments		133
Section 3: Managing marketing communications		135
8	Managing marketing communications	137
9	Marketing communications activities and measurement	159
10	Agencies and managing agency relationships	181
Section 3: Senior Examiner's comments		197
Section 4: Managing and achieving customers' service expectations through the marketing mix		199
11	Customer service and customer care	201
12	Managing key account customers	219
13	Sales and product information and relationship risks	233
14	Analysing the case material and preparing for the examination	245
Section 4: Senior Examiner's comments		255

1 Studying for The Chartered Institute of Marketing (CIM) qualifications

There are a few key points to remember as you study for your CIM qualification:

(a)   You are studying for a **professional** qualification. This means that you are required to use professional language and adopt a business approach in your work.

(b)   You are expected to show that you have 'read widely'. Make sure that you read the quality press (and don't skip the business pages), *Marketing*, *The Marketer*, *Research* and *Marketing Week* avidly.

(c)   Become aware of the marketing initiatives you come across on a daily basis, for example, when you go shopping look around and think about why the store layout is as it is; consider the messages, channel choice and timings of ads when you are watching TV. It is surprising how much you will learn just by taking an interest in the marketing world around you.

(d)   Get to know the way CIM write their exam papers and assignments. They use a specific approach (the Magic Formula) which is to ensure a consistent approach when designing assessment materials. Make sure you are fully aware of this as it will help you interpret what the examiner is looking for (a full description of the Magic Formula appears later).

(e)   Learn how to use Harvard referencing. This is explained in detail in our CIM Professional Diploma Assessment Workbook.

(f)   Ensure that you read very carefully all assessment details sent to you from CIM. There are strict deadlines to meet, as well as paperwork to complete for any assignment or project you do. You also need to make sure have your CIM membership card with you at the exam. Failing to meet any assessment entry deadlines or completing written work on time will mean that you will have to wait for the next round of assessment dates and will need to pay the relevant assessment fees again.

2 The Professional Diploma Syllabus

The Professional Diploma in Marketing is aimed at anyone who is employed in a marketing management role such as Brand Manager, Account Manager or Marketing Executive. If you are a graduate, you will be expected to have covered a minimum of a third of your credits in marketing subjects. You are therefore expected at this level of the qualification to be aware of the key marketing theories and be able to apply them to different organisational contexts.

The aim of the qualification is to provide the knowledge and skills for you to develop an 'ability to do' in relation to marketing planning. CIM qualifications concentrate on applied marketing within real workplaces.

The complete qualification is made from four units:

- Unit 1 Marketing Planning Process
- Unit 2 Delivering Customer Value through Marketing
- Unit 3 Managing Marketing
- Unit 4 Project Management in Marketing

CIM stipulates that each module should take 50 guided learning hours to complete. Guided learning hours refer to time in class, using distance learning materials and completing any work set by your tutor. Guided learning hours do not include the time it will take you to complete the necessary reading for your studies.

The syllabus as provided by CIM can be found below with reference to our coverage within this Study Text.

Unit characteristics – Delivering Customer Value through Marketing

This unit's primary focus is the development and execution of marketing activities that have been designed to achieve customer satisfaction and meet organisational objectives, through effective marketing mix strategies which deliver stakeholder value.

The unit includes the development of the product portfolio, managing marketing channels, managing the communications mix and managing the service expectations of customers.

The unit examines the use of the marketing mix to achieve an organisation's corporate and marketing objectives, and to deliver marketing activities which reflect the desired positioning of the organisation's products and services in addition to its brand values.

By the end of the unit, you should be able to apply the marketing mix and determine strategies that deliver highly effective and competitive marketing activities that meet customer needs and organisational objectives, in different organisational contexts and sectors. Students should be aware that the unit addresses marketing in the context of both domestic and international activities.

Overarching learning outcomes

By the end of this unit students should be able to:

- Develop and manage a brand and product portfolio in the context of the organisation's marketing strategies and objectives

- Develop and implement an effective and efficient channel management strategy which reflects the needs of stakeholders and considers the impact of the external environment

- Develop an effective and innovative communications strategy and plan which clearly delivers the organisation's proposition to the market, through effective segmentation and targeting of internal and external markets

- Utilise an innovative and effective integrated marketing mix to reinforce the organisation's brand values and overall marketing proposition and competitive advantage

- Determine customer requirements for product and service delivery to ensure the marketing proposition is customer focused, efficient and effective

The Chartered
Institute of Marketing

SECTION 1 – Product proposition and brand management (weighting 25%)

		Covered in chapter(s)
1.1	Critically evaluate the process for managing and developing an organisation's product portfolio to deliver best value products for customers in different market segments and achieve organisational and marketing objectives	1, 2
	■ Definitions of 'product' in the context of different sectors	
	■ Product management's contribution to delivering customer value. Competitive advantage and achieving organisational/marketing objectives	
	■ The rationale for managing and planning product portfolios for different market segments	
	■ Managing product profitability	
	■ Product life cycle	
	■ BCG matrix	
	■ General Electric model	
1.2	Critically evaluate the role of branding in the context of the product portfolio, recommending different branding strategies which are appropriate to a range of organisational contexts and sectors	3
	■ Role and importance of brand	
	■ Developing and building brand value	
	■ Rebranding	
	■ International and global brands	
	■ Brand strategies	
1.3	Critically evaluate the role and process of innovation and new product development including consideration of innovative, replacement, re-launched and imitative products and explain the strategic benefit in achieving best value	1
	■ Developing a culture of innovation across the organisation	
	■ The role of innovation in product management and new product development	
	■ Rejuvenating existing products	
	■ Generating new and enhanced product ideas	
	■ Developing new products	
	■ Standardisation versus adaption	
	■ Adoption	
1.4	Assess the links between product development, product positioning and pricing in terms of fit and alignment with an organisation's corporate and marketing strategies and customer requirements	1, 2
	■ Positioning new products	
	■ Positioning strategies	
	■ Repositioning existing products	
	■ Positioning of products against competitors	
1.5	Critically evaluate the importance of linking the product portfolio to price perception to ensure perceived value for money as part of the overall customer proposition	4
	■ The role of pricing in product management	
	■ Pricing in the context of value for money	
	■ Price sensitivity	
	■ The role of pricing in influencing customers	
	■ The impact of changes in pricing on customer perception	

		Covered in chapter(s)
1.6	Assess pricing frameworks that could be utilised by organisations to aid decision-making about product life cycles, product development and innovation ■ Understanding price versus cost ■ Determining pricing levels ■ Pricing in relation to customer satisfaction ■ Pricing in relation to competition ■ Pricing in relation to value ■ Pricing for international markets ■ The role of pricing in building market share ■ Pricing approaches and strategies	4

SECTION 2 – Channel management (weighting 25%)

		Covered in chapter(s)
2.1	Determine and prioritise the key principles and purposes of innovative and effective distribution strategies in order to deliver the organisation's business and marketing objectives in a range of different contexts and different sectors to maximise customer requirements ■ Different types of distribution channels ■ Establishing channel strategies ■ Establishing channel needs (appropriate to different customers, organisations, sectors and countries) ■ Developing distribution objectives ■ Approaches to international distribution; agent; strategic alliance; joint venture; in-country operation, virtual/digital channels ■ Different marketing tools required to give a co-ordinated marketing approach	5
2.2	Critically analyse the implications, challenges and constraints arising from internal and external environment in the context of the development of developing channel strategies ■ Internal factors which influence channel strategy ■ International and global factors influencing channel strategies ■ Ethical considerations ■ Intermediaries' engagement with competitors ■ Environmental considerations ■ Economic/financial considerations ■ Understanding and determining customer channel requirements ■ Analysing competitor channel strategies	5

The Chartered Institute of Marketing

		Covered in chapter(s)
2.3	Assess the nature and scope of intermediaries and determine criteria for selecting intermediary partners and the likely Return on Investment (ROI) they can achieve	6
	▪ Different types of intermediaries in distribution and the strengths and weaknesses of each	
	▪ Level of innovation and development demonstrated	
	▪ The roles and responsibilities of intermediaries in distribution	
	▪ Criteria for selecting intermediaries	
	▪ How intermediaries can influence profitability	
	▪ Impact of new and emerging channels	
2.4	Determine the level and scope of controls required for effectively monitoring and managing distribution channels	5, 6, 7
	▪ Setting objectives	
	▪ Monitoring performance of distribution channels	
	▪ Benchmarking of other sectors/organisations/countries	
	▪ Managing third party relationships in channel management, locally and internationally	
2.5	Assess the requirements for managing the various stakeholders' needs within the distribution channel, in particular reviews, reporting, communications and conflict management	6
	▪ Identification of the key stakeholders in channel management	
	▪ Determining stakeholders' needs in channel management	
	▪ The role of information in channel management	
	▪ The importance of communications in channel management, locally, internationally and globally	
	▪ Potential sources of conflict in local and international markets	
	▪ Reducing time to market	
	▪ Competitor conflicts	
	▪ Identifying, managing and resolving conflict	
2.6	Determine the contractual requirements and service level agreements for engaging intermediary partners within the distribution channel	7
	▪ Types of contracts and typical terms	
	▪ Implications of contracting with overseas	
	▪ Role of service level agreements	
	▪ Determining service levels based upon efficiency expectations	
	▪ Establishing and monitoring key performance indicators	
	▪ On-going management and review of service level agreements	

SECTION 3 – Managing marketing communications (weighting 30%)

		Covered in chapter(s)
3.1	Determine marketing communications strategy and objectives to align with and deliver the organisation's marketing strategy and plans	8
	■ The role of marketing communications	
	■ Legal aspects of marketing communications	
	■ Global/international aspects of marketing communications	
	■ Aligning communications strategy to corporate and marketing strategy	
	■ Utilising communications strategies to achieve competitive advantage	
	■ Strategic aims of marketing communications	
	■ The role of communications in achieving competitive advantage	
	■ The contribution of marketing communications in relationship marketing for all stakeholders	
3.2	Prioritise the internal and external marketing segments to be targeted for marketing communications in different organisational contexts and sectors	8
	■ Role of internal communications	
	■ Identifying key internal audiences	
	■ Internal communications methods, Intranet; notice boards; seminars; briefings, newsletters; portals; SMS	
	■ Identifying key external audiences	
	■ Role of marketing communications in different organisational contexts and sectors	
	■ Internal marketing as a key tool to aid and deliver service excellence	
3.3	Critically evaluate a range of communications mixes and recommend appropriate creative, innovative, sustainable and co-ordinated approaches to communications activities and creating the optimal mix for internal and external marketing activities	9
	■ Advertising, including writing and checking copy	
	■ Personal selling	
	■ Direct marketing	
	■ Online media	
	■ Media tools and media message	
	■ Sales promotions	
	■ PR, exhibitions and sponsorships	
	■ Online forums; blogs; social networks	
3.4	Develop and manage a co-ordinated marketing communications plan, in the context of the strategic marketing plan, in order to establish and build relationships appropriate to the needs of customers, stakeholders and prospects in different organisational contexts and sectors	8
	■ Developing a communications plan	
	■ Communications planning frameworks	
	■ The role of communications in building customer relationships and value	
	■ Role of communications in gaining new prospects	
	■ Communications planning and execution in different organisational contexts and sectors, (B2B, B2C, third tier, not-for-profit, international/global)	

The Chartered Institute of Marketing

3.5	Critically evaluate and select the most appropriate marketing communications agency for the utilisation of marketing communications capability against agreed criteria	10
	■ The role and value of agencies in marketing communications	
	■ The inclusion of innovative and effective means of communication	
	■ How agencies are structured	
	■ Criteria and process for selecting an agency	
	■ Fees and fee structures	
3.6	Recommend and justify an approach to managing agency relationships including reporting, monitoring and measuring performance	10
	■ Managing agencies locally and internationally	
	■ Conducting regular reviews against clearly defined service level agreements	
	■ Key information in managing agency relationships	
	■ Establishing objectives and measuring agency performance	
3.7	Recommend appropriate methods for measuring marketing communications activities and successful delivery of the marketing communications strategy	9
	■ Setting marketing communications objectives	
	■ Measuring the effectiveness of marketing communications activities	
	■ Benchmarking communication effectiveness against other organisations, sectors, countries and competitors	
	■ The role of market research, locally and internationally	

SECTION 4 – Managing and achieving customers' service expectations through the marketing mix (weighting 20%)

		Covered in chapter(s)
4.1	Develop clear objectives relating to the provision of service to customers	11, 12
	■ The importance of service	
	■ Identifying the needs and behaviours of customers	
	■ What constitutes 'service' to customers?	
	■ The role of service in building customer loyalty and competitive advantage	
	■ Organisational and financial benefits of customer acquisition and retention	
	■ Determining customer service requirements	
	■ The role of key account management in developing customer service excellence	
4.2	Develop a customer service plan and customer care programme, designed to support customer service requirements, including innovative communications; relationship management and development; support; and operations/process management	11, 12
	■ Identifying and evaluating key components of the plan/programme	
	■ Identifying, analysing and managing key issues	
	■ Use of resources	
	■ Effective implementation	
	■ Measuring and monitoring performance	
	■ Role of communications in delivering customer service	
	■ Importance of operations and processes in delivering customer service	

		Covered in chapter(s)
4.3	Assess the value, importance and financial implications of providing service level agreements to customers ■ Role of service level agreements with customers ■ Typical service level agreements ■ The costs of delivering against service level agreements ■ Benefits to the organisation of establishing service level agreements with customers	11
4.4	Determine the most feasible and viable approaches for managing key account customers for different organisational contexts ■ Criteria for and identification of key account customers ■ Different approaches for managing key account customers ■ Role of communications ■ The role of people in key account management and service provision ■ Key accounts in different organisational contexts and sectors	12
4.5	Assess the role and value to the organisation of sales/product information, including storage, retrieval and communication of information and its role in ensuring that revenue is increased or maintained for key account customers ■ Use and value of information and how it will be used ■ Managing information ■ Storing and accessing information ■ Using information to develop marketing activities ■ Role of information in revenue generation	13
4.6	Critically evaluate and assess the customer relationship for possible risks, problems and issues and prepare contingencies for dealing with those risks as they emerge ■ Likely risks, problems and issues in managing customer relationships ■ Contingency planning ■ Role of communications in dealing with problems	13

3 Assessment

The unit covered by this Study Text (Unit 2 Delivering Customer Value through Marketing) is assessed in a three-hour formal examination, with compulsory set tasks which are based upon pre-seen material. The pre-seen material takes the form of a company case study, which will be sent to you prior to the exam. As part of your exam preparation you will need to carry out a detailed analysis of the information contained in the case study, and condense this into PESTEL and SWOT analysis.

In order to help you revise and prepare for the exam we have also written a Professional Diploma in Marketing Assessment Workbook which is available either through your usual book retailer or our website www.bpp.com/learningmedia.

4 The Magic Formula

The Magic Formula is a tool used by CIM to help both examiners write exam and assignment questions, and you, to more easily interpret what you are being asked to write about. It is useful for helping you to check that you are using an appropriate balance between theory and practice for your particular level of qualification.

Contrary to the title, there is nothing mystical about the Magic Formula and simply by knowing it (or even mentioning it in an assessment) will not automatically secure a pass. What it does do, however, is to help you to check that you are presenting your answers in an appropriate format, including enough marketing theory and applying it to a real marketing context or issue.

The Magic Formula for the Professional Diploma in Marketing is shown below:

Figure A   The Magic Formula for the Professional Diploma in Marketing

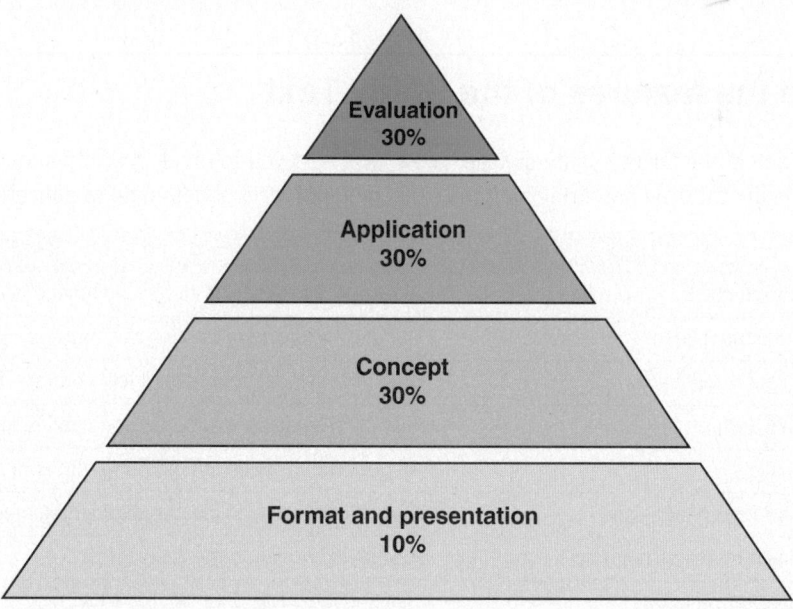

You can see from the pyramid that for the Professional Diploma marks are awarded in the following proportions:

- **Presentation and format – 10%**

    You are expected to present your work professionally which means that assignments and projects should **always** be typed. Even in an exam situation attention should be paid to making your work look as visually appealing as possible. CIM will also stipulate the format that you should present your work in. The assessment formats you will be given will be varied and can include things like reports to write, slides to prepare, emails, memos, formal letters, press releases, discussion documents, briefing papers, agendas and newsletters.

- **Concept – 30%**

Concept refers to your ability to state, recall and describe marketing theory. The definition of marketing is a core CIM syllabus topic. If we take this as an example, you would be expected to recognise, recall and write this definition to a word perfect standard to gain the full marks for concept.

- **Application – 30%**

Application based marks are given for your ability to apply marketing theories to real life marketing situations. For example, a question may ask you to discuss the definition of marketing and how it is applied within your own organisation. Here you are not only using the definition but are applying it in order to consider the market orientation of the company.

- **Evaluation – 30%**

Evaluation is the ability to asses the value or worth of something, sometimes through careful consideration of related advantages and disadvantages, or weighing up of alternatives. Results from your evaluation should enable you to discuss the importance of an issue using evidence to support your opinions.

For example, if you were asked to evaluate whether or not your organisation adopts a marketing approach you should provide reasons and specific examples of why you think they might take this approach, as well as considering why they may not take this approach, before coming to a final conclusion.

You should have noticed that for the Professional Diploma, you are expected to consider the equal weightings of concept, application and evaluation in order to gain maximum marks in assessments.

5 A guide to the features of the Study Text

Each of the chapter features (see below) will help you to break down the content into manageable chunks and ensure that you are developing the skills required for a professional qualification.

Chapter feature	Relevance and how you should use it
Introduction	Shows why topics need to be studied and is a route guide through the chapter
Syllabus reference	Outlines the syllabus learning outcomes covered in the chapter
Chapter topic list	Study the list, each numbered topic denotes a numbered section in the chapter
Key Term	Highlights the core vocabulary you need to learn
Activity	An application-based activity for you to complete
The Real World	A short case study to illustrate marketing practice
Exam tip/Assessment tip	Key advice based on the assessment
Chapter roundups	Use this to review what you have learnt
Quick quiz	Use this to check your learning
Further reading	Further reading will give you a wider perspective on the subjects you're covering

The Chartered
Institute of Marketing

6 Additional resources

To help you pass the Professional Diploma in Marketing we have created a complete study package. The **Professional Diploma Assessment Workbook** covers all four units of the Professional Diploma level. Practice questions and answers, tips on tackling assignments and work-based projects are included to help you succeed in your assessments.

Our A6 set of spiral bound **Passcards** are handy revision cards and are ideal to reinforce key topics for the Delivering Customer Value through Marketing exam.

7 Your personal study plan

Preparing a Study Plan (and sticking to it) is one of the key elements to learning success.

CIM has stipulated that there should be a minimum of 50 guided learning hours spent on each unit. Guided learning hours will include time spent in lessons, working on distance learning materials, formal workshops and work set by your tutor. We also know that to be successful, students should spend **approximately 100 hours** conducting self study. This means that for the entire qualification with four units you should spend 200 hours working in a tutor-guided manner and approximately 400 hours completing recommended reading, working on assignments, and revising for exams. This Study Text will help you to organise this 100-hour portion of self study time.

Now think about the exact amount of time you have (don't forget you will still need some leisure time!) and complete the following tables to help you keep to a schedule.

	Date	Duration in weeks
Course start		
Course finish		Total weeks of course:
Examination date	Revision to commence	Total weeks to complete revision:

Content chapter coverage plan

Chapter	To be completed by	Revised?
1 New product development and positioning		
2 Managing and developing an organisation's product portfolio		
3 The role of branding and branding strategies		
4 Pricing, pricing concepts and price setting		
5 Channel management, distribution strategies and control		

6 Channel intermediaries and stakeholders		
7 Contractual requirements and service level agreements (SLAs)		
8 Managing marketing communications		
9 Marketing communications activities and measurement		
10 Agencies and managing agency relationships		
11 Customer service and customer care		
12 Managing key account customers		
13 Sales and product information and relationship risks		
14 Analysing the case material and preparing for the examination		

The Chartered Institute of Marketing

Section 1:

Product proposition and brand management

Chapters 1 to 4 cover the part of the syllabus which relates to the role of products, the relationship with branding and the influence of pricing (product proposition and brand management). These are key tools available to a marketer when developing a product portfolio which meets the ever-changing needs of customers, and at the same time delivers corporate profitability.

This section will enable you reader to understand a number of techniques which have been tried and tested by a range of organisations to assist with effective strategic management of the product portfolio.

You will be introduced to a number of processes which will enable you to develop a better understanding of the product and its key elements, the reasons for managing products to maximise customer value and the tools available to achieve this. You will assess the advantages of strategic product management but at the same time learn to consider the limitations and how this might be managed.

A variety of different techniques will be explored including the product life cycle, BCG matrix, GE matrix and the new product development process. They will equip you with a number of options to achieve effective product management and this will be set in the context of opportunities both at home and abroad. The difficulties in developing products that eventually come to market and the key stages in the process will be explored and examples provided.

The marketing mix will be introduced as a concept which aids the strategic management of the product portfolio by developing an understanding of the role of the variable elements and the inter-relationship between them.

The role of branding will also be explored in the context of its critical role in shaping and positioning products with customers. We will look at a variety of strategies which can be explored with a view to maximising the attractiveness of the product range, the appeal to the customer and organisational profitability. Branding categories will also be considered and a view of how branding can be used to differentiate products explored. The role of branding in developing global products in overseas markets will be looked at particularly in relation to the degree of adaptation required.

Pricing will also be considered with a view to deepening the understanding of the impact that a variety of pricing strategies can have on the product position in the market. We will explore the ways in which pricing can be used to manage the product at various stages in its life cycle in order to maximise the appeal of the product and profitability. We will look at the importance of setting pricing objectives as a benchmark and to guide strategic product development. The role of the customers' view of different strategies will also be assessed, particularly in terms of the perception of value for money over which pricing strategies have significant influence. The role of pricing in building market share will also be considered as a key element of the marketing mix.

By the end of Chapter 4 you will have a greater understanding of the key variable of the marketing mix, a range of techniques available to manage product portfolios effectively and a variety of examples of how this has been achieved.

It must be remembered that the subject encompasses both the domestic and international markets and this is applicable across all the chapters. Similarly the context of the material needs to be understood in terms of different organisations or sectors, eg B2B, B2C, public and the not-for-profit sectors.

CHAPTER 1

New product development and positioning

Introduction

Products and services are the lifeblood of any organisation as they not only generate revenues and therefore ultimately profits for the organisation, they also create value for the customer. In this chapter we shall be exploring the components of a product, the process for developing new products, the importance of product positioning and the concept of product adoption.

Topic list

What is a product?   ①

Product categories   ②

New product development process   ③

Types of new product   ④

Product standardisation or adaptation   ⑤

Product positioning   ⑥

Product adoption   ⑦

Product innovation   ⑧

1.1	Critically evaluate the process for managing and developing an organisation's product portfolio to deliver best value products for customers in different market segments and achieve organisational and marketing objectives
	■ Definitions of 'product' in the context of different sectors
	■ Product management's contribution to delivering customer value. Competitive advantage and achieving organisational/marketing objectives
	■ The rationale for managing and planning product portfolios for different market segments
	■ Managing product profitability
	■ Product life cycle
	■ BCG matrix
	■ General Electric model
1.3	Critically evaluate the role and process of innovation and new product development including consideration of innovative, replacement, re-launched and imitative products and explain the strategic benefit in achieving best value
	■ Developing a culture of innovation across the organisation
	■ The role of innovation in product management and new product development
	■ Rejuvenating existing products
	■ Generating new and enhanced product ideas
	■ Developing new products
	■ Standardisation versus adaption
	■ Adoption
1.4	Assess the links between product development, product positioning and pricing in terms of fit and alignment with an organisation's corporate and marketing strategies and customer requirements
	■ Positioning new products
	■ Positioning strategies
	■ Repositioning existing products
	■ Positioning of products against competitors

1 What is a product?

> **Key terms**
>
> The **core product** comprises the functionality and key benefits of the product.
>
> The **actual product** comprises a range of 'add-ons' beyond the core product and offers potential for differentiation, eg product features, packaging and design.
>
> The **augmented (or extended) product** comprises potential customer value beyond the core and actual product elements, eg after sales service, guarantee, delivery and returns policy.

The terms 'product' and 'services' are used interchangeably but they do have precise definitions and implications which help marketers be more effective in carrying out their roles.

Kotler *et al* (2008, p500) define a product as 'anything that is offered to the market for attention, acquisition, use or consumption that might satisfy a need or want. Products include more than just tangible goods'. They go on to define a service as 'products that consist of activities, benefits, or satisfactions that are offered for sale that are essentially intangible and do not result in the ownership of anything'.

The Chartered Institute of Marketing

A product can be a physical good, service, idea or indeed a person. Lady Gaga, your favourite soup, or replacement parts for your car, all come within the definition of 'a product'. In other words a product is something which is capable of meeting customers' needs.

It can be the case that a product has tangible and non-tangible elements ie a combination of both product and service. Consider the purchase of a new software product by an organisation to streamline its payroll system. The software will be tangible, but its complexity means that an engineer needs to install it and then train staff on its use.

A product can be viewed from three levels:

- The core product
- The actual product
- The augmented (or extended) product

These levels are used by marketers to offer a range of benefits that will have a different meaning for each customer.

The anatomy of a product (the different levels) is shown as a series of concentric rings as illustrated in Figure 1.1.

Figure 1.1   Product levels

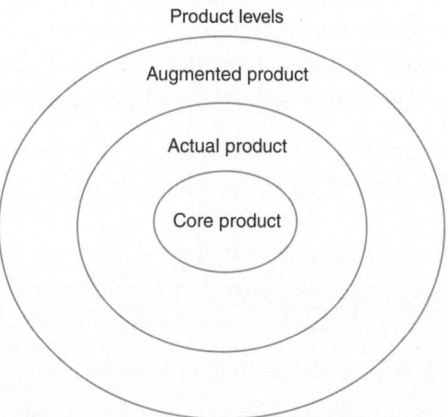

When marketers think about a product, its constitution is a little more complex than might be obvious and the various levels are summarised in Table 1.1.

Table 1.1   Summary of product levels

The core product	This is the basic product ie what the customer is buying. Marketers must be define the core product elements in terms which are meaningful to the customer.
The actual product	Is composed of several characteristics such as styling, brand, quality, and packaging.
The augmented product	Additional customer benefits and services are added. This could include things like warranties, guarantees, finance terms, or a dedicated helpline.

Very often, it is at the augmented level that most competition takes place. For example, having made a decision to purchase a new car and narrowed the choice of vehicles to two manufacturers, it may be the case that the decision is swayed by the three years' interest free credit deal offered by one of the brands. Organisations must constantly look to differentiate their product offers from the competition.

Identify three products that you have purchased which match the three product levels shown in Figure 1.1.

You can buy a laptop from PC World that comes as a basic product. Or you might prefer to buy one which includes security software and/or mobile broadband. You might also prefer a laptop which includes ongoing support. In addition, flexible payment terms might be attractive rather than paying outright for the laptop.

2 Product categories

Products can be categorised into consumer and business (or industrial) products. The key differentiator is the purpose for which the product is to be used. It is important for marketers to understand the different categories in order for the appropriate marketing mix to be developed. However, it is not always easy to differentiate between the two categories. For example, the owner of a company buys a laptop computer for home use. However, by clearly understanding the different purchasing intentions the marketing mix can be highly targeted.

Consumer products can be further subdivided into four categories and industrial products can be subdivided into seven categories (Dibb *et al*, 2005) which are shown in Table 1.2.

Table 1.2   Consumer products versus industrial products

Consumer products	Industrial products
Convenience products	Raw materials
Shopping products	Major equipment
Speciality products	Accessory equipment
Unsought products	Component parts
	Process materials
	Consumer supplies
	Industrial services

3 New product development process

▶ **Key term**

NPD: the new product development process comprises a number of recognised stages which enable an organisation to apply a structured approach to generating and evaluating ideas and deciding which ones to take through development and onto launch.

The new product development (NPD) process can be defined as the development of a new or an enhancement of an existing product involving a series of recognised stages prior to being launched in the market.

Developing new products is essential for any organisation if it is to be successful in delivering customer value. In particular, NPD:

- Reduces the possibility of product obsolescence, so that a range of products to meet customer needs will always be available

- Ensures the product range continues to remain relevant in the light of changes in the organisation's external environment

- Enables the organisation to compete in new and developing markets

- Can reduce the dependence on vulnerable product sectors; a range of products can weather changing economic conditions

- Can achieve long-term growth and profit by ensuring a better fit with customer needs and expectations

- Responds to changing customer needs and expectations

NPD is an expensive process and does not offer any guarantee that the product being developed will be financially successful, or will meet customer needs.

In a rapidly changing market, organisations sometimes seek to bring new products to market by buying a company which has the capability to launch quickly into the market. This can be because the organisation does not have the internal capability itself, but senses the gap in the market which it then fills by buying in the resources.

Sometimes failure can be down to timing, ie the market isn't yet ready for the product, or the product simply is not right for the market and insufficient research has been undertaken for an effective launch into the market.

There are several recognised stages in the NPD process, as shown in Figure 1.2.

Figure 1.2   The recognised stages in the NPD process

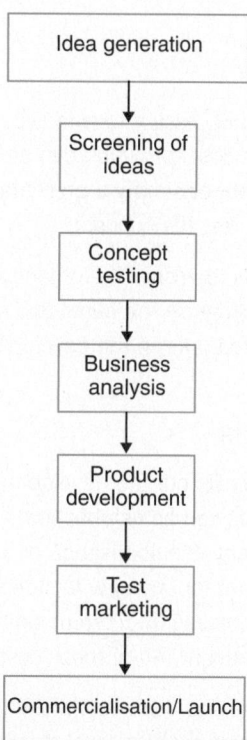

3.1 Idea generation

This is the first stage of the NPD process and there should be formal channels within the organisation to collect and collate the ideas generated. Organisations will generate ideas from many sources. These ideas need to be evaluated and moved on to the next phase or discarded.

Ideas can come from customers, who may have identified weaknesses in existing products or have made suggestions for new ones. Monitoring the competition through a sales team or research can also be helpful. Market research commissioned by the organisation will suggest gaps in the product range and possible product, or product features, that customers would be interested in. Staff who are in regular contact with customers can often offer useful market intelligence.

A number of organisations employ staff suggestion schemes where any member of staff can suggest a new idea which is rewarded in some way.

All the ideas generated must be properly collated and evaluated. It is usually the case that a significant number of ideas are generated, but very few move through to be commercially developed.

3.2 Screening

> ▶ **Key term**
>
> **Screening:** this is the process of evaluating all of the ideas that have been generated. It is necessary as not all of the ideas will be suitable, feasible and acceptable to the organisation. Criteria should be used in order to decide which ideas should progress to concept testing.

The second stage is to 'screen' the ideas. It is here that the ideas generated are evaluated to see if they should be taken forward. A systematic process should be in place to ensure that only ideas which match the organisation's mission and objectives should be progressed. Most ideas are rejected as being unsuitable when properly screened and analysed. Organisations have finite resources and only those products with the greatest potential for success can be developed.

3.3 Concept testing

Having got to this stage, it is necessary to establish what potential customers think of the idea, which now needs to be translated into a concept which can be visualised. This can take the form of samples, 'mock-ups' of the final product, a simulation, or simply a presentation. The concept can be tested with a focus group(s), or individuals can be invited to test the concept.

The idea of concept testing is to ensure the organisation is moving in the right direction and customers see the appeal of the product and recognise the benefits. Depending on the feedback at this stage, adjustments can be made before costs are incurred later in the development process.

3.4 Business analysis

Here, the organisation fully costs out the development and assesses the financial benefits to be derived from the product. Break even costs can be established with some certainty and sales will be estimated, taking into consideration the affects of any cannibalisation of any other products in the portfolio. Costs will be determined and these will need to account for any new facilities, such as premises or equipment which may be needed for launch. Additional staff, or those with different skills, may be required and there may be other costs associated with the development and launch. All of these costs must be fully explored.

Once the full financial picture has been established, an organisation must seek approval from senior management to gain the necessary high level commitment to proceed.

This is a crucial stage, for if the organisation proceeds and it subsequently transpires the estimates made were wrong, it could potentially bring financial ruin to the organisation, or might negatively impact on future development opportunities.

3.5 Product development

Once financial sign-off has been obtained, the organisation can now develop the concept into reality. What was presented as an idea at the concept testing stage must now be developed and a prototype or model produced.

This not only gives customers a clear picture of the product, but also allows the organisation to test whether the production and other costs, previously estimated, were realistic.

The organisation will now start to consider its marketing strategy and the deployment of an appropriate marketing mix (tailored to meet the precise requirements of the intended target market).

3.6 Test marketing

Prior to full roll out of the product, organisations will often undertake a 'test' in the real environment in a defined geographical area. This allows the organisation to fully roll out a sample of its marketing programme. The scale of the test depends on the importance of the product and the amount of the investment.

Customer response to the product and the marketing activity are evaluated and if any changes are needed they can be introduced now, rather than incur a costly launch only to make subsequent changes which could be embarrassing and very expensive.

It is important that this stage is concluded quickly as there is some vulnerability from the competition who can see what is being planned. Also if the test runs for a long period of time customers may get the impression that the product will never actually launch and lose interest.

3.7 Commercialisation/launch

Any changes needed will have been identified in the previous phase. The decision has been made to launch and now not only must the production and technical plans be fully developed and approved, the marketing programme must also be developed and the entire roll out plans co-ordinated.

Any investments identified and approved in the business analysis stage will have been initiated. Production commences and should be at such a level that demand can be met. An organisation launching a new product will need to ensure its call centre can handle the volume of customer calls, or that its website will not crash.

It is estimated that only 8% of new products launched by major organisations are successful (Dibb *et al*, 2005). The rigour of the NPD process must be sound to maximise the chances of commercial success.

---

4 Types of new product

The parameters of a product have been outlined. The characteristics of a new product have been explained. We have previously defined a product and now we should consider the different types of 'newness'. Brassington and Pettitt (2006) suggest that there are broadly four types:

- **New to company and market**: this is a totally new product which has never been offered before. At one time mobile phones, when they were first developed, would have come under this category.

- **New to company, significant innovation for market**: the core product is already familiar to the customer, but an additional feature has been added. An example is the addition of the Facetime (video calling) capability to iPhones.

- **New to company, minor innovation for market**: the burden now is on the company and the launch of the product is unlikely to have a significant impact on the market, but it may be important for the company in order to fill a gap in its product range and therefore retain customers.

- **New to company, no innovation for market**: 'me too' products fall into this type when a market follower launches a product into the market, effectively replicating a competitor's offering.

5 Product standardisation or adaptation

Organisations that operate beyond their domestic market must consider the implications for standardising or adapting its products to meet the needs of the market it intends to serve.

Where the product is standardised, the organisation will offer the same product in each of the markets it serves, whereas with adaptation the product will be changed according to the needs of each market.

Having decided to enter an overseas market, an organisation needs to adopt the 'best' strategy to serve the target market and there are three product strategies an organisation could employ which are summarised in Table 1.3.

Table 1.3   Three product strategies an organisation could employ in an overseas market

Strategy	Summary of strategy
Keep product the same worldwide (standardisation)	The product is exactly the same worldwide, ie there is no product development required.
Adapt the product for each market (adaptation)	The product is changed for each market to meet local needs.
Develop a new product	Create a new product for each overseas market.

5.1 Product standardisation

An organisation may prefer to offer the same product, because it can be cheaper in terms of production and because the cost of adapting the product cannot be justified in terms of the potential income. Equally the costs of product development and research are reduced through standardisation. Sometimes the overseas market may prefer the product not to be adapted eg HP sauce which is quintessentially British. IKEA is a good example of an organisation that offers the same product across each of its markets.

Keeping the product the same worldwide has some advantages, such as no additional product development or research because no changes are anticipated or implemented. The ability to actually achieve this may be restricted because the product name does not translate well (may cause offence), or simply has a different meaning. Therefore it is not always possible to export a brand in its existing form.

5.2 Adaptation

Here it is assumed the product would benefit from being tailored to the needs of the local market.

A product's size and packaging may have to be modified to facilitate shipment or to conform to possible differences in engineering or design standards in a country or in regional markets. Product adaptations may even include changes in one or more combinations of brand name, colour, size, taste, design, style, features, materials, warranties, after sale service, technological sophistication and performance.

On occasions there is no choice but to adapt the product to meet the differing needs of the market. In addition to social and cultural factors, this may also be driven by local legal or regulatory requirements, eg to meet health and safety standards.

Car manufacturers have to produce the same model in left- and right-hand-drive versions. Electronics companies need to produce products to accept different electricity voltages. McDonald's needs to offer halal

meat options. Soft drinks manufacturers need to change the formulation of their ingredients to satisfy the particular tastes of each market.

ACTIVITY 1.2

Consider the criteria which might be used by a consumer organisation to evaluate and select the best ideas to progress through the NPD process.

6 Product positioning

Positioning is 'arranging for a product to occupy a clear, distinctive and desirable place relative to competing products in the minds of target consumers' (Kotler *et al*, 2008, p157). This means the product must be clearly positioned against the competition and must have a distinct image in the market.

Kotler *et al* (2008, p432) say that 'products are created in the factory, but brands are created in the mind'. Clearly, positioning has a key role to play in achieving this.

THE REAL WORLD

MINI is positioned as 'a MINI adventure' to reinforce an element of 'fun' associated with the brand. For a number of years HSBC has positioned itself as 'the world's local bank' reinforcing its knowledge of local markets and customs, suggesting, perhaps, that other banks may not have the same credentials. For many years, Stella Artois was positioned as being 'reassuringly expensive', although this slogan was dropped a few years ago. The product is now positioned as 'A thing of beauty'.

6.1 How to position new products

▶ **Key term**

Positioning: Kotler *et al.* (2008, p432) say that 'products are created in the factory, but brands are created in the mind'. Positioning is all about perception and how products and brands are thought about by consumers.

Perception maps are used to show a consumer's perception of a brand and its perceived attributes. Each circle in Figure 1.3 shows the perceived position of eight brands mapped against two variables, in this case quality and price. The size of each circle represents the relative market share held by the brand. We can see that in the low price/high quality quadrant that two brands are competing and brand '6' has the higher market share. In the low price/low quality market only brand '8' is competing and there is potentially a gap in the market (big circle) where an organisation may potentially want to compete because there is no competition and it represents the ideal positioning ie relatively low price, with relatively low quality.

Figure 1.3   Perceived position mapped against quality and price

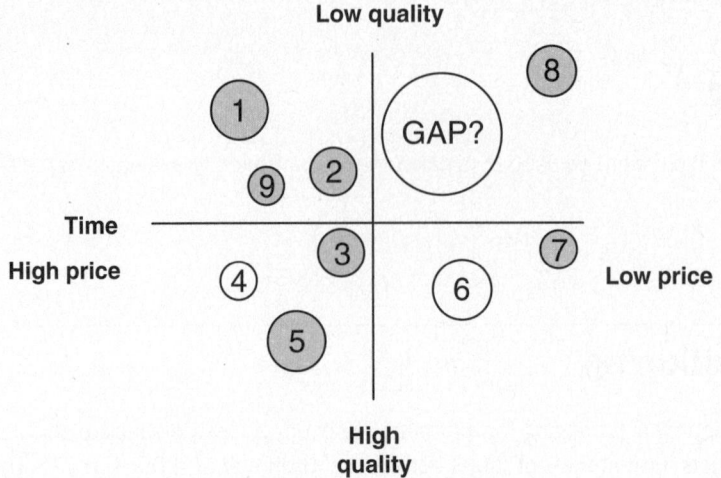

Dibb *et al* (2005) suggest there are six options available when developing a positioning for a product:

1   Identify the product features or attributes that are superior or desirable and matched by few, if any, competitors, or

2   Identify the key customer benefits achieved as a result of using the product, or

3   Emphasise specific occasions when the product might be used

4   Identify and depict user groups

5   Adopt a head-to-head positioning

6   Have a clear point of differentiation from the competition

7 Product adoption

Product adoption refers to the various stages a consumer goes through as part of the process of adopting a new product.

For the marketer it is important to understand the customer journey so the most effective communication strategies can be developed to move the consumer through each stage as rapidly as possible.

The journey consists of five stages as shown in Table 1.4.

The Chartered
Institute of Marketing

Table 1.4   Production adoption stages

Product adoption stages	Summary
Awareness	At this stage the consumer becomes aware of the product, but lacks information on it.
Interest	The consumer now seeks information on the product and this could be around features and benefits.
Evaluation	Is the product worth trying? Will it meet the needs of the consumer?
Trial	The consumer will now try the product; this could be by free sample, special promotion, free trial or through a one-off purchase.
Adoption	The consumer tries to make full use of the product, although even at this stage there is no guarantee of loyalty.

7.1 Product adoption categories

▸ **Key term**

Diffusion of innovation: this is a concept which was first introduced by Rogers and it relates to the rate at which consumers 'adopt' products. Rogers identified five main adopter categories (innovators, early adopters, early majority, late majority and laggards).

Consumers do not take up a new product at the same rate and we can group them into categories reflecting the rate at which the product is adopted. However, not everybody takes up a new product and some people will adopt the product just at the time its replacement is being introduced.

Rogers (1962) identified five separate customer categories reflecting the rate at which they adopt a product. It should be noted that because a person is an innovator for example in respect of mobile phones, it does not necessarily suggest they will be innovators for other product types.

Knowing where customers are in the 'model' shown in Figure 1.4 allows a marketer to develop an integrated marketing mix which is targeted at each stage.

Figure 1.4   New production acceptance innovation/diffusion model

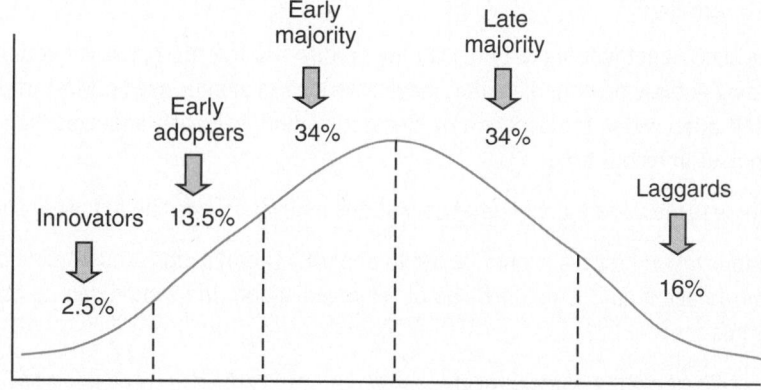

7.1.1 Innovators

Innovators are the first people to try the product. They enjoy trying new things and like to be at the forefront of new development. They are a small group of people who help get the product launched. They are generally, but not always, young, confident and well educated.

7.1.2 Early adopters

Early adopters enter the market early and take their lead from the innovators who are taking the risk. Once the early adopters enter the market, the product's rate of growth (of adoption) accelerates. Although early adopters are 'followers', they remain alert to new developments in the market.

7.1.3 Early majority

At this stage the mass market is starting to build. The group is more risk adverse than previous ones and will seek reassurance that the product will work. Relatively well educated, they tend to have above-average incomes.

7.1.4 Late majority

The late majority is content to watch and see how the market develops; competition may be building, so they will have a range of products to choose from. Initially, when the product was launched, they may have been hesitant for financial reasons. The product may be reaching maturity by the time the late majority take it up.

7.1.5 Laggards

Laggards are the last to be converted. They are usually reluctant to change and may have attitude or economic issues preventing them from taking up the product sooner. There is little risk now to them in taking up the product as the manufacturer will have rectified any faults and issues by this time. Prices are now starting to fall and innovators are already purchasing the next product.

---

8 Product innovation

The process and technical aspects of developing new products, managing their position in changing markets and the relationship with the dynamic needs of customers has been considered. However, innovation brings these processes to life and enables excellent NPD and management. Innovation comes from a variety of sources:

- Customers
- Front line staff
- Executives
- Advisers

Innovation is not just about bringing new products to the market. It is about reinventing business processes and building entirely new markets that meet untapped customer needs. Most important, as the internet and globalisation widen the pool of new ideas, it is about selecting and executing the right ideas and bringing them to market in record time.

There is some debate about what constitutes innovation and the following should offer some help.

The innovation process cannot be left to chance. Organisations must gear up to the opportunities for innovation and embrace it as it is the lifeblood of the organisation. Innovation can be achieved in different ways, for example:

- Co-operating with suppliers
- Responding to changing customers' needs
- Accepting that product failure, on some occasions, is inevitable
- Building an innovation culture within the organisation
- Identifying and responding to market opportunities for new or enhanced products

There are a number of ways to categorise innovation. Utterback (1994) suggested the following:

- **Product innovation**: making changes to the products offered by the organisation, eg the enhanced functionality which has been introduced by Sky TV over the years such as SKY Plus.

- **Process innovation**: changing the way products are created and delivered, eg online banking

- **Position innovation**: changes to the context in which products are introduced, eg mobile phones which combine email, internet, music, radio, satellite navigation, in addition to the ability to make phone calls

- **Paradigm innovation**: changes in the underlying attitude of an organisation, eg Northern Rock which was originally a small regional building society in England which converted to bank status and grew into one of the largest mortgage lenders in the UK (now nationalised at the time of writing).

We can also add to the list:

- **Organisational innovation:** ie outsourcing or combining business function with other organisations
- **Management innovation**: business process re-engineering
- **Marketing innovation**: new delivery channels

As the above suggests, innovation is not to be regarded as a one-off process never to be repeated, it is ongoing and customers welcome new products. Equally organisations often have to stimulate demand to encourage purchase.

It has been noted that not all new product ideas survive, in fact most are rejected at some point in the NPD process and then for those that do get launched, the majority will be unsuccessful. Therefore organisations need to have a mechanism or criteria in place to encourage successful innovation. Hooley *et al* (2008) suggest three conditions:

- **Closeness to customers**: ie understand their needs very well

- **Cross-functional communication**: ie an effective communications procedure is in place between the key functions within the organisation

- **Multi-functional team work**: most innovation comes about through teams working effectively together rather than people working alone

8.1 The innovation process

Innovation can be achieved through small incremental changes or a 'big bang' or radical changes. Most organisations will follow an incremental process, as the 'big bang 'approach requires a radical organisation.

Hooley *et al* (2008) suggest six broad approaches that can be adopted by organisations to encourage and develop innovation, as seen in Table 1.5.

Table 1.5   Six broad approaches that can be adopted by organisations to encourage and develop innovation

Approach	Commentary
Functional approach	People from the different business units within the organisation undertake the requisite tasks with a representative from each unit meeting with the other units to progress development. This is usually an additional activity beyond the normal day-to-day tasks.
Taskforce	A group of individuals will be selected to progress development. The team should be selected on the basis of individual skills and it is likely that the individuals will be able to allocate more time to the project than with the functional approach. However, they will still have their normal duties to attend to.
Functional matrix	Here team members will be expected to spend around 50% of their time on the project and the rest on their normal activities although insufficient time is usually available to undertake them.
Venture teams	People are released from their normal activities and spend their entire time on the project.
Spin-outs	Used by large organisations to support high risk projects which do not fit in with the organisation's core activities.
Inside-outside venture	Teams from different organisations come together to develop the project combining the skills from both organisations.

8.2 Radical and incremental innovation

Much of the innovation that is witnessed today is 'incremental' innovation rather than 'radical'. Incremental innovation involves making smaller changes, which are often more palatable within the organisation as they carry lower levels of risk. Radical innovation is much more transformational and therefore carries a far greater level of risk, although, of course, the rewards can be considerable.

Being perceived to be innovative can have a significant impact on positioning and may be important in order to appeal to the intended target market.

Opportunities to innovate are created through a number of sources, some from within the organisation (internal) and others through changes in the organisation's marketing environment (external). These are summarised in Table 1.6.

Table 1.6 Sources of innovation

Internal sources
Structural change
Increased budgets
Change of ownership
Change of strategy
New management / staff
External sources
New technology
Demographic change
Changes in customer needs / behaviour
Competitor activity
Changes in legislation / regulation

8.3 Benefits of innovation

To adapt and evolve, ie to be successful, an organisation must innovate. It is hard to find examples of successful companies where they have not been innovative. As we have seen, innovation can be incremental or radical, its benefit or purpose is to launch a new product into the market to gain a competitive and improve sales.

THE REAL WORLD

Apple

Apple Computer was created in 1976 by Steven Wozniak and Steven Jobs, who had been friends in high school and who both shared an interest in computer design. The company sold its computers quite successfully but on a relatively small scale. In the early 1980s Apple experienced difficult trading conditions, resulting in a number of redundancies. In 1981 Job's became Chairman and around the same time Apple started work on its new 'Mackintosh' personal computer.

In response to both customer and market changes, Apple focused on enhancing the Mackintosh product and in 1987 launched the Mac II. Initially a major success, Apple found itself moving in a different direction to the market, which was now saturated with PCs using the Microsoft operating system. Apple, however, was still viewed in some markets as having superior functionality, for example in the creative and design industry.

Growth at Apple was transformational in the 1990s and more recently as it focused on improving the functionality of its existing products and has it embarked on a programme of new product development. Famous now for a wide range of groundbreaking

technology-driven products, it has built a vast and loyal customer base, in a fiercely competitive market, many of who are eagerly awaiting not only the next releases of iPhone and iPad, but can only speculate what the next new product from Apple will be.

ACTIVITY 1.3

Identify three different organisations and consider how each is perceived in the market in terms of its approach to innovation.

▶ **Exam tip**

In December 2009, Black & Decker case study, Task Two required students to:

'Examine the key stages in the process that the Black & Decker Corporation should follow in order to identify and develop a new product for existing consumers.'

Better answers identified each of the recognised stages in the new product development process, as set out earlier in this chapter. The important consideration when answering this question was for students to ensure that the content focused on Black & Decker. Weaker answers simply described the NPD process in a general way rather than relating the content to the issues encountered by Black & Decker. Students should have identified these issues ahead of the examination through the analysis of the case material. Weaker answers made little or no use of this pre-prepared analysis. Better students fully applied this pre-prepared analysis within their answer. 'Application' means that the pre-prepared analysis was used to reinforce and support points made. Simply 'referring' to it is not sufficient.

- Products can be viewed from different levels – the core, actual and augmented/extended product.

- Understanding the ultimate use of the product enables the marketer to categorise the product, eg by consumer and industrial usage.

- New product development is vital to an organisation to ensure that its product portfolio remains applicable to the target audience and reflects changes in the marketing environment.

- There are recognised stages in the NPD process – idea generation, screening, concept testing, business analysis, product development, test marketing and commercialisation/launch.

- There are different types of 'new product', ie not all new products are totally new to the market.

- A key decision for an organisation which has decided to enter a new market, especially internationally, is whether to adopt a standardisation or adaptation approach.

- Product positioning can have a significant impact on the success of a product.

- Organisations use marketing activities to attempt to influence how consumers perceive their products, in particular, how they are perceived versus competitor products.

- The concept of product adoption is important as consumers will not all take-up new products at the same time.

- Rogers defined five adoption categories – innovators, early adopters, early majority, late majority and laggards.

- Innovation has become important to most organisations today.

- Not all innovation is 'transformational'. 'Radical' innovation involves significant change, however 'incremental' innovation involves much less significant change. As a result it may be easier to achieve as it is perceived to be less risky.

FURTHER READING

The following paper, while now quite old, sets out Rogers' thinking around the diffusion of innovations concept:

Rogers, E.M. (1976) New product adoption and diffusion. *Journal of Consumer Research*, Vol 2 (4), pp290-301.

REFERENCES

Brassington, F. and Pettitt, S. (2006) *Principles of marketing*. Harlow, FT Prentice-Hall.

Dibb, S. *et al* (2005) *Marketing: concepts and strategies*. 5th European edition. Boston, Houghton Mifflin.

Hooley, G. *et al* (2008) *Marketing strategy and competitive positioning.* 4th edition. Harlow, FT Prentice-Hall.

Kotler, P. *et al* (2008) *Principles of marketing.* 5th European edition. Harlow, Pearson Education.

Rogers, E.M. (1962) *Diffusions of innovation*. New York, The Free Press.

Utterback, J. (1994) *Mastering the dynamics of innovation*. Boston, Harvard Business School Press.

 The Chartered Institute of Marketing

1   Give examples of how a motor manufacturer can compete at the augmented (or extended) product level.

2   Why is the development of new products essential to the ongoing success of an organisation?

3   What is a key product consideration for a company when entering a new market, especially internationally?

4   Identify and explain the recognised stages of the NPD process.

5   Why do think the success rate for new products is low?

6   What do you understand by the term 'innovation'?

7   What are the adopter categories identified by Rogers' diffusion of innovation model?

8   Why is Rogers' model useful to marketers?

9   Describe the main characteristics of an 'innovator'.

10   Define 'product positioning'.

Activity 1.1

The answer will very much depend on the products which have been chosen. For each product there should be consideration of the 'levels', which are shown in Figure 1.1, ie the core product, actual product and augmented (or extended product).

Activity 1.2

The criteria used will vary depending on the organisation's strategy, objectives, available finance, return requirements and risk culture. Typically criteria might include:

- Is it feasible for us to develop and launch?
- Will it generate potential for competitive advantage?
- Is there sufficient demand for the product?
- How competitive is the market, ie do our competitors already have the same or similar product?
- Will it 'fit' within the current range?
- How much will it cost?
- How much income/profit will it generate?

Activity 1.3

This will depend on which organisations are chosen. How innovative an organisation is, in reality, might be difficult to assess, but it is possible to make an assessment based on perception. For example, how frequently does the organisation launch new products? Importantly, does it withdraw products which are out of touch with its customers? What do the brand image and marketing communications portray about the organisation?

QUICK QUIZ ANSWERS

1   At the augmented (or extended) level the product features extend beyond what customers might regard as 'natural add-ons'. This is an area where the manufacturer can add value to the customer proposition and also attempt to create competitive advantage. For example, the manufacturer might offer an extended warranty (say five years), free servicing and free credit terms. The challenge for marketers however is that these added extras soon become accepted as the 'norm', especially when other providers have followed suit, so maintaining differentiation is not easy.

2   Product development is important for a number of reasons. First, products have a life cycle and most, eventually, will need to be withdrawn. Therefore, the organisation needs to replace these with new products. New products are also required to meet changing customer needs. NPD can also have a positive impact on the organisation's brand, leading to improved customer retention and customer satisfaction.

3   The key decision is adaptation or standardisation, and not just the product but the entire marketing mix should also be considered.

4   The recognised stages of the NPD process are idea generation, screening, concept testing, business analysis, product development, test marketing and commercialisation launch.

5   The success rate for new products is low because many of the ideas generated will not meet the key criteria determined by the organisation, for example return, payback and fit with strategy. Some ideas

may also simply be too expensive or too difficult for the organisation to develop and implement. Finally, the organisation is unlikely to have sufficient resources to properly analyse and evaluate all of the ideas generated.

6   Innovation means different things to different organisations and people. However, it is recognised that there are two types of innovation – incremental and radical. Incremental innovation involves smaller changes, possibly enhancements to existing products. Radical innovation involves more transformational change. Innovation tends, often, to be associated with 'risky', however, the risks can be reduced by adopting a more incremental approach to change.

7   The categories are innovators, early adopters, early majority, late majority and laggards.

8   It is useful to marketers for a number of reasons. First, customers in the 'innovator' category can be specifically targeted by marketing campaigns when a product is launched as they are the most likely to buy first. Other potential customers can be identified and campaigns tailored to suit their characteristics. For example, the 'newness' of the product needs to be emphasised in order to attract the innovators and early majority. The marketing mix may need to be adjusted to attract the early/late majority, for example pricing may need to reduce.

9   Innovators are consumers who like to own the latest products and place a high value on being first to own a product. They will be the very first people to buy a new product.

10   Positioning is concerned with how a consumer perceives a product or brand, and how they view it in relation to rival products/brands. Typically, positioning focuses on quality and price, although other characteristics could also be considered. The organisation's marketing mix and branding approach will have a significant impact on the product's/brand's positioning.

CHAPTER 2

Managing and developing an organisation's product portfolio

Introduction

In this chapter we will look at the advantages of strategic product management and, at the same time, consider the limitations and how this might be managed. A variety of different techniques will be explored including product life cycle, BCG matrix, and the GE matrix. These offer a number of options to achieve effective product management and will be set in various contexts.

Topic list

The importance of product management   ①

Product management process   ②

Customer value   ③

Product portfolio management tools   ④

1.1	Critically evaluate the process for managing and developing an organisation's product portfolio to deliver best value products for customers in different market segments and achieve organisational and marketing objectives
	▪ Definitions of 'product' in the context of different sectors
	▪ Product management's contribution to delivering customer value. Competitive advantage and achieving organisational/marketing objectives
	▪ The rationale for managing and planning product portfolios for different market segments
	▪ Managing product profitability
	▪ Product life cycle
	▪ BCG matrix
	▪ General Electric model

1 The importance of product management

▶ **Key term**

Product management: the organisational function which has ultimate responsibility for the product range. Key goals will include growing income and profit from the portfolio and ensuring that the organisation's products align with the marketing environment.

According to Jobber (2010, p389) product management 'entails the assignment of product managers to product lines. These managers are then responsible for their success (ie the products') and have the task of co-ordinating functional areas, eg production, sales, advertising and market research'. 'Product success' can be determined in many ways, but realistically, in today's environment, product managers are most likely to be focused on a number or priority areas:

- Increasing product profitability
- Generating new revenue streams
- Delivering and supporting products in a cost-effective way
- Retaining existing (valuable) customers
- Cross-selling and up-selling to existing customers
- New customer acquisition

2 Product management process

Organisations generally try to offer customers a range of products suited to their particular needs based on their knowledge of the market. Very few organisations have just one product to offer their customers and a range of products allows for segmentation, targeting and positioning (STP) of the portfolio, leading to a greater market share, higher levels of customer satisfaction and increase resilience for the organisation.

Additional products cannot be added to the portfolio without considering the impact on other products and how they are performing (eg financially, or by market share) and therefore a range of portfolio management tools must be utilised to ensure the portfolio is effective. Products need to be managed effectively so that customers receive a best in class product and the organisation maximises its opportunities for profit.

Additional products must be added in a systematic and logical way.

Product management is integral in creating value for customers, it does this through the effective management of the marketing mix in order to satisfy customer needs – see Table 2.1.

Table 2.1   The extended marketing mix

Marketing mix	Commentary
Product	The right product(s) available to meet current customer needs (added value). The product range can be expanded or collapsed as needs change.
Price	It is important to understand how customers perceive price, so the organisation must be clear on exactly how to price its products and the relationship with any other products within its portfolio.
Promotion	A range of tools is available to support the product, create customer satisfaction and loyalty through careful positioning in the customer's mind. Branding reinforces the product image with the consumer.
Place	It is necessary to get the products to customers where they want to purchase not where you would like them to purchase.
Physical evidence	Where services are concerned, some tangibility needs to be provided to support the overall proposition. This could range from brochures to the decor of the office where the service is delivered.
People	Arguably the most important element, who need to be consistent and professional and reflect the brand.
Processes	It is important to train staff and have defined processes in place to support staff in delivering a consistent and a high quality service.

Effective management of the marketing mix process allows an organisation to effectively meet a range of customer needs as categorised below.

Table 2.2, based on Blythe (2006), suggests five customer needs.

Table 2.2   Customer needs (Blythe, 2006)

Needs	Summary
Current product need	Identified through research, are the key features and benefits of the product acceptable or do they need to be enhanced?
Future needs	Identifying future demand levels and product functionality is difficult, but effective management of the product life cycle supported by ongoing research will assist.
Pricing levels	While customers may want to buy at the 'best' price, this is often based on quality v cost issues and the balance must be understood.
Information needs	What information does the customer need to commit to the purchase? How can this information be conveyed?
Product availability	Customers generally want the product available to them in a readily accessible way and therefore the choice of distribution channel and channel's members is crucial.

ACTIVITY 2.1

Identify the main responsibilities of a product manager working for a major organisation.

New products cannot simply be added to the organisation's product portfolio in a random way; Table 2.3 sets out how an organisation's portfolios can be categorised.

Table 2.3   How an organisation's portfolios can be categorised

Product mix	This is the total of all products (and variants) that an organisation offers to its customers.
Product line	Here the product mix is divided and grouped into products which are related to each other for internal (production or technical reasons) or external reasons as they all offer a similar solution to the consumer.
Product item	The product line is further divided into individual products which meet a specific customer need.

Effective product management will develop sufficient product variants to meet the needs of the different groups of customers with specific needs which must be satisfied.

An example of a product mix for a typical university is shown below in Figure 2.1.

Figure 2.1   Product mix for a typical university

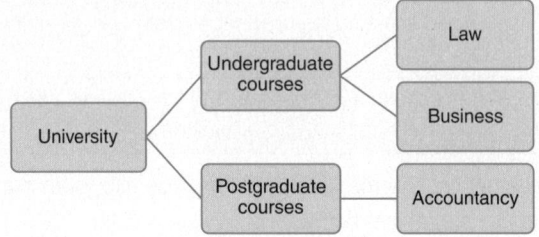

The university may want to expand its law programmes, ie want to expand its product mix width and it may offer:

- Law with Spanish
- Law with French
- Criminal Law
- Child Law

And within each programme it could offer short courses, foundation degrees, full degrees, etc. Consequently it has a larger product mix.

3 Customer value

Customer value is derived from a customer-centric organisation that understands its customers. The better it understands them, the better value achieved through the deployment of the marketing mix. It is customers who define value, not the organisation, and organisations must stay close to the dynamic nature of this definition in order to keep the product portfolio relevant to customer needs.

Value is derived either directly or indirectly through better customer services, brand reputation, market coverage and technology, pricing or cost savings.

4 Product portfolio management tools

Marketers have a range of tools available to them to help them make strategic choices when developing and managing a product portfolio. Strategic planning tools help marketing managers understand the current position or help to devise future strategies to improve efficiency, performance and profitability through a better understanding of customers.

The Chartered
Institute of Marketing

4.1 Product life cycle (PLC)

> ▶ **Key term**
>
> **Product life cycle (PLC):** this concept is based on the principle that once products are developed and launched they will all, broadly, follow a similar pattern of demand that flows through growth, maturity and then onto decline.

Products are considered to have a finite life, this life is referred to as the PLC and the 'classic' view is shown in Figure 2.2. The PLC helps marketers to develop their marketing strategies as well as monitoring the progress of the product from launch.

Marketers will want any newly launched product to have as long a life as possible in order to generate an accepted level of profit for the organisation after the costs of development have been recovered.

It is difficult to predict the life of the product and consequently the shape of the PLC can vary as modifications or changes are made to the product throughout its life.

A temporary period of unusually high sales volumes driven by consumer enthusiasm and immediate product or brand popularity (Kotler *et al*, 2008) otherwise known as a 'fad' or 'novelty' will shorten the PLC. A good example would be the 'must have' toy for Christmas. Parents will spend a considerable amount of money (and time) ensuring they get the product only to find that after Christmas it is being discounted and quickly moves off sale.

Marketers want to effectively manage each stage of the PLC and while the concept receives criticism it is undoubtedly a useful tool. As will be seen below each stage of the product's life will be monitored, so that the appropriate strategies can the developed. Pricing, product features, promotion (repositioning, rebranding) and distribution strategies will be reviewed at each stage and adjustments made as necessary.

Some organisations will find they have a majority of their products in the maturity stage and much time will be spent advertising the products, but with thought being given to rebranding, repositioning or product modification. The changes made at this stage can be quite dramatic, or subtle in delivery. As an example, Mercedes Benz changed the shape of the headlights on its modules to a 'tear drop' shape which attracted new sales.

The PLC in Figure 2.2 shows sales and revenue plotted against time.

Figure 2.2　　Product Life Cycle

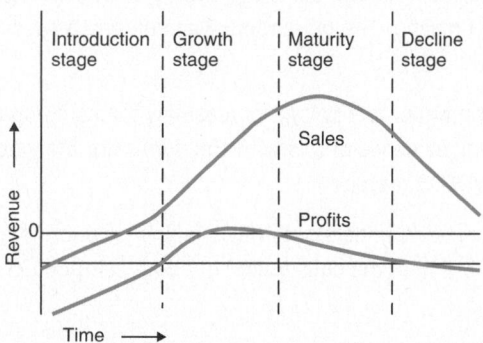

There is a critical relationship between the analysis of a product's life cycle and the ability to develop, generate and maintain customer value through a deeper understanding of the customers changing needs over time.

The four key stages of the PLC are introduction, growth, maturity and decline. We now look at these in more detail.

4.1.1 Introduction

Generally it takes time for a product to be accepted and sales can be slow at this stage. Depending on the investment, profit can be negative. However, the role of the marketer is to raise the level of sales with the target

audience and widen distribution into the market to develop the product through to the next stage. Depending on the marketing objectives a skimming or penetration pricing strategy can be adopted.

4.1.2 Growth

Sales start to rise quickly, possibly because there are now competitors in the market and more consumer awareness. The original product may be improved through the addition of new product features to compete more effectively and maximise profit.

Profit is starting to rise at the growth stage and promotional activity needs to focus on brand building to encourage customers to purchase with less focus on price.

Brand building needs to be effective to encourage new customers to switch, to build a strong position in the market and generate customer loyalty.

4.1.3 Maturity

Maturity tends to be the longest stage of the PLC, but sales now start to plateau and then fall. Profits come under pressure as the organisation focuses its marketing effort on countering competitive activity. However, the market becomes saturated and some of the weaker competitors will leave as profitability drops steeply. While many products at this stage remain unchanged, it is here that organisations develop enhanced versions of the product or launch new ones. Innovative use of the marketing mix can extend the maturity stage ie prolong the life of the product, but eventually it will move into decline.

4.1.4 Decline

The decline stage can be a little unpredictable; sales can drop off dramatically, or follow a slow but steady downturn. The marketer has to decide on the most effective way of dealing with this by slowing down sales or by withdrawing marketing support and letting the product 'die'.

Depending on the product, there is always the possibility of repositioning it in the customer's mind and developing new markets or customers. Take for example Lucozade which is the name for a range of energy and sports drinks. Originally a drink for people who were unwell, designed to provide a source of energy, it was sold in glass bottle with an orange cellophane wrapper. In 1983, the slogan was changed from 'Lucozade aids recovery' to 'Lucozade replaces lost energy' along with a change in packaging. The glass bottle and wrapper was replaced with plastic. The rebranding was deemed a success as sales over a five-year period were reported as having trebled.

The rapid development of technology increasingly forces manufacturers to consider letting the product die. We are currently seeing evidence of this with the demise of the video recorder and video tapes and with CD players being replaced by MP3 players.

Organisations do need to understand that a failing product not only affects the organisation's profitability, but can diminish the brand in the consumers' minds if competitors are launching 'newer' or more advanced products.

ACTIVITY 2.2

Identify products at each of the PLC stages. At each stage consider what you would do, as the product manager, to maximise profitability of the product.

4.1.5 Product enhancement

Careful management is necessary at all stages in the PLC, but particularly at the growth stage. Competition is increasing as more organisations are coming into the market and similarly many customers may now be ready

The Chartered Institute of Marketing

to make repeat purchases. Consequently serious consideration needs to be given to any changes which may be felt necessary to maintain the competitive edge and not lose market share at this early stage.

Rather than compete just on price, new product features or enhancements can be introduced to ensure customers stay loyal to an organisation. After all, the investment in developing the new product may not have been recovered and threat of intermediaries stocking and distributing competitor products, along with retailers giving additional space to the competitor product, will threaten the financial investment made.

THE REAL WORLD

Mobile phone companies are continually enhancing their offering in an attempt to build customer loyalty. While lengthy contracts of 18 or 24 months keep customers locked in, there is intense competition between the phone companies and, therefore, increasing pressure for them to add additional features and benefits.

Many commentators argue that making enhancements to the product at maturity stage is of little value as the product has run out of power and argue that new products should be introduced and the current one left to move into decline.

4.1.6 The PLC and the marketing mix

For those organisations operating across countries it should be remembered that a product can occupy different positions on the PLC in different countries and that the PLC will be different for each country in which the product is offered. Table 2.4 shows the role of the marketing mix throughout the PLC.

Table 2.4   The role of the marketing mix throughout the PLC

Marketing mix	Introduction	Growth	Maturity	Decline
Product	Basic product, but quality assured and any legal protection needed is in place	Additional product features may be added or existing features enhanced	More variety	Maintain, harvest or discontinue
Price	Skim or penetrate the market	Maintain	Maybe lowered to match or beat the competition	Maintain
Place	Selective or limited	Increasing in line with demand	Now reaching critical mass	Now declining
Promotion	Build awareness or tell people how to use the product. Often high impact/awareness	Broader audience which may be for building image or encouraging repeat purchase	Now about reminding and encouraging purchase	Reminding may also be confirming discontinuation

4.1.7 A critique of the PLC

The PLC is a useful tool to deepen understanding of the product portfolio but it is not a forecast of future sales, and for many organisations the PLC extends well beyond the planning timeframe which could be from one year to five years.

We have seen how 'fads' can change the PLC and different patterns will develop depending on the nature of the product, the management or modifications made to it and environmental conditions, so it is difficult to know how long each stage will last. The PLC will vary according to the industry in which the product operates and the nature of the competition.

4.2 Boston (BCG) matrix

Developed by the Boston Consulting Group in the 1970s, this is generally regarded as an important model of marketing and strategic planning (Brassington and Pettitt, 2006). The model helps organisations to identify potential opportunities and problems associated with a product. It does this by categorising the organisation's products into four categories (see Figure 2.3).

Figure 2.3 BCG Matrix

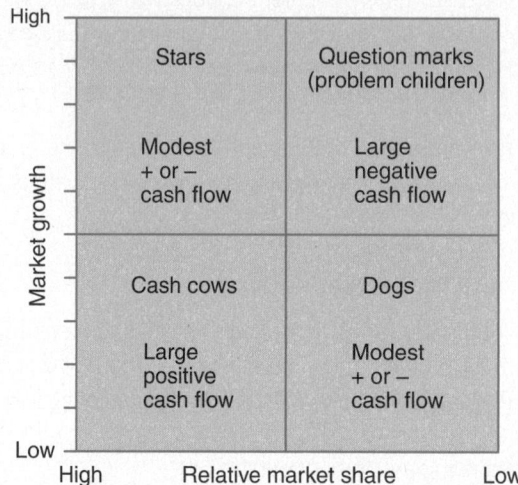

The purpose of the BCG matrix is to help marketers develop their forward planning by suggesting strategy for the future development of the range; selectively invest in problem children; invest in and grow stars; maintain cash cows; and evaluate dogs removing them as necessary (McDonald, 2007). Many organisations, particularly those with large numbers of products may find they have a large number of dogs.

The BCG matrix can operate at a number of levels including:

- Corporate
- Product
- SBU (Strategic Business Unit)

It is based on the principle that cash, not profits, drives a product from one box to another within the matrix (McDonald, 2007) and helps an organisation to develop its growth strategies. It is based on two dimensional variables:

- Relative market share
- Market growth rate

Market share is measured against the product's nearest competitor, ie the degree of dominance the competitor enjoys, while market growth reflects the potential market opportunities and also indicates the organisation's likely cash needs.

The need which prompted this idea was, indeed, that of managing cash flow. It was reasoned that one of the main indicators of cash generation was relative market share, and one which pointed to cash usage was that of market growth rate.

For each product, a circle can be plotted on the matrix to pictorially represent the value of sales in the category as well as likely cash flows.

However, when each product is plotted on the matrix, the organisation can see how balanced the portfolio is. Too many dogs and the business will be losing cash rapidly. While it is important to have some stars amongst the portfolio the importance of having sufficient cash cows cannot be over stated. Those organisations without

cash cows might find it difficult to generate sufficient and regular revenues and can experience cash flow problems. Ultimately, this might be a contributory factor in the business going into liquidation.

An analysis of the product portfolio will also help with the planning process. For example, it would be unrealistic for an organisation to want to increase sales by 10% in the coming year when the portfolio consists of mainly dogs.

Equally products can be in different quadrants if they are made available by the organisation in different countries and this must be considered when reviewing the portfolio as must the direction of travel of the products between the quadrants.

4.2.1 The quadrants of the BCG matrix

Dog: A dog maintains a low market share in a low growth market and is likely to be cash neutral or consuming a modest amount of cash flow and resources. A dog may have been a solid performer, but has subsequently declined in terms of performance. Given its low market share and lack of growth potential the organisation will generally want to remove the product from the portfolio ie divestment, unless the cash flow is strong in which case the product could be harvested.

Stars: A star occupies a high growth share in a high growth market. It generally requires a substantial investment to support expansion, but it is cash neutral and generally regarded as a potential investment for the future. Existing market share should be protected, or a larger share of new consumers should be sought.

Cash Cows: A cash cow maintains a high market share in a low growth market. It generates cash which can be used to support other products. Market position or pricing should be maintained, or the profits used to invest in new processes.

Problem child: Sometimes referred to as question marks, problem children can occupy a low market share of a high growth market. A problem child consumes cash just to maintain its market share and requires cash to support product development. Strategies for a problem child include divesting, harvesting, or removing from the portfolio. Looking externally another strategy is to buy a competitor in order to build a large market share.

4.2.2 A critique of the BCG matrix

Like the PLC, the BCG matrix is not without its critics. It is generally accepted that any analysis undertaken on the matrix will result in an over simplification of the position because it is based on just two dimensions.

Organisations do not just launch products with the intention of being a market leader, often products are launched for strategic reasons, ie to position against the competition.

The BCG matrix should not be seen as a single tool; it has individual merits which can be utilised most effectively as part of a tool of techniques to deepen the understanding of the customer's needs in the context of the business.

4.2.3 Product strategies

There are four main strategies that product managers should consider using for products within the BCG categories and at different stages in their life cycle:

1   **Build:** here the product manager will invest (in marketing activities) in an attempt to increase market share, eg to move a problem child product into the star category.

2   **Hold:** here the product manager will invest just enough in order to keep the product in its present category, eg to maintain a cash cow.

3   **Harvest:** here the product manager will reduce the amount of investment in order to maximise the short-term cash flows and profits from the product, eg this may be sufficient to maintain a cash cow or may be appropriate for a star which is nearing the end of its life cycle.

4   **Divest/withdraw:** here the product manager decides that investment is no longer justified and the decision is taken to 'wind down' support for the product, with a view to withdrawing it from the market altogether, eg typically used for dogs.

4.3 General Electric (GE) matrix

▶ Key term

General Electric (GE) matrix: a useful product management tool, which is often used alongside the BCG matrix. The GE matrix enables the products to be categorised based on industry attractiveness and business strengths.

Another tool available to marketers is the GE matrix that, like the BCG matrix, uses a two dimensional approach. Both models can be used as an aid to future planning or to evaluate an existing portfolio or the current level of investment in a SBU.

The GE matrix uses two dimensions: industry attractiveness and business strength. In contrast to the BCG matrix these dimensions are broken down into other factors which are rated and combined into an index of industry attractiveness. Business strength also uses an index which is then ranked into strong, average or weak.

To use the GE matrix an organisation would need to identify key factors which would make the market attractive to it. These factors would include:

Industry attractiveness:

- How large is the market now and in the future?
- What is the expected annual growth of the market?
- What are the expected profit margins?
- How easy is it to enter the market?
- What is the competition?

Business strengths:

- Current market share
- Organisation's current rate of growth
- Ability to influence the market
- Available resources
- Current profit margins

Having compiled its strengths and ranked them strong, weak or medium, the organisation can then map them across industry attractiveness. This will then produce a position on the matrix (see Figure 2.4).

Figure 2.4 GE Matrix

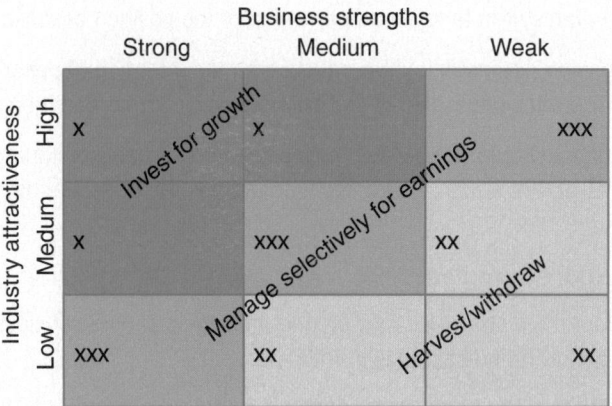

The positioning on the matrix then offers three potential strategic options.

Where the organisation has identifies strong or medium business strengths and the industry has been medium to high attractiveness (indicated x on the matrix) it should invest for growth.

Having identified a market with low to medium attractiveness, linked with medium to weak business strengths (indicated xx on the matrix) then the consensus would be to withdraw from the market or harvest.

The remaining positions ie weak strengths linked with medium to low industry attractiveness (xxx) on the matrix should be managed selectively. Careful consideration is needed here to establish the most appropriate strategy.

 The Chartered Institute of Marketing

Take an organisation with which you are familiar and one of the markets it operates in. From the perspective of the GE matrix, consider its business strengths and the attractiveness of the industry as a whole.

THE REAL WORLD

An overseas business school may identify a growing market for the provision of MBA programmes in the UK and has ranked the industry as highly attractive. However, it has also recognised that at the current time its 'business strength' is weak as it does not have sufficient lecturers (along with other limitations) to deliver the programme. Therefore the overall attractiveness is regarded as medium and the business school would need to improve its strengths in order to move into that market and for the time being should concentrate on its existing markets.

Where an organisation has significant business strengths and identifies a highly attractive industry the decisions are much more straightforward.

Kotler *et al* (2008, p143) state that one of the objectives of portfolio analysis is 'to direct firms away from investing in markets that look attractive, but where they have no strength'.

THE REAL WORLD

The motor industry

There is no better industry to use as an example of how products are managed than the motor industry. There is a seemingly endless production line of new vehicles each with enhanced features and improvements compared with 'last year's model'. Of course, it is a fiercely competitive market, with several brands all competing in the same segments and so sustainable differentiation is difficult to achieve. Hence, the manufacturers invest heavily in communications activities to tempt would-be purchasers and to extend the life of their models.

Extended product life cycles in this industry are vital given the high levels of investment in manufacturing. To create a completely new model is expensive and might require new plant, machinery and processes. So, the decision to 'withdraw' a model from the market will not be taken lightly.

The original Mini is perhaps the best example of having an extended life cycle, surviving in production from 1959 to 2000, a considerable time, during which its life cycle no doubt had been extended on numerous occasions through manipulation of the marketing mix. The original Mini was withdrawn from production in 2000 but was re-launched in 2001 as the MINI, since when the car has yet again been a dominant and iconic brand in the market.

Over the years, there have been some very brave decisions by the manufacturers to withdraw highly successful models and to replace them with new ones, with no guarantee of success for the new model. There is no better example of this than Ford, which, over the years, has manufactured some of the biggest selling models and has taken the decision to withdraw them before sales fell too steeply. Ford examples include the Cortina, Escort and Sierra.

▸ **Exam tip**

When answering questions in the examination about product portfolio management it is vital that you go beyond just describing the tools. Remember to relate the content of your answer to the case material. Too many students are clearly familiar with the various tools and models but do not go on, in the examination, to apply them properly. When you analyse the case material, if you are provided with sufficient information, use the PLC, BCG matrix and GE matrix. Remember, also, to consider the business strengths and industry attractiveness when you undertake your analysis ahead of the examination.

- Product management is a vital function, to ensure that profitability is maximised and that products remain 'fit for purpose', ie are adapted to meet changes in the marketing environment and satisfy customers' needs.

- There is a structured approach to product management and the role features the use of a number of recognised tools, most commonly product life cycle analysis, the BCG matrix and the GE matrix.

- A key focus of the product manager is to ensure that the organisation remains focused on delivering and improving customer value.

- The product life cycle (PLC) is a widely used tool which enables product managers to ensure they have a balanced product portfolio. Products and services progress through recognised stages – introduction, growth, maturity and decline.

- Marketers will seek to extend a product's life where appropriate to do so. This can be achieved through use of the marketing mix.

- The BCG matrix is another product portfolio management tool. It is used to identify a product's position within the overall portfolio in relation to its relative market share and the market growth rate.

- The BCG product categories are cash cows, dogs, stars and problem children (also referred to as question marks).

- The GE matrix is also a product portfolio management tool. It takes into account business strengths and industry attractiveness.

- There are recognised product strategies which can be used in conjunction with these tools – build, hold, harvest and divest/withdraw.

- All three tools have their critics – the most common criticisms being that each features only two dimensions and that it is difficult, often, to identify precisely where products should be plotted. They are nevertheless highly popular amongst marketers and can play an important role in the decision-making process.

FURTHER READING

This article challenges the concept of the product life cycle:

Moon, Y. (2005) Break free from the product life cycle. *Harvard Business Review*, Vol 83 (5), pp86-94.

While this article was written in 1983 it provides a useful summary of the uses and limitations of the BCG matrix:

Hax, A.C. and Majluf, N.S. (1983) The use of the growth-share matrix in strategic planning. *Interfaces*, Vol 13 (1), pp46-60.

REFERENCES

Blythe, J. (2006) *Principles and practice of marketing*. London, Thomson.

Brassington, F. and Pettitt, S. (2006) *Principles of marketing*. Harlow, FT Prentice Hall.

Jobber, D. (2010) *Principles and practice of marketing.* 6 th edition. London, McGraw-Hill.

Kotler, P. *et al* (2008) *Principles of marketing.* 5th European edition. Harlow, Pearson Education.

McDonald, M. (2007) *Marketing plans: how to prepare them, how to use them.* 6th edition. London, Butterworth-Heinemann.

QUICK QUIZ

1   What are the main responsibilities of a product manager?

2   What are the four elements of the traditional marketing mix?

3   What additional three elements are added to the '4Ps' to make the extended marketing mix for services?

4   Identify three tools which are commonly used in product portfolio management.

5   Describe some of the components of 'customer value'.

6   What are the two dimensions which are used to identify where products sit within the BCG matrix?

7   What are the recognised stages that a product will go through during its life cycle?

8   What are the four product strategies which a product manager can apply to products within a portfolio?

9   How does the GE matrix differ from the BCG matrix?

10 What are the four product categories highlighted by the BCG matrix?

ACTIVITY DEBRIEFS

Activity 2.1

The precise responsibilities of a product manager will vary between organisations. However, typically, the product manager will be responsible for a specific product range. They are likely to be responsible for the profitability of the portfolio and for driving income growth. This will be undertaken through deployment of the marketing mix, in particular the pricing and promotion elements. The product manager will develop the communications plan for the portfolio. They will also be responsible for monitoring changes in the market and feedback from customers. They will also closely monitor competitor activities. They will be responsible for new product development.

Activity 2.2

One of the frequently quoted challenges/limitations of the PLC is that it can be extremely difficult to pinpoint precisely at which stage products are during their life time. The development stage, of course, is easy to identify because this is pre-launch. The introduction stage is also easy to identify as the product will be new to the market. Maximising profit here will depend on the strategy, the nature of the product and the market. For a premium product which is unique in the market a high price can be used for launch and maintained (skimming/premium pricing). Where there are competing products a low entry price may be required to encourage consumers to switch (penetration pricing). As the rate of growth accelerates (the growth stage), possibly because the product has unique features which are unavailable elsewhere in the market, pricing can be maintained and promotional activities carried out to continue to stimulate demand. As demand begins to slow (maturity) pricing may need to reduce; perhaps promotional offers might stimulate consumers to buy more. As demand continues to fall (decline) the product manager needs to decide whether to continue supporting the product or to withdraw from the market. Changing product features during the latter stages may extend the product's life cycle.

Activity 2.3

The business strengths and industry attractiveness will depend on the organisation/industry selected. Typical business strengths might be derived from its scale (market share and resources), reputation (brand), products, systems etc. The attractiveness of the industry will be influenced by its size, the number of competitors, the ease with which new entrants can compete, future growth rates, complexity etc. Porter's five forces tool is useful for helping to analyse the competitive dynamics within the industry.

QUICK QUIZ ANSWERS

1   The product manager is responsible for product performance and profitability, awareness of the external environment relevant to the product range, applying the marketing mix, managing the portfolio, developing new products, tracking customer feedback.

2   Product, price, place, promotion.

3   People, processes, physical evidence.

4   Product life cycle (PLC) analysis, BCG matrix and the GE matrix.

5   Quality of service, reliable and up to date products, brand reputation, market coverage, pricing, benefits achieved through product/service usage.

6   Relative market share and market growth.

7   Introduction, growth, maturity and decline. Some writers also consider 'development', ie the pre-launch activities.

8   Build, hold, harvest, divest/withdraw.

9   The GE matrix considers business strengths and industry attractiveness, whereas the BCG matrix considers relative market share and market growth.

10   Stars, dogs, problem children (also known as question marks) and cash cows.

The Chartered Institute of Marketing

CHAPTER 3

The role of branding and branding strategies

Introduction

There is probably as much written about brands, branding and brand management as there is about all of the other marketing activities combined. In the eyes of the target audience the brand 'is' the organisation. Unlike other areas of marketing, which are often effectively processes and where frameworks exist, branding is much more about emotion. Brands with powerful and positive images are highly valuable. However, brands which are perceived negatively can have a very serious (negative) impact on the organisation's success.

Significantly, branding removes anonymity and provides an identity for the organisation, even where the customer might have no 'physical' relationship with the organisation, as so often happens in services businesses. Often, people will have an instant reaction to brands and it is this which impacts on the organisation's positioning and, ultimately, determines its success in the market.

Topic list

Branding – a definition   1

Branding categories   2

Building a brand   3

Branding strategies   4

Rebranding   5

Global branding   6

1.2	Critically evaluate the role of branding in the context of the product portfolio, recommending different branding strategies which are appropriate to a range of organisational contexts and sectors
	▪ Role and importance of brand
	▪ Developing and building brand value
	▪ Rebranding
	▪ International and global brands
	▪ Brand strategies

1 Branding – a definition

> ▶ **Key term**
>
> **Brand:** a name, term, sign, symbol or design which has been created in order that customers can identify the product in the market and differentiate it from other products in the market.

Kotler *et al* (2008, p511) suggest a brand is 'a name, term, sign, symbol or design, or a combination of these that identifies the maker or seller of the product or service. Consumers view the brand as an important part of a product and branding can add value to the product'. Importantly, branding plays a key role in differentiating the organisation, and its products, from the competition.

Blythe (2006, p89) defines branding as 'the culmination of a range of activities across the whole marketing mix leading to a brand image that conveys a whole set of messages to the consumer about quality, price, expected performance and status'.

The role of the brand is to create a position of differentiation in the mind of the consumer, so that the brand is understood (see brand values) and clearly differentiated from the competition to encourage purchase.

Such is the power of branding that most products are branded. Branding has a number of advantages for the consumer, the manufacturer and retailer:

- Customers will be attracted to a product because of its branding, sometimes totally to the exclusion of other brands
- It creates an image in the customer's mind that can be hard to replicate in other brands
- The risk associated with the purchase is reduced because of the known qualities associated with the brand
- Pricing can be higher because of the positioning
- Loyalty towards the brand will generate additional sales
- Customers will be attracted to a store which stocks a particular brand, it also gives an indication of the service that can be expected
- Branding can help with market segmentation ie developing new products for different segments

Successful brands create strong, long-term and lasting impressions with consumers. However, it should be noted that an individual can have an impression about a brand without actually experiencing it.

In financial services when asked to describe, say, Coutts & Co and NatWest consumers will undoubtedly view them very differently. Coutts & Co is highly exclusive, with very few branches and is clearly targeted at high net worth individuals (it is widely known in the UK as 'the Queen's bank'). NatWest, on the other hand, is highly visible, both on the high street and in the media. It clearly targets young people, families, the elderly, businesses and as a result its positioning is very different to that of Coutts & Co.

2 Branding categories

Dibb *et al* (2005) suggest three types of brand:

- Manufacturer (corporate brand)
- Own-label
- Generic

2.1 Manufacturer

This is a brand type where the manufacturer sells the goods under their own name. The product is clearly associated with the manufacturer although it may be sold in a range of different outlets, for example, Cadbury's and Coca-Cola.

2.2 Own-label

The manufacturer's name does not appear on the product. The manufacturer has sold the product to an intermediary who has given it its own name, known as an own-label brand. An example is Sainsbury's Own brand.

2.3 Generic

The number of generic brands ie brands that do not have a brand name, or any other identifying terms, has been falling dramatically because of the growing importance of brands to the consumer.

3 Building a brand

▶ **Key term**

Brand management: marketing activities which aim to both protect and grow the brand and, ultimately, lead to the organisation achieving its desired positioning for the brand. Typically, this will involve monitoring changes in the organisation's marketing environment, especially competitor brands, and deploying an appropriate communications mix to support the brand.

A successful brand is an identifiable product, service, person or place, augmented in such a way that the buyer or user perceives relevant unique, sustainable added values, which match their needs most closely (De Chernatony and McDonald, 1998).

Building a brand (De Pelsmacker *et al*, 2004) means that an organisation will invest significant sums of money building a brand's favourable image and position in the marketplace, such that long term benefits will be achieved both in brand awareness (recognition) and brand value (financial).

To become successful a brand must meet a number of criteria. Figure 3.1 shows the key factors in developing a successful brand.

Figure 3.1 Successful brands (based on De Pelsmaker *et al*, 2004)

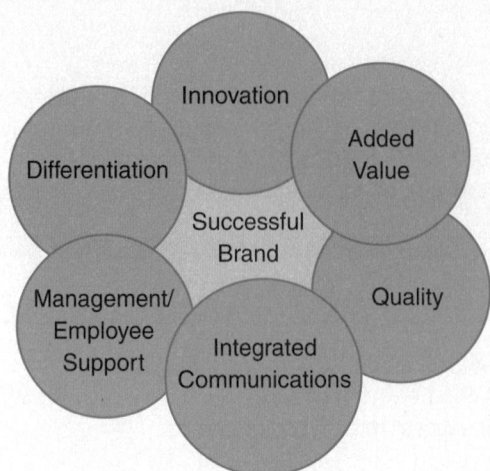

- **Differentiation**

  It needs to be clear to the consumer what the unique benefits of the product are. Brand values play an important role here.

- **Innovation**

  Brands must constantly respond to the changing needs of their customers or they will become irrelevant to the consumer. This is equally true of new and established brands.

- **Added value**

  What additional value does the consumer receive from buying the product? This can encompass a range of attributes from service, status, confidence or making things simple.

- **Quality**

  'Top' brands are usually considered being of high quality within their category and the quality will need to extend to any intangible aspects of the product. Service dimensions are usually much harder to replicate by competitors.

- **Integrated communications**

  Consistent, regular and targeted communications need to be developed. Consumers can easily forget about the brand, or be exposed to competitor brand messages and therefore constant communication is needed to ensure 'front of mind' with the consumers.

- **Management and employee support**

  Internal marketing is crucial to success. It is a waste of resources to communicate with external customers if the internal dimension is overlooked. Staff must be clear on the importance of the brand and act as 'brand ambassadors', but this requires motivation and training.

3.1 Brand values

> ▶ **Key term**
>
> **Brand values:** an effective brand depicts the philosophy and beliefs of the organisation, which are reflected, to the consumer, through the values portrayed within the brand and how it is positioned. Examples of values are quality, reliability, innovation, fun, safety and value for money.

Brand value is established through emotional connectivity with the customer, with the brand itself reinforcing, to the customer, reassurance and creditability while also portraying the specific brand attributes. Brand values support the more visible attributes that organisations demonstrate in their brands, and are often vitally important when the

The Chartered Institute of Marketing

consumer is thinking of making a purchase. So, it is important that the organisation's values are understood and align with the purchaser's own values.

3.2 Brand equity

This chapter has made the case for the importance of brands. In the 1980s it became increasingly important to agree on some measure of a brand's worth from a consumer or financial perspective, or both, and that is what brand equity seeks to measure. We need to be clear on what is being measured and brand equity is generally referred to as **the value of possessing a specific brand name compared to a generic brand of the same type in the same category**. Some organisations view the concept of brand equity from an economic perspective which is considered to be **the sum of the future profit associated with the brand discounted over time**. The actual value is not 'set' but can and will vary over time depending on how well the brand is managed.

In a take-over or merger situation the value of the brand becomes important. BMW in the UK sold off the Rover Group for a nominal £1, but kept the 'Mini' brand which has been an outstanding success and not just in the UK, but as far afield as the USA. Huge sums of money are paid for brand portfolios (De Pelsmacker *et al*, 2004).

A brand can now have more financial worth than the organisation's tangible assets such as property and equipment. As we have already seen, a brand can be a powerful thing and therefore it needs to be managed with care and attention if it is to survive in the long term.

We can look back at brands such as Midland Bank (for so long a dominant brand in the global financial services market, but no longer exists, although the organisation was taken over by HSBC); the high street retailer Marks & Spencer has experienced the 'ups and downs' of brand management; and, one of the most famous branding success stories, Skoda has seen the benefit of effective brand management.

ACTIVITY 3.1

Take a major organisation of your choice as an example. What are the factors that are likely to have influenced its branding decisions?

---

4 Branding strategies

Any strategy must start from the point 'do we want to put our brand name on the product?' It can be argued that for some product categories, there is little point in branding. This is often true for undifferentiated or homogeneous products such as aluminium foil. However, this trend is reducing with organisations opting to name the brand as branded goods are generally easier to sell. When an organisation looks to develop its brand range it can adopt the following strategies:

4.1 Brand stretching

Stretch the brand (brand extension) typically into a new or modified product in a similar category. All brands will carry the same name, an example being Caterpillar moving into clothes from its traditional association with earth moving equipment.

4.2 Line extension

Here the organisation develops a new product closely related to an existing product by developing a new form. This is quite common as it is a low-cost and generally low-risk approach to increasing sales within the same market. There is always the fear that the consumer can become confused with the choices available. A classic example is Kit Kat, a chocolate bar produced by Nestlé which for many years remained unchanged. Then in no particular order, orange and dark chocolate versions appeared, chunky milk chocolate and peanut chunky versions followed along with Kit Kat minis and Kit Kat ice cream.

4.3 Multi branding

Organisations often introduce additional brands within the same category. Royal Bank of Scotland (RBS) offered car insurance under the Churchill, Direct Line and Privilege brands, with each appealing to a different target audience. In the fast-moving consumer goods (FMCG) market, a range of brands will often secure important space on the supermarket shelf. As well as offering the benefits of segmentation, it also means the competition has to compete across a number of brands. Equally, multi-branding allows an organisation to remove a brand which is underperforming quickly and without a serious impact on the existing owned brands.

4.4 New brands

Sometimes an existing brand will not fit in a new product category. Toyota introduced Lexus to position the new luxury brand away from the existing and very successful mass market range of cars. NatWest offered a new range of (cheaper) credit cards branded Lombard to maintain the premier pricing on its other range of credit card products.

The choice of branding strategy depends on what the organisation is trying to achieve.

THE REAL WORLD

Motorway service areas now commonly show the logos of the brands available on signs outside the service area. This is to show motorists the choices available and indicate the quality they can expect when they pull in.

---

5 Rebranding

> ▶ **Key term**
>
> **Rebranding**: where an existing brand in the market is either adapted or changed completely. This can be an expensive exercise and might be undertaken simply to 'rejuvenate' the brand, or to appeal to a new/wider audience. It may happen where the original brand is perceived negatively or where a merger or acquisition has taken place.

Rebranding can take place at both the organisational and product level.

Rebranding is the process by which an organisation changes the way a product is marketed or distributed using a different brand. This usually involves changes to the brand's logo, name, image, marketing strategy or advertising, but this is not always the case. The changes are generally aimed at the repositioning the product in the market.

Kaikati and Kaikati (2004) have identified proactive and reactive reasons for wanting to carry out a rebranding exercise. In practice any rebranding undertaken can encompass aspects of both elements.

An organisation may over the years have developed or acquired a number of regional brands and may want to bring them together as one global brand.

JIF, a cleaning product, became CIF in the UK; similarly Opal Fruits (confectionery) became Starburst. Marathon, a chocolate bar, became known as Snickers. The rationale in each case was to enable the organisation to introduce economies of scale when marketing the one brand across the different markets.

Sometimes it is necessary to reposition a product in the mind of the consumer and this can be for a variety of reasons ranging from price differentiation to expanding into overseas markets. It can be done to overcome perceived service problems, or position the product more correctly in the consumer's mind.

New products, mature products, or even products still in development phase can be rebranded. Mergers and company takeovers can often involve the need to rebrand a product, especially if more than one of the companies involved offers the same or similar products.

Organisations can also rebrand themselves in an attempt to change their image or move into different markets, but care needs to be exercised.

ACTIVITY 3.2

Why might an organisation decide to rebrand?

THE REAL WORLD

Santander

Santander, the Spanish banking giant, bought the Abbey (formerly Abbey National) and the Bradford and Bingley in 2004 and 2008 respectively. It also bought Alliance and Leicester in 2008. All three financial services organisations had long histories and large customer bases.

In mid-2009 Santander announced a major rebranding exercise under which the names of the individual organisations would become 'Santander'. The rationale for this decision being to offer a more consistent approach to its customers and wider accessibility. In addition, Santander escaped the banking crisis relatively unscathed and had grown into a considerable global banking force. This reputation and status was perceived as critical to adding a high degree of trust, vital in the savings market especially in view of the meltdown of a number of other financial institutions.

In late 2010, Santander agreed to increase its UK presence further through the acquisition of 318 Royal Bank of Scotland branches at a cost of £1.65 billion. The deal involves around 2 million customers and is scheduled to go through in 2012, bringing the size of Santander's UK network to more than 1,500 branches. This will provide significant coverage for customers and significantly raise Santander's profile on the UK high street.

(Adapted from the Telegraph, 2009, 2010)

6 Global branding

Standardisation of products generally produces economies of scale, which, given the high costs involved in product development, encourage expansion beyond the home market into initially a few, then an ever-increasing number of overseas markets. However, organisations take different approaches to branding; some believe the benefits of a single global brand outweigh the benefits of country-specific brands with their own brand identities.

Arguments in favour of global brands (Yeshin, 2006) are:

- Economies of scale through standardisation across each market
- Developing technology ensures similar product use
- Rapid and readily available communication channels such as the internet and satellite TV
- Increasing similarity between segments across countries
- Global brands can be seen as better quality than local brands

However, it should be noted that that the product (as opposed to the brand) does not need to be exactly the same. So, as discussed in the previous chapter, the organisation may decide to adapt the marketing mix supporting the product/brand internationally, even though the brand itself is still the same. This can be clearly seen in fast food restaurants around the world, for example Burger King, KFC, Pizza Hut and McDonald's. The brand looks the same however the menus will vary according to local tastes.

Byfield and Caller (1996) suggest three categories of global brand:

- Long-term international brands which are exploiting a universal heritage
- New products developed with the global market in mind
- Brands which have been exported to other markets

Table 3.1 indicates the differences between the adaptation and standardisation approaches.

Table 3.1   Adaptation versus standardisation

Adaptation	Standardisation
Different customer needs	Large number of buyer similarities
Infrastructure variation	Easier to control campaigns from a central source
Varying levels of education	Technology advances allow consistent brand image to be maintained
Economic, cultural and political conditions vary	Economies of scale
Inconsistent local management experience	
Abilities and skills	

There are a number of annual surveys to rank global brands (eg Interbrand). These surveys take into account a number of factors about the brands, including their profile and visibility around the world and the estimated value that the brands themselves deliver for the organisation. The rankings of these global brands (including for example Coca Cola, IBM, Microsoft, Apple, McDonald's, Disney, Toyota, Nokia, Oracle and Honda) do change over time, demonstrating the challenge for management to ensure that global brands are managed effectively.

ACTIVITY 3.3

Visit the Interbrand website http://www.interbrand.com and look at the list of top global brands for 2011. Consider why the ranking for some brands might have changed over the previous year.

The Chartered
Institute of Marketing

In December 2010, Prostate Cancer Charity case study, Task Two required students to:

'Evaluate the role of branding and the factors that the charity should consider in relation to branding decisions as it seeks to gain a larger share of the "donations market".'

The question contained two elements, ie the role of branding and the factors, both of which should have been addressed. The role of branding is critical to any organisation including a charity as it strives to gain broader recognition and appeal in a very crowded market. As with all organisations, branding is important as it reflects the values of the organisation and attempts to build an emotional connection with the consumer.

The factors which should be considered have already been addressed in Activity 3.1. For the Prostate Cancer Charity it is vital that the brand reflects its values. It is also important that its brand 'stands out' in the market. This needs to be achieved on a relatively low budget, which would be a major consideration.

The most common failing on this question was the lack of 'evaluation' provided within answers. Most students who fail do so because their answers are far too 'descriptive' rather than 'analytical' or 'evaluative'. At this level of qualification descriptions are inadequate to achieve a pass, so answers must be detailed and points made must be fully supported. There should also be a strong connection between the answer and the issues in the case material. The student's pre-prepared analysis must be properly applied in answers.

CHAPTER ROUNDUP

- Branding is of critical importance to most organisations and is used to establish differentiation in the market and to encourage consumers to 'recognise' the organisation's products.

- There are many factors that might influence branding decisions.

- There are clear criteria for successfully building a brand.

- Brand values are important and can establish an emotional connectivity with the consumer.

- Brand equity is the value placed on an organisation's brand and will grow based on positive brand attributes. Unlike other assets, brand value can be virtually lost overnight, in the event of bad news.

- Branding is achieved primarily through marketing communications activities although the brand values may be portrayed through other elements of the marketing mix.

- Organisations adopting a corporate branding approach will clearly associate the company's name with its products.

- There are a number of recognised branding strategies, including stretching, line extension and multi-branding.

- Rebranding is a way of repositioning the brand/organisation and reflecting new values. It is also common following merger and acquisition activity.

- Global branding can be expensive to build, but once established economies of scale should be achieved.

FURTHER READING

Interbrand (2011) 2011 Ranking of the top 100 brands. Interbrand,http://www.interbrand.com/en/best-global-brands/best-global-brands-2008/best-global-brands-2011.aspx [Accessed on 9 February 2012]

This paper offers an interesting perspective on managing and developing brands:

Keller, K.L. (2011) How to navigate the future of brand management. *Marketing Management*, Vol 20 (2), pp36-43.

REFERENCES

Anon (2009) Abbey, Alliance & Leicester and Bradford & Bingley to be rebranded Santander. The Telegraph, http://www.telegraph.co.uk/finance/newsbysector/banksandfinance/5392621/Abbey-Alliance-and-Leicester-and-Bradford-and-Bingley-to-be-rebranded-Santander.html [Accessed on 9 February 2012]

Anon (2010) Santander pays £1.65bn for 318 RBS branches. The Telegraph, http://www.telegraph.co.uk/finance/newsbysector/epic/rbs/7925781/Santander-pays-1.65bn-for-318-RBS-branches.html [Accessed on 9 February 2012]

Blythe, J. (2006) *Principles and practice of marketing*. London, Thomson.

Byfield, S. and Caller, L. (1996) Building brands across borders. *Admap*, 31 (6) pp19-24.

De Chernatony, L. and McDonald, M. (1998) *Creating powerful brands*. Oxford, Butterworth-Heinemann.

De Pelsmacker, P. *et al* (2004) *Marketing communications: a European p*erspective. 2nd edition. Harlow, FT Prentice Hall.

Dibb, S. *et al* (2005) *Marketing: concepts and strategies*. 5th European edition. Boston, Houghton Mifflin.

Interbrand (2011) 2011 Ranking of the top brands. Interbrand, http://interbrand.com/en/best-global-brands/best-global-brands-2008/best-global-brands-2011.aspx [Accessed on 9 February 2012]

Kaikati, J.G. and Kaikati, A.B. (2004) Identity crisis: the dos and don'ts of brand rechristening. *Marketing Management*, January/February.

Kotler, P. *et al* (2008) *Principles of marketing.* 5th European edition. Harlow, Pearson Education.

Yeshin, T. (2006) *Advertising*. London, Thomson.

QUICK QUIZ

1 Define 'a brand'.

2 What is the role of a brand?

3 What is a corporate brand?

4 What are some of the criteria for a successful brand?

5 What is brand stretching?

6 Define 'brand values'.

7 What is brand equity?

8 What is line extension?

9 Give an example of a multi-branding approach.

10 What are some of the benefits of having a global brand?

ACTIVITY DEBRIEFS

Activity 3.1

Its corporate objectives and strategy will have a significant impact on branding and so too will its desired segmentation, targeting and positioning. In addition it will have a clear branding strategy, which will be evident from its current products and approach. Its target market will also be a factor as will the competition. The brand will need to reflect the organisation's values and so these must be taken into account. The budget available, to establish and maintain the brand, will also be a factor.

Activity 3.2

There could be a number of reasons why an organisation has decided to rebrand. Perhaps, over time, its values have changed and so its existing brand no longer reflects the company's current image. Maybe it has decided to enter new markets, perhaps internationally, and the existing brand is considered to be inappropriate (or ineffective) to achieve this. Maybe the organisation has decided to appeal to a different market segment. Often, rebranding occurs after a merger or acquisition has taken place. Alternatively rebranding might be necessary to reposition the product/brand in the market place.

BPP
LEARNING MEDIA

Activity 3.3

Brand value can be influenced by a number of factors. During the year the amount of media coverage can have a significant impact, ie has there been more good rather than bad news featuring the brand? Succeeding in entering new markets will have a positive impact on brand value. Brand value can also be influenced through association with other brands. For example, a joint venture or collaboration with a weaker organisation might devalue the brand. Alternatively, association with a well known, high quality organisation might increase brand value.

QUICK QUIZ ANSWERS

1   A brand is a name, term, sign, symbol or design which has been created in order that customers can identify the product in the market and differentiate it from other products in the market.

2   Branding is key in achieving differentiation in the market. It is also important in positioning, driving sales and building customer loyalty.

3   A corporate brand is where the product carries the name of the organisation, eg Coca-Cola.

4   Differentiation, innovation, added value, good quality, management/employee support, communications support.

5   Brand stretching is where the organisation decides to move the brand into a new market, for example Virgin (which began life as a record shop in London) has 'stretched' into several different markets including trains, air travel, financial services and technology.

6   Brand values represent an emotional connectivity with the customer. Positive brand values will provide, to the customer, reassurance and creditability while also portraying the specific brand attributes.

7   Brand equity is the asset value placed on a brand and is based on positive brand attributes.

8   Line extension is where the product range is extended but into markets which are more naturally associated with the original product. For example, a perfume manufacturer might launch a range of shampoos and soaps.

9   With multi-branding the organisation has taken the decision to use different brands for its products/businesses. Each brand is viewed, by customers, as 'stand-alone' and not connected to the parent organisation. Procter & Gamble would be a good example as it produces several different types of detergent but each marketed under a separate brand.

10   Having a global brand, eg HSBC, should achieve economies of scale as there is only one brand to support. It also provides the opportunity for greater consistency and builds recognition, especially as many people now are frequent international travellers. Companies which are global brands are often viewed as being powerful and more trusted because of their global acceptability.

The Chartered Institute of Marketing

CHAPTER 4

Pricing, pricing concepts and price setting

Introduction

Pricing will now be considered with a view to deepening the understanding of the impact that a variety of pricing strategies can have on the product position in the market. We will explore the ways in which pricing can be used to manage the product at various stages in its life cycle in order to maximise the appeal of the product and profitability.

We will consider the importance of setting pricing objectives as a benchmark and to guide strategic product development. The role of the customers' view of different strategies will also be evaluated particularly in terms of the perception of value for money over which pricing strategies have significant influence. The role of pricing in building market share will also be considered as a key element within the marketing mix.

Topic list

The role of pricing in product management   ①

Pricing decisions   ②

Building market share   ③

Pricing for new products   ④

Pricing frameworks   ⑤

Price elasticity of demand   ⑥

Pricing in international markets   ⑦

Services pricing   ⑧

Managing price changes   ⑨

Perceived product value   ⑩

1.5	Critically evaluate the importance of linking the product portfolio to price perception to ensure perceived value for money as part of the overall customer proposition
	■ The role of pricing in product management
	■ Pricing in the context of value for money
	■ Price sensitivity
	■ The role of pricing in influencing customers
	■ The impact of changes in pricing on customer perception
1.6	Assess pricing frameworks that could be utilised by organisations to aid decision-making about product life cycles, product development and innovation
	■ Understanding price versus cost
	■ Determining pricing levels
	■ Pricing in relation to customer satisfaction
	■ Pricing in relation to competition
	■ Pricing in relation to value
	■ Pricing for international markets
	■ The role of pricing in building market share
	■ Pricing approaches and strategies

1 The role of pricing in product management

According to Doyle (2000, p116) price is 'the amount of money that customers pay for the product. It includes discounts, allowances and credit terms'. Price is the value that someone is prepared to pay for the product or service. It is also the one element of the marketing mix that generates revenue, income and profit for the organisation, ie it has a direct impact on the bottom line and needs careful management.

While organisations do not compete with each other on price alone, it can be an important consideration for the consumer when choosing to make a purchase. Different organisations selling a (very) similar product can charge different prices, which are often brought about by internal calculations of 'cost'. Different costing approaches will make a difference to the price which can be charged to the consumer if an acceptable profit is to be made by an organisation.

Setting prices is a strategic decision that must be reflected in the other elements of the marketing mix. Potential consumers will have a perception about price in relation to the organisation's promotion style, including the brand, the product itself and where it can be purchased.

1.1 Product management considerations

While pricing decisions must reflect the organisation's business objectives, they must also take into consideration value for money, customer satisfaction, and the level of competition in the market. In other words pricing must be co-ordinated with indirect and non-price competitive strategies.

While organisations view price as a revenue generator, customers view it in a different way; for example they will ask how the quality compares with a similar brand, or simply regard the product as too expensive and leave the organisation with lower than expected sales.

The Chartered Institute of Marketing

2 Pricing decisions

There are six key factors summarised in the table below to consider when making pricing decisions:

1   **Pricing objectives**: What are the pricing objectives which will support the business objectives?

2   **Buyers' perception**: What does the price mean to the customer?

3   **Perceived value for money**: What benefit will the customer receive as a result of buying the product?

4   **The competition**: How are competitors pricing their products?

5   **Marketing mix**: Does our pricing reflect the other elements of the marketing mix? Does the marketing mix reflect the price?

6   **Channel members**: What are the implications of price for the members of the distribution channel?

Taking each consideration in turn:

2.1 Pricing objectives

Pricing objectives represent the measurable goals a company wants to achieve through its pricing policy. Dibb *et al* (2005) set out different objectives which are summarised in Table 4.1.

Table 4.1   Pricing objectives (based on Dibb *et al*, 2005)

Pricing objective	Summary
Survival	Here the organisation simply wants to ensure it remains in business.
Profit	Organisations generally like to increase profits on a year-on-year basis. Therefore taking into account potential sales a specific profit level will be anticipated.
Market share	Here it is the share of market that is important (ie market leader) and therefore an organisation will be willing to reduce price(s) to maintain its market position.
Cash flow	Cash generation is very important in some organisations and the price is set to bring cash into the organisation quickly.
Status quo	An organisation may simply want to retain its position in the market compared with the competition, ie be content to be the 'number 2' in a particular category and therefore while it may match the price offered by the competition it has no intention of beating them on price.
Product quality	Here the organisation wants to offer the 'best product' in terms of quality. In terms of the price paid it could be considerably be more expensive than similar products. However, if reliability is more important to the purchaser because breakdowns mean lost income which potentially would be well in excess of any quality premium, then a high price can be justified.

2.2 Buyer perceptions

Organisations must interpret what the customer response to the price will be. Dibb *et al* (2005) suggest that an organisation needs to understand:

- What messages that price communicates to the customer and how they respond to it
- The degree to which the price will improve their satisfaction with the product

Often a low (relative) price will convey low levels of satisfaction which may be unfounded. Bringing the price more into line with the competition may generate more sales. Similarly higher prices would suggest higher levels of satisfaction. Organisations need to recognise the price versus quality decision as determined through regular marketing research and respond accordingly.

Customers will often refer to an internal reference price based on their previous experience, ie this should cost around £x. For example, a customer is considering the purchase of a drink and some sandwiches before

embarking on a train journey. They could have planned ahead and bought it at the supermarket for, say, £3. Failing that, the purchase could have been made at the railway station prior to boarding the train for £4.50. Having done neither, the purchase can be made on the train for £6. While each price point could be considered expensive, experience may suggest the price is reasonable for the circumstances and pleasure derived for the customer at different points.

Where there has been little previous purchasing experience in the category the consumer may refer to external information such as that provided by a retailer, manufacturer, service provider or adviser, friend or colleague.

2.3 Perceived value for money

This is the benefit the customer derives from the purchase of the product. The organisation needs to understand the value that the customer places on the benefits received and then price the product accordingly. Effectively, customers assess the price and measure the benefits received. The benefits can be measurable and real or associated with confidence, or status. An example is the cost of a 'Black credit card' which is offered to customers by invitation only. The price may be £250 per year which the customer justifies on the status the card confers alone.

Other factors which affect the perceived value of the product include:

- Service and after-sales service quality
- Level of differentiation from competitor products
- Quality of any packaging
- Product functionality
- Any substitute products which maybe available

Ultimately it is the customer and not the organisation who decides on the value received.

2.4 The competition

Organisations do not operate in a vacuum and must be alert to any competition in the market. That does not mean that the prices need to be the same. Understanding competitors' objectives such as market leader, follower, or profit maximisation will enable an organisation to establish its own pricing position. Competition should not simply be based on price alone. For example, if organisation A reduces its price to below competitor B (which has more financial resources), then it may well be able to retaliate by offering deeper discounts. This ultimately has a cost to both organisations, which will be difficult to sustain beyond the short term.

Sometimes the published price is not the price actually paid as discounts can be offered for:

- **Volume purchases**: when a purchase over a specific quantity will trigger a price reduction
- **Trade discount**: a discount is offered to an intermediary such as a wholesaler because of the role they play in the market
- **'One off' discounts**: because of seasonality, or the state of the market
- **Loyalty discounts**: given because of the length of time seller and buyer have had a relationship

2.5 Marketing mix variables

While the price charged affects the other elements of the marketing mix, the other mix elements also affect price. It would generally be considered that a Rolex watch will attract a premium price reflecting its positioning in the market place. Rolex is generally distributed through a highly select range of retailers. Imagine therefore if Rolex were to take advertisements out in the national press offering a 70% discount! This would cause confusion with the consumer who may question if the offer was genuine considering to Rolex's overall image. However, if Next, a UK clothes retailer, were to advertise a similar discount, shoppers would have no hesitation to rush into the shops to take advantage of the offer.

The Chartered Institute of Marketing

2.6 Channel members

Organisations (or individuals) involved in the distribution channel will have profit expectations, such as volume discounts, or income for performing value-added activity.

ACTIVITY 4.1

Take an organisation of your choice, with which you are familiar, and consider the factors that might have influenced its pricing decisions.

3 Building market share

An essential element of pricing is its relationship with the product life cycle (PLC).

An organisation will seek to maximise revenue through a carefully managed pricing strategy that may change at each stage of the PLC in order to build market share in line with its stated objectives.

When a new product is introduced into the market, the most difficult task is to set a price. There are two options at this stage; price high to attract a specific segment, or price low to appeal to a wider market.

As the product continues its journey into the growth stage, competitors enter the market and consequently one of the considerations is how to price the product. While the focus may be on product improvements, often it is necessary to price aggressively which may involve price cuts.

At product maturity when sales growth is slowing, organisations now start to consider price reductions as some competitors start to leave the market.

When the product moves into the decline stage, the organisation has a number of pricing options. It can increase the price in order to 'milk' the product. Alternatively, a price reduction could be initiated to slow the rate of decline.

4 Pricing for new products

Organisations can adopt two generic pricing strategies for new products: skimming and penetration. A comparison is shown in Table 4.2.

Table 4.2   New product pricing strategies

Skimming	Penetration pricing
High price charged	Low initial price charged
Focus on the innovators	Attracts large sales volumes quickly
Some product differentiation is required	High sales volumes reduce costs
	Economies of scale achieved

4.1 Skimming

▶ **Key term**

Skimming: a pricing strategy for new products where the product has a clear advantage in the market at the time of launch and therefore a high launch price can be achieved.

Skimming is where a high initial price is set to 'skim' income from those buyers who are prepared to purchase at this price. Buyers will be from small and profitable market segments. Apple launched its iPhone

in this way (and continues to do so when new versions are launched), a high price was set and product availability was through a specific telephone network (rather than being available on all networks).

4.2 Penetration pricing

Instead of charging a high price, the price is set below the price of any competing brands that may be in the market or about to enter the market. The intention here is to attract a large number of buyers in order to achieve a substantial share of the market quickly, or take share aware from competitors, or a combination of both.

5 Pricing frameworks

There are four broad pricing strategies, summarised in Table 4.3. These strategies help an organisation decide on the most appropriate way to price its existing products.

Table 4.3   Pricing strategies

Pricing strategies	Summary
Cost based	Includes cost plus and mark-up pricing and breakeven analysis
Customer based	This includes: psychological pricing, differential, product-line and promotional pricing
Competitor based	Pricing near or away from the competition
Professional pricing	The price does not relate to the time taken providing the service

5.1 Cost based pricing

Here a specific sum of money or percentage is added to the cost of the product. This can be cost-plus, or mark up.

5.1.1 Cost-plus

No account is taken of market needs. Costs are established and an amount of money (£) or percentage (%) is added.

Cost-plus pricing is a simple and common method of pricing particularly in the commercial environment where costs can be difficult to identify with certainty. It also has the advantage that any changes in the cost of materials can quickly be reflected in the price.

5.1.2 Mark-up

Here the price is calculated by adding a fixed percentage (the mark-up) to the production and other costs incurred by the seller. It is a method often used in the high street, or when purchasing wine in a restaurant and can be displayed as a percentage of cost or sales.

 The Chartered Institute of Marketing

Many high street retailers apply mark-up in order to calculate their selling prices, in this way providing assurance in terms of how much profit is made. Mark-up and profit margin are frequently confused or the terms are applied interchangeably, which is a mistake. They are quite different. A retailer produces an item for £600 and decides to apply a mark-up of 25%, making their profit £150. As a result, the selling price is £750. While the profit is £150 in both calculations, profit margin is calculated as a percentage of the selling price and so, in this instance the margin is 20%.

Mark-ups vary according to the industry sector, but it is not unusual to see a 100% mark-up on a bottle of wine purchased in a restaurant.

This method also has the advantage of simplicity as the mark-up can easily be calculated. However, it does not take into account any competitive pricing aspects nor how much the customer may be willing to pay.

With cost-plus pricing no changes are made for volume or volume changes. To overcome this we need to understand the relationship between cost, price and volume; a concept known as breakeven analysis.

5.1.3 Breakeven analysis

Breakeven analysis identifies the level of output where total revenue equals total cost, ie no profit or loss is sustained at this point. This is the break even point. Sales or output beyond this level starts to generate profit.

A small manufacturer sells a product for £200. Its fixed costs are £200,000 per year while its variable costs are £100 per unit. Its breakeven point is 2,000 units per year.

This is calculated by total fixed costs/unit price minus variable costs, or £200,000/£200 minus £100.

5.2 Customer based pricing

This is based on the perceived value as seen by the customer.

There are a number of pricing methods, as seen below.

5.2.1 Psychological pricing

The price says something about the product that makes the purchase an emotional rather than a rational purchase. The prime purpose of psychological pricing is to influence a customer's perception of price in order to make the product appear more attractive. Everyday low prices or a price point of £9.99, or £19.99 can achieve this. Alternatively pricing high can have the same effect, eg a £100 bottle of wine becomes attractive to some segments because it reflects status, or makes the purchaser feel confident.

5.2.2 Promotional pricing

Products are sold at below their usual price for a specific period of time to raise the level of sales. This is usually temporary and can take a number of forms from the special event approach, eg a discount is offered for all purchases made on the night, to the supermarket selling a product below cost, in order to encourage sales on other (higher margin) products.

5.2.3 Differential pricing

A different price is charged to different purchasers of the same product, ie the price can vary.

A standard price for the product is clearly easier for the purchaser to understand. However, differentiated pricing is commonly used. Consider the purchase of a holiday overseas, this will typically be much more expensive during the period of school holidays. Leisure facilities may charge less for those aged over 60.

5.2.4 Product-line pricing

Here the price is set in relation to the total number of products contained within the product line.

5.3 Competition

Organisations need to consider the structure of the market, ie number of competitors and the customer's perceived value of the product.

The more the product is seen to be unique by consumers, the greater the opportunity to raise the price.

Some organisations want to be price leaders and set the prices in the market, others prefer to be followers and have others set the prices which they look to as the benchmark or point of reference. Organisations can then choose to price near or away from the competition.

5.4 Professional pricing

Professional pricing is used in situations where the provider of the service has a particular skill and may be regarded as an expert in their field. Professional pricing covers a wide range of situations and can be applied in a number of ways.

Doctors and consultants (of all types) operating outside the NHS, ie in the private sector, may charge a standard fee for a consultation irrespective of the time taken. Typically an initial consultation may take 10 minutes but the 'standard' fee is £200.

The legal profession operates in a similar way, buying or selling a house commands a standard fee irrespective of the work which needs to be carried out.

Auctioneers and estate agents tend to work on a percentage basis, ie do not set a fixed fee but charge 2.5% of the price of the property or goods sold.

In some situations professionals will charge on a daily rate which reflects the nature of the particular contract, or if the work will take an extended period to complete they may charge a fixed price for completion. Consequently with a fixed price if the work takes longer than expected the profit margin will be smaller and may turn into a loss. Conversely if the job is finished earlier the profit margin will be increased.

Builders like to charge on a day rate so that if unexpected problems arise during the course of the work, they simply keep charging for the work undertaken. In this case the client's final bill may be much more than they were expecting or had budgeted for.

ACTIVITY 4.2

Identify two or three products which have been recently launched and consider which pricing strategy the organisation has adopted for each and why.

The Chartered Institute of Marketing

6 Price elasticity of demand

▶ **Key term**

Price elasticity of demand: the relationship between price and demand. Where demand is 'elastic' even a small change in price might have a dramatic impact on demand. However, where demand is 'inelastic' the product is relatively insensitive to changes in price.

Price elasticity of demand is a measure of consumer sensitivity to changes made to the price of a product, and organisations need to understand the relationship in order to manage demand.

There are three forms of elasticity of demand:

- Products are said to have **elastic demand** where a small increase in price produces a large percentage decrease in demand.

- **Inelastic demand** is where a small percentage increase in price produces a very small percentage change in demand.

- **Unitary demand** is where the percentage change in price results in an identical change in the demand.

The higher the level of price elasticity, the more sensitive the market. However, different situations affect price elasticity in different ways.

Products which represent a small proportion of a consumer's overall spending are likely to be inelastic as the price increase is likely to appear insignificant. Where the product enjoys high brand awareness, inelasticity may well be higher because of the loyalty that may be attached to the brand.

The importance of price sensitivity needs to be fully understood if price is to be used effectively (ie optimised) and in relation to the rest of the marketing mix.

The UK government uses price to encourage motorists to consider more fuel-efficient cars by levying a higher duty on cars that emit high levels of pollution.

ACTIVITY 4.3

Identify six products and determine whether they have elastic, inelastic or unitary demand. For products that have a similar level of elasticity try to identify if they have any similar characteristics.

7 Pricing in international markets

Pricing for international markets offers the same options as the domestic market, but there are other factors that need to be taken into consideration.

The international distribution channel is going to be more complex than an entirely domestic one and this must be recognised when considering pricing and a whole channel perspective needs to be evaluated.

It is recognised that distribution channels vary in length and complexity and between countries. However, in some markets, not only do marketers have to set the prices, but they may also have to arrange the finance for some of the intermediaries.

An organisation can choose to offer a product at different prices in each of the markets it operates, or set a uniform price worldwide in relative currency terms.

Setting a uniform price may have some benefits, but it could also mean that the product is simply too expensive for some markets and will not be able to compete with the local competition. However, if there is no local competition a uniform price can be set. Airbus sells aeroplanes at the same price across all markets.

Most organisations will price the product in accordance with the needs and conditions of the local market, taking into account cost considerations.

Factors which need to be taken into consideration when setting different prices for each market include:

External

- Economic conditions, which may allow a greater (or lower) price to be charged
- Level and strength of competition in each market
- Currency exchange rates operating between markets
- Legal implications, ie selling below cost price on the overseas market

Internal

- Marketing objectives for each market
- Customer perceptions of your brand
- Products position within the PLC

Doole and Lowe (2008) suggest the following additional factors that need to be considered as part of the international pricing decision:

- Economies of scale should reduce the product costs
- Markets can be cross-subsidised
- Different segments require the marketing mix to be adjusted
- Global trading requires a continuous need to source products at the lowest cost from around the world

8 Services pricing

The pricing of services can be difficult; not only has customer perception to be taken into consideration, but there is also value, costs and regulations to be considered.

We have already seen how different professionals set prices, but if we now take a broader view of services we can understand the problems. Chapter 11 will outline the difficulties of services ie the fact that they cannot be owned, stored or touched, and are often produced in advance of the purchase.

Sometimes prices are set by external organisations such as the NHS or regulated by consumer bodies. Prices can also be set in accordance with supply and demand, eg consider a marketing consultant who had a full client list in 2010, and has since found business has slowed down he might reduce his fees to secure business.

Prices can reflect seasonality; a family holiday will cost more during the school holidays.

The price of a hotel room would typically be offered at the standard or 'rack' rate for bookings made in advance, and reduced nearer to the date if available, as the hotel would not want to be left with an empty room. Flights were similarly priced until the advent of Ryanair and easyJet when the model changed; flights booked in advance were cheaper and got more expensive as the date neared. This helps manage availability and rewards people for forward planning. The same principles now apply to many railway companies.

9 Managing price changes

The price charged for a product does not remain constant over time. Inflation often causes minor price changes which can immediately be passed on to the customer, or absorbed within the organisation. This decision can be made in order to protect the level of sales and offer a potential advantage against competitors. However, the effect could be to reduce profitability.

Sometimes it is necessary to increase the price of a product because consumers (wrongly) assume that the low price reflects low quality rather than value for money.

The Chartered Institute of Marketing

The timing of the price change also sends an important message to the market; the first organisation to reduce prices may be perceived as the most customer orientated, similarly with the last to increase prices.

Apart from the financial impact, price changes can signal important messages to the market. A small price reduction could be seen as the organisation simply passing on to consumers the price changes taking place through the supply chain. Examples of this would be, the garage that reduces the price of petrol, because of the price change in the wholesale market, or the bank that reduces the price of borrowing as a result of a change in the Bank of England base rate.

There are three main reasons for cutting prices as suggested by Brassington and Pettitt (2006):

9.1 Capacity utilisation

Where there is excess capacity in the market, an organisation may lower prices to encourage consumer take-up. The price reduction may be sufficient to enable the production lines to be maintained (although at a smaller capacity), rather than close them down completely.

9.2 Market dominance

If an organisation already enjoys a strong position in the market for price and cost, for example Ryanair or easyJet, it may want to further strengthen its position by offering 'deep' price cuts. However, it will need to consider whether its strengthened position would contravene current legislation in the UK or overseas.

9.3 Market defence

Where demand becomes weak, compared to alternative products which could be purchased, then a price reduction could be initiated to reduce the impact. It is important to avoid a 'price war' as this generally has a negative impact on the players in the market as they make price reductions which impact on profitability.

---

10 Perceived product value

Beamish and Ashford (2008) suggest the perceived value of a product has a major impact upon the customer's decision to buy. Key factors that affect perceived value include:

- **Life cycle of the product**: customers will generally be happy to pay extra for 'new' products but will expect to pay less as the product moves through the PLC. Consider mobile phones and laptop computers as they became more mainstream.

- **Service and technical support**: should a product break-down, then the availability of 'experts' will be an important consideration. Consider after-sales for computers.

- **Prestige and status** are key factors. The purchase of a prestigious brand does not always offer better quality, but it will confer confidence and status to the user or wearer of the product which may be of much greater importance. Consider the fashion brand Hackett.

- **Packaging which reflects the status of the product**: eg consider the difference in packaging between Sainsbury's 'taste the difference' range and Sainsbury's 'basics' range.

- **Ease of use**: the more straightforward a product is to use, then the less time that has to be spend getting accustomed to the product. Consider the purchase of a new mobile phone, or computer.

- **Availability of competitor products**: the fewer substitute products, the greater the perceived value.

Aldi (Case Study)

This short case study focuses on Aldi the food retailer, which now operates in many countries around the world. Its approach to pricing is unashamedly 'low price'.

Aldi Wins The Grocer Gold Awards 2011: Discounter of the year

The food industry is highly competitive and is dominated by a relatively small number of major players. Whilst a number of retailers have entered the 'value' food and drinks market, quality and service have always been recognised as key elements of the organisations' offering to customers.

The Aldi brand, however, is recognised for offering 'no frills' service and low price products, basing its differentiation mostly on price. Its 'Like Aldi, like the Price' strapline has delivered on its promises and, over the years, the organisation has won numerous awards for its competitive pricing. As a consequence, Aldi has established a strong (and in many markets growing) customer base, largely due to its low price approach.

It provides an excellent example of an organisation which has adopted a clear pricing strategy, which is used to establish differentiation in the market and which is key to its positioning. This, in particular, is vital in the retail industry where, frequently, brands are highly visible and the key to success for the organisation is the ability to demonstrate how it is different from its competitors.

(The Grocer, 2012)

▶ **Exam tip**

In March 2010, Eskom case study, Task One B required students to:

'Examine the relationship between price and perceived value for money to all Eskom's customers, following the increase in tariff agreed by the South African Government'.

To answer this question students needed to understand the dynamics of the market that Eskom operates in, which was set out in the case material, ie power supply in South Africa is a virtual monopoly and so customers have very little choice. In addition, the word 'customers' needed to be explored, because it's not just the consumers and businesses which Eskom supply directly who are their customers, Eskom also supplies to Local Authorities who act, effectively, as re-sellers. While pricing is important, especially for consumers, it is part of the overall customer value package and, as a result, is closely linked to service. A further consideration is that price is relative, ie in comparison with other goods and services. Pricing elasticity should also have been considered, ie demand is likely to be relatively inelastic. Other macro environmental factors should also have been considered, for example the general state of the economy and consumer disposable income.

- Pricing is the element of the marketing mix that specifically generates revenues and so it is vital that it is managed properly.

- Developing appropriate pricing objectives is also vital (remember that all objectives must meet the SMART criteria).

- The likely customer response to pricing, and price changes needs to be properly evaluated by the organisation.

- The area of customer perception is important, especially as pricing has a significant impact on the customer's view of value for money (with the consequent impact on positioning).

- The competitive environment can have a major impact on pricing decisions (Porter's five forces tool may prove helpful in analysing the competitive dynamics in the market).

- There are different pricing strategies and approaches and these need to be fully considered before implementation.

- Skimming involves setting a relatively high price at launch.

- Penetration pricing is where the launch price is set relatively low.

- Mark-up is a commonly used approach in the retail sector.

- Price elasticity of demand is a key consideration when evaluating pricing options.

- Pricing for international markets is often more complex and requires deeper and broader analysis.

- The pricing of services can also have additional challenges compared with pricing goods, given the intangible nature of supply.

FURTHER READING

This is a paper on applying pricing policies:

Baker. W. L. *et al* (2010). Do you have a long-term pricing strategy?
McKinsey Quarterly,
https://www.mckinseyquarterly.com/Marketing/Pricing/Do_you_have_a_long_term_pricing_strategy_2682
[Accessed on 11 June 2012]

REFERENCES

Beamish, K. and Ashford, R. (2008) *Marketing planning*. Oxford, Butterworth-Heinemann.

Brassington, F. and Pettitt, S. (2006) *Principles of marketing*. Harlow, FT Prentice Hall.

Dibb, S. *et al* (2005) *Marketing: concepts and strategies.* 5th European edition. Boston, Houghton Mifflin.

Doole, I. and Lowe, R. (2008) *Strategic marketing decisions*. Oxford, Butterworth-Heinemann.

Doyle, P. (2000). *Value-based marketing*. Chichester, John Wiley & Sons Ltd.

The Grocer (2011) The Grocer Gold Awards 2011: Discounter of the year. The Grocer,
http://www.thegrocer.co.uk/companies/the-grocer-gold-awards-2011-discounter-of-the-year/218937.article
[Accessed on 21 January 2012]

1   A company is launching a new product which has a clear advantage over its rivals. It is a high quality product. What pricing strategy is likely to be used at launch?

2   A company is launching a new washing powder. It is a fiercely competitive market but the company has set itself an objective to build market share quickly. What pricing strategy is likely to be used at launch?

3   The price of a product is £500. It costs £300 to manufacture and the profit is £200. What is the mark-up percentage?

4   The price of a product is £500. It costs £300 to manufacture and the profit is £200. What is the margin percentage?

5   Give an example of psychological pricing.

6   What is differential pricing?

7   Where demand is said to be inelastic and there is a price change what is likely to happen to demand for the product?

8   Where demand is said to be elastic and there is a price change what is likely to happen to demand for the product?

9   Why might adopting a cost-based approach to pricing be problematic from a marketing perspective?

10 Give an example of promotional pricing.

ACTIVITY DEBRIEFS

Activity 4.1

There are many factors, and these might vary depending on the organisation you have chosen. The organisation's pricing objectives will have a significant impact, so too will its customers (eg how much disposable income do they have?). Competitor pricing will also be a significant factor. Factors from within the organisation's marketing environment are also likely to have had an impact (students should consider applying PESTEL analysis and Porter's five forces model). Pricing elasticity will also be a key factor.

Activity 4.2

Where prices are lower than the market, at launch, the organisation has adopted a penetration pricing strategy. Where pricing is relatively high, compared to the market, they have adopted a skimming strategy. Where they have priced the products in line with the market they have adopted a market-based pricing approach.

Activity 4.3

The answer to this activity will depend entirely on the products selected. Where the consumer has choice and there are alternative (substitute) products available then demand is likely to be elastic, ie if one, of a number of companies increases its pricing, even if only by a little, then demand may change considerably. The opposite of course applies if one company reduces its prices, in which event demand for its products will increase. Where there is little or no choice, or where the product is used by habit, eg cigarettes, the sensitivity of demand to price changes will be limited.

The Chartered
Institute of Marketing

1   Skimming

2   Penetration pricing

3   66.6%

4   40%

5   Psychological pricing aims to influence the customer. An example might be a car which is priced at £9,999.99, rather than £10,000.

6   Differential pricing is where a product is priced differently for different segments.

7   With inelastic demand a price change is likely to have only a small impact on demand.

8   With elastic demand a price change is likely to have a significant impact on demand.

9   Costs are inwardly focused, for the organisation, and, it could be argued that organisations should be outwardly focused (ie on customers and the market) to succeed. In addition, while costs are important, the organisation needs to be aware of affordability, ie what the consumer is prepared to pay for the product.

10   Any pricing discount is an example of promotional pricing, including BOGOF (buy one get one free) which is effectively a reduction in price of 50%.

Section 1:

Senior Examiner's comments

By the time that students have completed Section 1 they should have a detailed knowledge and understanding of:

- How and why products/services and product portfolios are managed
- How and why new products are developed
- The different branding strategies available to organisations and the considerations when implementing branding (both domestically and in international markets)
- The meaning, role and importance of positioning in product management; and
- The importance of pricing; the pricing approaches and strategies commonly used and the factors that influence pricing decisions (domestically and in international markets).

Importantly, students must be able to apply what they have learnt to organisations in various sectors, including business-to-business, business-to-consumer, goods, services, public sector and not-for-profit. Students must also be able to apply learnings to organisations trading domestically, in overseas markets and globally.

Students are urged to find their own examples, for instance from reading their local and national media, and from case studies. Students are also urged to apply the various theoretical tools, models and concepts that have been examined in this section to gain a deeper insight into the practical application of theory.

Students should also examine how the tools, models and concepts which have been examined in Section 1 have been deployed successfully by organisations to achieve key marketing goals, for example income generation, customer retention and new business acquisition.

Section 2:

Channel management

This section of the syllabus introduces the concept of channel management (also known as 'distribution' and 'distribution channels'). While touching on the concept of the physical management of the goods from manufacture to the consumer, it is more concerned with the information flows that pass between the different members of the channel. In Chapters 5, 6, 7 we will explore how effective distribution channels work, why they are chosen, what makes them effective, and how they can be monitored.

Distribution channels are an important consideration for any organisation and, as we will see, the relationship between the various parties can be complex and extend beyond the formal channel relationships into a wider network which still has to be managed.

Chapter 5 focuses on the different types of channels and how they are used domestically and overseas.

Channel management, distribution strategies and control

Introduction

We are now moving on to consider the 'place' element of the marketing mix. This focuses on how products are distributed to customers. Channel management, as 'place' is more widely known, is arguably one of the aspects of business which has altered the most in recent years, driven by technological change, the need for greater efficiency and demands from customers for greater choice, flexibility and convenience.

Topic list

Distribution channels	1	Channel profitability	10
Distribution strategy	2	Competitor strategies	11
Influences on channel strategy	3	Benchmarking in channel management	12
Channel structure	4	Ethical considerations in channel management	13
Overseas distribution considerations	5	Channel innovation	14
Managing channel relationships	6	New and emerging channels	15
Marketing tools in channel management	7	Criteria for selecting new channel partners	16
Role of communications in channel management	8		
Evaluating channel options	9		

2.1	Determine and prioritise the key principles and purposes of innovative and effective distribution strategies in order to deliver the organisation's business and marketing objectives in a range of different contexts and different sectors to maximise customer requirements
	▪ Different types of distribution channels
	▪ Establishing channel strategies
	▪ Establishing channel needs (appropriate to different customers, organisations, sectors and countries)
	▪ Developing distribution objectives
	▪ Approaches to international distribution; agent; strategic alliance; joint venture; in-country operation, virtual/digital channels
	▪ Different marketing tools required to give a co-ordinated marketing approach
2.2	Critically analyse the implications, challenges and constraints arising from internal and external environment in the context of the development of developing channel strategies
	▪ Internal factors which influence channel strategy
	▪ International and global factors influencing channel strategies
	▪ Ethical considerations
	▪ Intermediaries' engagement with competitors
	▪ Environmental considerations
	▪ Economic/financial considerations
	▪ Understanding and determining customer channel requirements
	▪ Analysing competitor channel strategies
2.4	Determine the level and scope of controls required for effectively monitoring and managing distribution channels
	▪ Setting objectives
	▪ Monitoring performance of distribution channels
	▪ Benchmarking of other sectors/organisations/countries
	▪ Managing third party relationships in channel management, locally and internationally

1 Distribution channels

> ▶ **Key term**
>
> **Distribution channel:** the means through which the organisation delivers its products and services to the end customer.

Distribution channels refer to a group of individuals or organisations (intermediaries) that move goods from the producer to the consumer or industrial user of the product. In other words a distribution channel is the way an organisation gets its product to the consumer.

Sometimes distribution channels are referred to as marketing channels.

Distribution channels do not just involve physical products, but can equally apply to services which tend to have a shorter channel. Channels can extend beyond geographical boundaries and have an important role to play in overseas markets.

Without an effective distribution channel, products, even the best products, are more likely to fail, so organisations are continually looking to develop cheaper and faster ways of selling their products.

Organisations use distribution channels for a variety of reasons including the need to reduce cost, maximise sales and customer satisfaction. However, in return for reaching a wider market, there are often challenges to be faced through the management of the various channel members and a particular issue for most organisations is the loss of control over elements of the channel which could include pricing and promotion.

The distribution of products to consumers has two main management components:

■ Getting the tangible or physical products to the customers (the supply chain)
■ Controlling the flow of communication between the various parties that make up the distribution channel

Our focus is on the distribution channel, but an example of the supply chain is shown in Figure 5.1.

In Figure 5.1 we see the flow of materials from suppliers to customers, but we need to note that information flows in the other direction and has been referred to as the 'information highway', where all the partners in the chain have access to the same information.

Figure 5.1   The supply chain

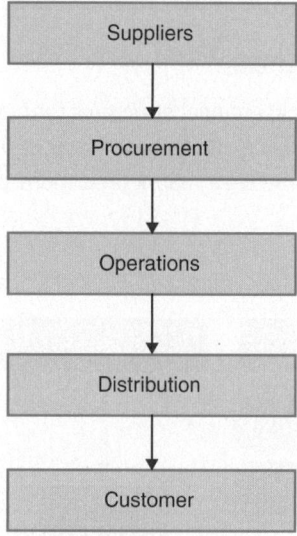

1.1 Functions of a distribution channel

There are a number of key functions of a distribution channel which are summarised in Table 5.1.

Table 5.1   Functions of distribution channels

Functions	Summary
Creating utility	This refers to time, place, possession and form. ■ Getting the product to the customer at a time when they actually want it. ■ Making the product available where the customer wants to buy it. ■ Giving the customer the legal right to use the product. ■ Assembling the product to the format wanted by the customer.
Facilitating exchange efficiencies	Using intermediaries can reduce the distribution costs by eliminating (for example) many of the journeys that would take place. A manufacturer of washing machines would save costs by using an intermediary (also distributing products for other manufacturers) to get the product into the various retailers.
Alleviating discrepancies	Discrepancies break down into two: quantity and assortment. ■ Discrepancy in quality: organisations need to produce in bulk to generate cost efficiencies. Many operate production runs turning out hundreds of thousands of the product each and every day. Consumers may only want 'one' and retailers (depending on size) will want smaller quantities. ■ In other words, the manufacturer produces far more products the typical customer can use.

Functions	Summary
	A discrepancy in assortment relates to the fact that a consumer generally wants a number of products which constitute an assortment. However, a manufacture may only produce a small range of products (assortment) which produces the discrepancy.
Standardising transactions	Products, packaging, pricing, delivery is standardised through the channel.
Customer service	The intermediary will be providing service to other members of the channel or the end user.

Wholesalers will be expected to advise the retailer on any technical issue. Retailers or distributors will be expected to deal with customer enquiries and deal with any issues that may arise. |

1.2 Channel structures

Figure 5.2 shows the typical channel structures for business-to-business channels. However, depending on the nature of the business being conducted, members of the channel may be called dealers, distributors, agents, outlets, or partners. It can be seen that organisations can go 'direct' to customers and this is typical in financial services.

Figure 5.2   Typical channel structures for business-to-business channels

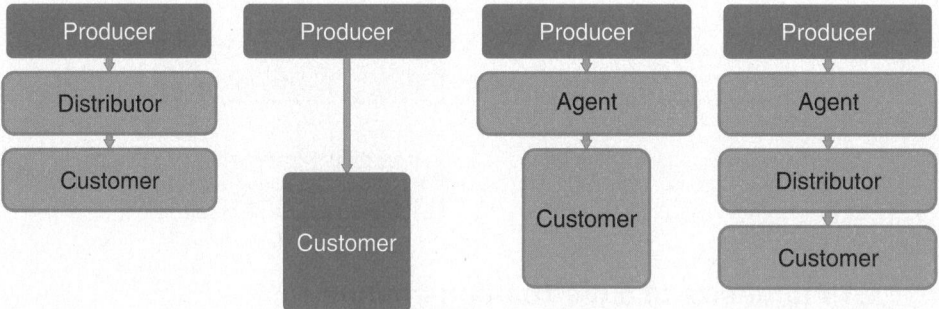

Within the table there are four channel structures from direct to the longer channel where agents, distributors and customers are involved. Each member of the channel has a role to play in ensuring the efficient movement of the product to the end user.

Figure 5.3 shows a typical channel structure for the consumer (B2C) market.

Figure 5.3   Typical channel structure for B2C market

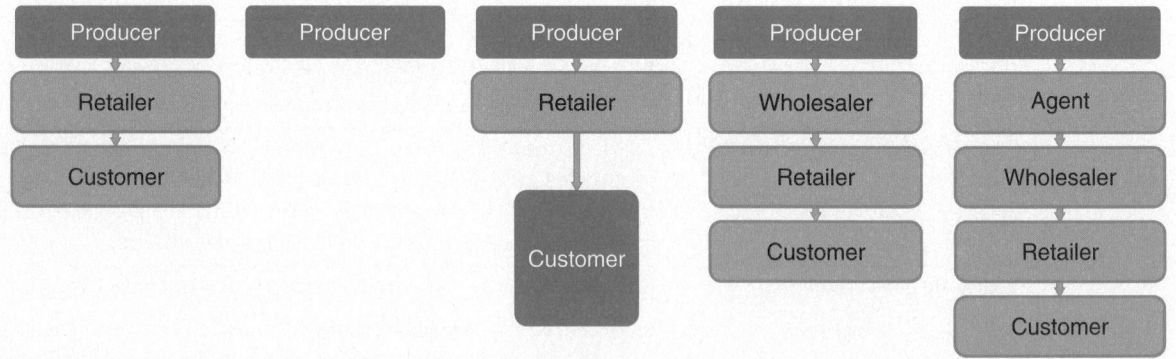

As we will see later, an organisation will often use multiple channels to get the product to the customer, such as that shown in Figure 5.4.

The Chartered Institute of Marketing

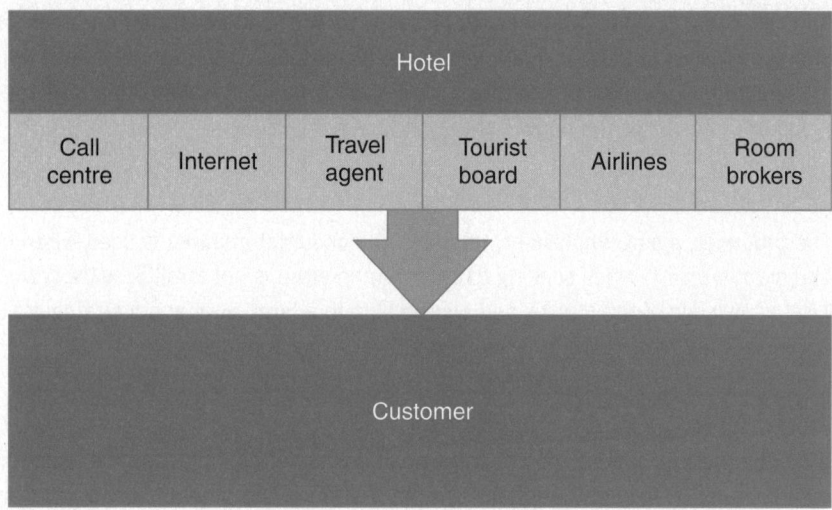

1.3 Channel objectives

The structure and the objectives for the channel depend on the need of the end user, and this in turn is affected by the nature of the end user, ie consumer or industrial products.

Channel objectives must be set which must be SMART, ie specific, measurable, achievable, realistic and time bound. Usually objectives are set which meet customer needs at the most effective price.

The structure of the channel will depend the capabilities of the organisation, ie how large is it? What resources does it have available? What are its key skills?

Kotler *et al* (1999) suggest that objectives should be set in terms of the levels of services to be provided.

However, this does not mean the same levels of service have to be provided to all customers. Different customer segments can have different service levels attached to them and should reflect the value of the customer.

1.4 Consumer channels

1.4.1 Short distribution Channels

Where goods are moved directly between the producer and the consumer there are advantages for both parties as the intermediary is eliminated. The producer has control and the consumer can be in direct contact with the manufacturer so that customer service, queries and complaints can be dealt with.

There are various forms of 'direct', but the increasing popularity of the internet and sophisticated databases make this channel more popular and another way for customers to access the product.

Amazon, for example, has made a great success of this channel, but others have been less than successful as they need to rely on other parties to actually get the product to the customer, and this part of the distribution channel has not worked well.

Interestingly we are now seeing the internet disintermediate other channels.

Another short distribution channel is the producer to retailer to consumer. This channel is the most common one where the manufacturer produces the product in bulk which is sold to the large retailers in typically large numbers, who then sell to the end consumers who purchase in much smaller numbers. This channel only works where the retailer has a large turnover and can sell the product to the consumer quickly and in small quantities. A good example is a supermarket.

1.4.2 Producer, wholesaler, retailer, consumer

A longer channel is the **producer, wholesaler, retailer and consumer channel**. The manufacturer still produces in bulk and sells in smaller quantities to the wholesaler. This channel is also appropriate for smaller manufacturers who cannot sell direct to retailers. The wholesaler also brings together a wide range or deep range of products for the benefit of the end user or retailer.

1.4.3 Producer, agent wholesaler, retailer, consumer

The **producer, agent wholesaler, retailer** and **consumer channel** is used when overseas business is involved. The manufacturer, when seeking to enter a market he is not familiar with, will appoint an agent who will have local knowledge of the market and will be able to advise on channel strategies. However, in return for local knowledge the manufacturer loses control over aspects of delivery.

1.4.4 B2B

B2B channels tend to be much shorter than consumer channels, as the users prefer the dialogue with the manufacturer in view of the (often) complex nature of the products involved. Consider the building of the Olympic village in the UK and the importance of having key components at exactly the right moment. Similarly with Airbus and the building of their aeroplanes; components are built across Europe to be assembled in France. Each component, wings, fuselage, etc must arrive at the factory for assembly at just the right time, otherwise the knock-on effect is considerable.

1.4.5 Direct

A short channel categorised by direct contact between the manufacturer and the user, **direct channels** are generally used for complex or expensive products. The method is preferred as there is direct access to the manufacturer's technical help team, which is particularly important for non-standard products. However, there is often a need for the manufacturer to maintain a direct sales team along with some representative offices.

1.4.6 Manufacturer, distributor, user

This channel can be likened to the wholesaler approach for the consumer market. Large quantities of the product are sold to distributors who sell them in smaller quantities.

1.4.7 Manufacturer, agent, user

An agent is used where it would not be economic for a manufacturer to deal directly with the user. The agent will have expertise in the products, and knowledge of the local market, but equally depending on the agreement between the parties may also act as agent for a competitor product.

There are attractive cost advantages to be achieved as the agent will usually be paid on a commission basis so there will be no fixed costs.

1.4.8 Manufacturer, agent, distributor, user

The longest channel, but again one used when selling to overseas markets. The agent has market knowledge which is used to supplement the role of the distributor who will be responsible for ensuring product availability at a point where the customer wants it.

ACTIVITY 5.1

For your own organisation, or an organisation of your choice, identify the channel structures adopted and the rationale for this decision.

2 Distribution strategy

A key element of channel management strategy is ensuring adequate market coverage for the organisation's products, and this can be achieved in many ways. Brassington and Pettitt (2007, p284) suggest that market coverage is 'about reaching the end customer as cost effectively and efficiently as possible, while maximising customer satisfaction'. Stern et al (1996) identify three potential approaches to achieve market coverage:

2.1 Exclusive distribution

▶ **Key term**

Exclusive distribution: the organisation has very few outlets, reinforcing the exclusive nature of the brand.

With this approach, the organisation adopts a very narrow and highly focused strategy for distribution. The fact that there are few outlets strongly supports the exclusive nature of the product/brand. Exclusive cars, eg Ferrari and Aston Martin would be good examples of this approach.

2.2 Selective distribution

▶ **Key term**

Selective distribution: there are a relatively small number of outlets; generally associated with 'premium' brands.

With this approach, the organisation carefully selects the number and location of its outlets. Products are available on a more widespread basis than with the exclusive strategy adopted above, but the range of outlets is still low. Waitrose would be a good example of this approach.

2.3 Intensive distribution

▶ **Key term**

Intensive distribution: products are available on a widespread basis from many different outlets.

With this approach, the organisation is seeking blanket coverage, ie as wide a market exposure as it possibly can. Many FMCG are in this category as they are widely available from many shops.

ACTIVITY 5.2

Identify three organisations which have adopted each of these three distribution strategies and consider why each approach has been chosen.

THE REAL WORLD

Compared to its food retailing rivals, Waitrose has been careful to protect its high quality reputation by adopting a selective approach to its stores. There are significantly fewer Waitrose outlets than Tesco, Sainsbury's and Asda, for example. In addition, the location of Waitrose stores is carefully managed to ensure they are within the catchment of consumers from higher socio-economic groups.

3 Influences on channel strategy

We have seen the various ways a channel can be constructed: direct, indirect, business to consumer, business to business and the roles that each intermediary can undertake. Organisations then select the most appropriate channel, or channels, as they are not restricted to one. This is because they can use multi channels, ie many different routes to market which can include direct and indirect channels.

The actual choice of channel or channels can be influenced by five factors (Brassington and Pettitt, 2007): the product, organisational objectives, market size and location, consumer behaviour, changing environment (Figure 5.5).

Figure 5.5   The actual choice of channels can be influenced by five factors (Brassington and Pettitt, 2007)

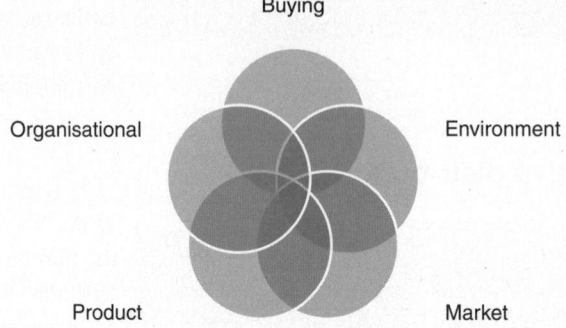

3.1 The product

We have seen that where complex or expensive products are involved, the end user will often prefer to be in direct contact with the manufacturer so that any technical or design issues can be discussed or resolved without the need to go through an intermediary. Similarly once the product has been installed any after-sales issues can be dealt with direct.

3.2 Objectives

Organisational objectives determine the overall channel approach. If the brand has an 'exclusive' image then it may want to open a new channel rather than use an existing one. Sometimes an organisation will reduce the number of distributors in order to reposition the brand in the mind of the consumer.

One of the key concerns for organisations at the moment is consideration for the environment and how distribution channels can become 'greener'.

While channels need to be designed with the consumer in mind, the channels also need to be aligned with the organisation's stated objectives.

An organisation that was initially established to service a small niche market, finds it now wants to expand and consequently its distribution strategy would move from exclusive to select.

Objectives change over time and need to be reflected in the distribution channel. More effective distribution channels may require new or different intermediaries eg Tesco home delivery. Customers no longer need to visit the store to purchase; they can have the groceries and more delivered direct to their home within a two-hour time period.

The Chartered Institute of Marketing

3.3 Market size and location

Where there is a substantial market for the product, an organisation may choose a direct channel and, in the case of an overseas operation may open an office or presence, and this will cut out the need for intermediaries. The organisation retains complete control over all activities.

If the market is small, the use of intermediaries may be necessary as the organisation can rely on intermediaries to get the product to market without the need to invest heavily in a new infrastructure, as the intermediary will already have it in place.

Similarly, the market for the product may be located some distance from where it is produced and the cost of a physical presence would be too expensive to justify. An intermediary could be used to manage the distribution and represent the organisation through its own network.

Where the size of the market is small and does not warrant a large distribution chain, for example expensive designer label clothing, the channel will be short, with few outlets (exclusive).

Newspapers on the other hand will require a highly complex channel if the reader is to be able to purchase at a convenient location and time.

3.4 Consumer behaviour

For some general 'low involvement' purchases a consumer may be happy to make the purchase from a general retailer such as Argos. However, when considering the purchase of, say, a TV which incorporates the latest design and technical features, it may be more appropriate to visit a specialist retailer. The retailer will be able to add value to the purchase through detailed product knowledge as well as being able to offer a wide product range to choose from.

Many consumers like to purchase from out-of-town stores with the convenience of easy parking and a small range of stores, but large range of products. Equally some consumers prefer to travel into town, wander around the shops and enjoy a coffee before making a purchase.

3.5 Changing environment

The changing business environment needs to be reflected in new and evolving distribution strategies.

Organisations need to recognise the importance of being 'green', which includes the distribution of goods; something that should increasingly involve environmental considerations.

Working with intermediaries can lead to reduced fuel and pollution costs through more efficient vehicles and distribution methods. Sharing of best practices will also contribute to efficiencies.

While there are usually a number of channel strategies to consider, it can be the case that external environmental considerations affect the availability of channels.

Technology has fundamentally changed the nature of distribution channels, allowing more direct channels, more self service options and the intermediation of many channel partners.

4 Channel structure

We have suggested that a distribution channel is a group of individuals that move goods to the consumer. This ignores the relationships that exist between the channel members. Often the members will be independent of each other, or there may be some connection such as ownership. Equally the channel member can also be a member of another channel which may be a competitor. Relationships and potential conflicts can easily occur within the channel. Therefore it is necessary to define the structure of the channel so that all members are clear on their roles and responsibilities, are willing to co-operate with each other and will maximise the benefits of being a member of the channel.

4.1 Vertical Marketing System (VMS)

In a conventional channel, as identified above, role and responsibilities can be confused, or blurred (Figure 5.6).

Figure 5.6   Conventional channels versus vertical system

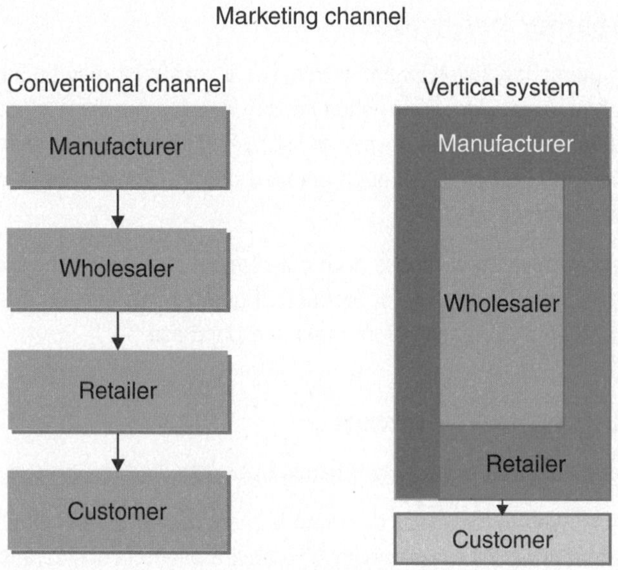

Marketing channel

Conventional channel

Manufacturer

Wholesaler

Retailer

Customer

Vertical system

Manufacturer

Wholesaler

Retailer

Customer

To overcome this, the VMS was introduced and is broken down into three types:

- **Corporate VMS**: Here an organisation can own and operate intermediaries within the channel and the dominant member of the channel may in fact not be the manufacturer. For example, TNT Post, a competitor to Royal Mail, collects mail from clients and distributes them into Royal Mail's central depots which are then responsible for delivery to offices and offices in the UK. Another example is Sainsbury's petrol; it is Sainsbury's who owns the petrol tankers and the filling stations, but no other part of the channel.

- **Contractual VMS**: Where members of the channel retain their independence, written agreements are put in place to specify the exact role and responsibility of each member. It will be clear, for example, as to who is responsible for pricing, promotion, stock levels, finance packages, delivery dates, manufacturer, etc. Franchising comes under this category and is commonly perceived as an example of best practice as the key details of the relationship between franchisor and franchisee are clearly specified.

- **Administered VMS**: There is not usually a legal agreement between the channel members; rather there is a dominant member who assumes responsibility for the co-ordination of the other channel members. This domination could come about because of their position in the channel or the nature of their business.

5 Overseas distribution considerations

Many organisations are content to operate in their home market. However, for a variety of reasons and circumstances, an organisation will look to operate or sell their product overseas.

Working with an organisation's home market is less risky than venturing overseas. Within the UK laws are generally the same, language is known and distribution channels understood. There is no need to worry about currency fluctuations, and PESTEL factors are generally very well appreciated and changes can be anticipated. Nevertheless there are often good reasons to consider entering into an overseas market.

An organisation that wants to enter an overseas market must consider the most appropriate entry method. They include:

- A saturated domestic market, where sales are slowing down and the competition is becoming stronger.
- Efficiencies of scale, where the opening of an overseas market reduces the unit cost of production
- Existing customers may be expanding overseas and there is an opportunity to support them

Paliwoda (1993) suggests six factors to be taken into account:

- **Speed**: How quickly does the organisation want to enter the market and what share will it obtain in the timescale?

- **Cost**: What are the costs of the entry methods and which represent better value?

- **Flexibility**: How much flexibility is needed? ie what are the alternatives if things do not proceed to plan?

- **Risk**: What is the organisation's view on risk, including financial, reputation, economic and social?

- **Payback**: How quickly does the investment need to generate a profit, or what level of profit is needed by a certain date in time?

- **Long term profit objectives**: What are the long term plans for the market?

Having considered the key factors, the organisation can select from a variety of distribution channels.

Although the international channels of distribution are broadly similar to domestic channels they are more complex in their management and culture forms an important part of the relationship.

5.1 In-country operation

An organisation can choose to produce goods in the home country and export them to the overseas country. It can achieve this through 'indirect exporting' where an agent is appointed in the home country with specialist knowledge of the overseas market(s). Alternatively the producer can export the goods direct to the overseas country (direct exporting).

Direct exporting brings options. An organisation can manage its exporting operation from within the domestic market by establishing an exports division or department. Alternatively it could set up an overseas office to handle sales, distribution and potentially marketing (see Figure 5.7).

Figure 5.7   Overseas options

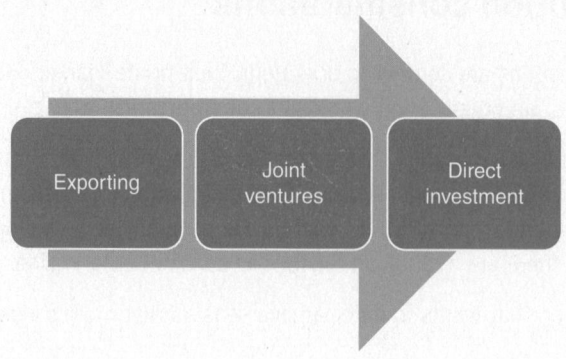

5.2 Strategic alliances

A strategic alliance is a commitment between a number of organisations (a minimum of two) that agree to work together for a specific purpose(s). It is a collaborative agreement where organisations work with each other to develop, or improve a product, or exploit a specific market. There is similarity with joint ventures (see below), but while the number of strategic alliances is increasing, they are not without their problems or risks.

The strategic partner(s) must be carefully selected and have similar aims or objectives. The technology industry has seen many strategic alliances that have successfully developed new products or opened up new markets through new distribution channels which individually the partners would not have been able to do. However, as we have seen already, trust and commitment are essential requirements for members of a channel and in a very challenging environment, members of a strategic alliance could quickly find that they are competitors for the same market, leading to the breakdown of the alliance. Finally, strategic alliances are often formed for a short period of time; there is no sense of long-term commitment necessarily.

5.3 Joint venture

A joint venture shares many similarities with a strategic alliance, but differs in the sense that it is more formal; a joint venture will usually involve establishing a jointly owned business with an overseas partner. The overseas partner(s) will help the domestic organisation in a number of ways:

- Share distribution channels
- Expert knowledge of the market
- Build synergy

The relationship can also hasten the time needed to get into a new market as the organisations will be working jointly together for a common purpose, rather than possibly competing with each other.

5.4 Digital/virtual channels

Electronic channels open up new markets and opportunities for organisations of all sizes; smaller organisations can now access markets that previously could not have been reached and it gives larger organisations an alternative channel for supplementing existing channels. In many instances the need for a physical presence has been reduced along with the associated costs.

While the presence of a website supports the buying process, e-commerce is necessary to facilitate a truly integrated channel. E-commerce provides the capability to accept and make payments across the internet.

Cost reduction is a key motivator for the use of digital channels and the electronic and instant nature of the channel means that transactions are processed more quickly and payment received faster leading to improved efficiency.

Even before an organisation looks to an overseas market, the internet is a rich source of information, saving time and cost, in areas such as:

- Key financial statistics
- Exporting terms and conditions
- Media availability

No longer do brochures need to be sent out by mail to potential customers, they are made available online. Customers visiting a website are also a valuable source of information that can be used to improve existing channels.

A two-way dialogue can be established where any queries can be dealt with immediately. Errors are reduced as it is often the purchaser who keys in their requirements.

Larger organisations develop extranets, where suppliers, distributors, joint venture partners, any channel intermediary or end user can have access to a specific area of the organisation's website.

In the extranet each user would see a website customised to their needs and the key purpose includes:

- Raising awareness for new products or procedures
- Facilitating purchase and payment
- Sharing sensitive information in advance
- Rapid response to changing market conditions, so price changes can be communicated

The internet has benefits for most organisations, but like all other channel choices should be used appropriately in line with organisational objectives and customer needs. Complex and expensive products will rely on traditional channels, but technical information can be made available on the web or extranet to support other channels.

For the smaller business, the web will remove barriers, give access to a wider range of overseas suppliers and may become the sole distribution channel.

5.5 Agent

An agent can be used where it is not viable or practical for an organisation to have a physical presence. An agent will not own the goods but may stock them and buy and sell on behalf of the principal. The agent will have been carefully selected for their knowledge of the market or for their network of contacts in the overseas market and will often sell through distributors.

An agent is generally paid on a commission only basis and does not contribute to the fixed costs, but can be a substantial variable cost depending on the commission terms agreed between the parties.

6 Managing channel relationships

> ▶ **Key term**
>
> **Cateora's 5Cs:** coverage, character, continuity, control and cost. A useful framework for the evaluation of options in channel management and the performance of channel partners.

In selecting a new channel or evaluating an existing channel the organisation will have carefully considered the cost incurred in setting up the channel, the ability of the channel to effectively distribute the products, the characteristics of the product and of course the customer.

While organisations understand the importance of managing costs, it is only one of a range of measures that can be used to monitor the performance of channels.

Cateora (1993) offers a framework for evaluation based on 5 Cs that are applicable to both the domestic and international markets.

- **Coverage**: How well the channel performs in achieving sales, or market share, or penetration of the market.

- **Character**: Compatibility of the channel with the organisation's desired positioning for the product.

- **Continuity**: How loyal the various channel members are and the length of time they have been a part of the channel.

- **Control**: How well the organisation is able to control the marketing programmes within the channel; this can be of particular concern where long international channels are involved.

- **Cost**: This will cover the cost of investment, variable costs, and expenditure.

ACTIVITY 5.3

Can you identify any other considerations beyond Cateora's 5Cs which might help when identifying and selecting new channel partners?

7 Marketing tools in channel management

To be effective, an organisation must design the marketing mix to offer synergy and consistency with its channel members.

Where the organisation also has overseas markets, there is the additional dimension of whether to standardise, ie use the same strategy across all the markets it operates in, or adapt the strategy, ie have a different marketing strategy for each country.

The effective use of the marketing mix will:

- Build profitable and different relationships with intermediaries
- Establish one-to-one communications and dialogue

Marketing mix considerations include:

- **Product**: can be a physical product, idea or service.

- **Price**: usually negotiated for channel member, but may be set for end user.

- **Place**: a range of channels depending on whether B2B or B2C. The internet can be used to cross both channels. The length of channel will depend on the nature of the product.

- **Promotion**: branding and heavy advertising is necessary in the FMCG sector, along with push and pull strategies. More complex products would require trade advertising and extranet support.

- **People**: a high degree of training with carefully selected and accountable staff.

- **Process**: clear processes which are well documented and have clear timescales for completion.

- **Physical evidence**: the internal and external appearances of any buildings need to reflect the product qualities, so do brochures and the web.

When considering the international dimension the following should be noted:

- **Product**: may need to be adapted to the needs of the local market and the product positioning may be different. For example Coca-Cola alters its recipes for different countries.

- **Price**: other currencies make pricing more complex, but should reflect the positioning in the overseas country.

- **Place**: reflects the different entry strategy, eg joint venture, in-country operation, etc. E-commerce is worthy of specific consideration reflecting the immediacy of the channel in ordering goods.

 The Chartered Institute of Marketing

- **Promotion**: may need to be adapted for cultural, ethical and taste reasons.

- **People**: a high degree of training with carefully selected and accountable staff, but recognising some of the difficulties this may cause depending on the market.

- **Process**: clear processes that are well documented and have clear timescales for completion.

- **Physical evidence**: the internal and external appearances of any buildings need to reflect the product qualities, so do brochures and the web.

We have already seen the importance of channel members and the importance of the role they play. The roles, activities and function they perform are integral to the success of the channel. However, even though distribution channels are generally portrayed as a linear process, they are far more complex than this and stakeholders can form complex relationship networks through collaboration, joint ventures and alliances. This is known as the 'extended enterprise'.

8 Role of communications in channel management

While it sounds like a cliché, poor communication often lies at the heart of channel conflict; mixed or confused messages are communicated through the channel or only communicated to certain members and then often in reaction to an event which has occurred. Proactive and clear communication should be the norm in distribution channels.

Fill (2006, p132) offers a succinct definition of communications which is: 'marketing communication is an audience-centred activity designed to encourage engagement between participants'.

In other words the needs and motivations of each channel member must be understood as well as the environment in which the message is being delivered and received. The nature of the relationship between the channel members also needs to be recognised and appreciated.

Consequently, marketing communications will need to convey not just product information, but relationship building through trust and commitment. This is best done using the DRIP model:

- **Differentiation**: messages explaining how the organisation is different from others in the industry and the competitive advantages it confers.

- **Reminding**: reminding, or reinforcing the importance of the relationship and benefits that the parties accrue from each other as a result of being part of the channel.

- **Informing**: sharing with others exactly what the capabilities of the organisation are. Common or potential areas for misunderstanding can be dealt with in a proactive manner.

- **Persuading**: messages to encourage potential channel members, or encouraging existing members to continue with the relationship.

The DRIP model is a useful framework from which communication tools and media can be deployed effectively. This can range from regular email updates, to monthly sales meetings to an annual meeting.

For any communication strategy to be effective there must be a basis of trust between the parties, otherwise any messages conveyed will be ignored or dismissed. Trust is formed by the parties in the channel agreeing to a culture of mutual commitment, co-operation, understanding, openness and a willingness to rectify mistakes rather than adopt a 'blame culture'. A lack of trust inhibits the development of the channel and can lead to conflict becoming a constant feature of the channel.

9 Evaluating channel options

An organisation will evaluate a number of channels and select one or multiple channels that will best meet its business objectives.

When selecting the 'best' channel the organisation could use the following three criteria (Kotler *et al*, 1999).

9.1 Economic

An estimate of the potential sales, investment and channel costs will be made for each channel. Different scenarios will be modelled to understand the effects of variations from any central estimates to see the potential effect on income.

Identifying the most effective channel now and in the future can be difficult. The measure of profit must be established; this could vary from ROI (return on investment) to shareholder value and will need to consider:

- Any assets which may need to be shared
- Replacement of existing assets to meet the needs of the channel
- Redundant assets, no longer needed in the channel
- Exit costs of leaving the channel

9.2 Control

In order to widen distribution of the product and made it more accessible to customers, intermediaries are used which dilute the overall control over product marketing. Procedures should be put in place to clearly define responsibility of the intermediary to avoid a lack of overall control.

9.3 Adaptive

Establishing a channel usually involves a long-term commitment which goes beyond financial dimensions and the channel needs to be able to respond to changes in the market. This could involve changes to purchasing behaviour, the introduction of new technology, environmental issues and economic conditions. A channel that readily adapts will be often able to secure a competitive advantage.

10 Channel profitability

We have outlined the key selection criteria for channel members. We have looked at how channel selection ensures the right product is available to the right customer at the right time. It should also be at the right price.

An organisation will want to maximise its return on investment (ROI). This determines the price that needs to be charged to produce a specific return on the organisation's investment. To calculate ROI an organisation needs to clearly establish not only its costs, but potential revenue streams which will flow through.

Channel members are an important contributor to overall profit as they:

- Generate long-term relationships which produce 'repeat' business.
- Reduce inefficiencies by combining activities or undertaking activities they are uniquely skilled to carry out.
- Reduce cost, by having highly structured processes and systems which mean the time from when the product is manufactured to the time it is sold is much faster.
- Add value at stages of the process.

The Chartered Institute of Marketing

Clearly the value added by channel members has to be more than the cost of carrying out that activity and this must be continually monitored.

11 Competitor strategies

It is usually expected that competition for an organisation's products would come from outside of its own distribution channel. However, the often complex nature of distribution channels and the interconnectivity between channel members, who may also have relationships with customers and suppliers through other distribution channels, can bring about competition from within the channel as well as beyond it.

Palamountain (1955) suggests four types of competition shown in Figure 5.8.

Figure 5.8   Palamountain (1955) suggests four types of competition

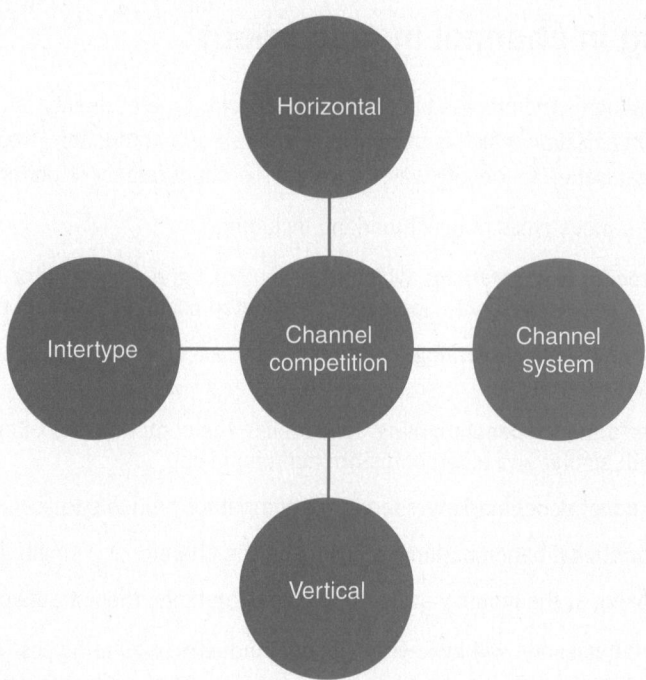

11.1 Horizontal competition

This is where competition occurs between intermediaries of the same type, eg wholesalers where each may seek to develop marketing or product strategies to gain a competitive advantage over the other. Some may chose a broad range of products, with little choice within the category; others may choose a small but deep product range.

11.2 Intertype competition

Here competition takes place at the same level in the channel, eg a bicycle manufacturer wants to make its bicycles available to a broad range of customers. It has a choice of selling through high street retailers, small local shops, or national chains which operate out of town.

The manufacturer would need to develop different strategies for each outlet, but overall it must be seen to be fair and even-handed. Unnecessarily favouring one outlet leads to frustration in the channel, and also customer dissatisfaction if they find they cannot make the purchase from their chosen outlet, possibly because the manufacturer makes stock available to the larger retailer in preference to the small independent retailer.

11.3 Vertical competition

Competition takes place at different levels in the channel, eg between wholesaler and retailer.

11.4 Channel system competition

In channel system competition a channel of distribution is in competition with another, but parallel, distribution channel.

This is now common in the motor industry. Tyre manufacturers compete with each other so that each wants to be the first choice for the consumer (or retailer). They will want to ensure adequate stock is always in place, that the marketing messages encourage purchase and replacements are readily available. The competition will be looking at the other channels and will similarly want to make sure their channel is performing better.

---

12 Benchmarking in channel management

Benchmarking is the process of comparing the cost, time or quality of company products against that of another organisation which is usually best in class or a competitor. Knowing how you compare is a useful way for an organisation to identify ways to improve product quality or performance in order to gain more business.

There are various types of benchmarking including:

- **Process benchmarking**: which involves looking at a competitor's processes and identifying best practice. It is also necessary to apply some estimated costings to the processes being observed.

- **Financial benchmarking**: undertaking a financial evaluation in order to establish and assess your overall competitiveness.

- **Performance benchmarking**: to establish the competitive position by evaluating competitor products with similar and different distribution channels.

- **Product benchmarking**: identifying competitor products to secure ideas for new products of your own.

- **Functional benchmarking**: focusing on the channel or a single aspect of it such as finance or logistics.

When looking at the industry sector or overseas markets, then strategic benchmarking could be employed.

Often an organisation will look within its own industry to identify 'best in class'. However, it is often unwise just to look within the industry. Looking outside will identify world class organisations and improve procedures.

An organisation can choose to benchmark any aspect of its process in order to improve its performance. Table 5.2 provides some examples.

The Chartered Institute of Marketing

Table 5.2   An organisation can choose to benchmark any aspect of its process in order to improve its performance

Marketing mix	<ul><li>Product: sales by segment, warranty claims, market share</li><li>Price: price by segment, discount levels</li><li>Place: channel costs, channel volumes, stock levels, delivery time</li><li>Promotion: cost per contact, media coverage, sales per telephone call</li></ul>
The organisational structure	<ul><li>Number of employees</li><li>DMU constitution</li><li>Staffing structure</li><li>Roles and responsibilities</li></ul>
Resources	<ul><li>Utilisation of plant and equipment</li></ul>
Financials	<ul><li>ROI</li><li>Profitability</li></ul>

Camp (1989) suggests that an organisation that benchmarks itself derives the following benefits:

- Best practice from other industries can be adapted and implemented as part of the organisation's own systems and procedures

- Benchmarking provides motivation to improve organisational processes.

- Reluctance to change can often be overcome. People are often more receptive to change when it originates outside their own organisation or industry.

- A technological breakthrough can occasionally be achieved.

13 Ethical considerations in channel management

Marketing ethics are the principles and standards that define acceptable marketing conduct as determined by the various stakeholders, including government regulators, private interest groups, consumers, industry as well as the organisation itself. An ethical issue has been defined as an identifiable problem, situation, or opportunity requiring a choice between several actions that must be evaluated as right or wrong.

Increasingly organisations are being viewed not just on the products sold, but on their ethical credentials. Many organisations publish a code of ethics, so stakeholders are aware of the standards that they can expect to be adhered to. There is generally an understanding that being ethical is the norm and in line with customer expectations.

Given the nature of distribution channels the following outlines a range of ethical considerations:

- Does the channel result in higher prices for the end user?
- Are prices open and transparent?
- Is the product fit for purpose?
- Are staff sufficiently trained to ensure staff provide reliable and informed information?
- Changes to terms and conditions?

For e-channels the American Marketing Association (AMA) has developed a code of ethics. This *inter alia* refers to:

- Ethical practices being applied to stakeholders
- The rights and privacy and access to information
- Risks and polices relating to internet marketing

Marketing is concerned with delivering value through longer-term relationships. Organisations therefore need to behave in such a way that stakeholders will want to continue working or buying from each other.

Organisations need to be aware of the ramifications of their actions and a formal process of Corporate Social Responsibility (CSR) needs to be established.

Figure 5.9 (Carroll, 1991) recognises the different stages an organisation goes through or remains at and is used to recognise and measure the dimensions of its Corporate Social Responsibility (CSR) policy.

Figure 5.9   The different stages an organisation goes through or remains at

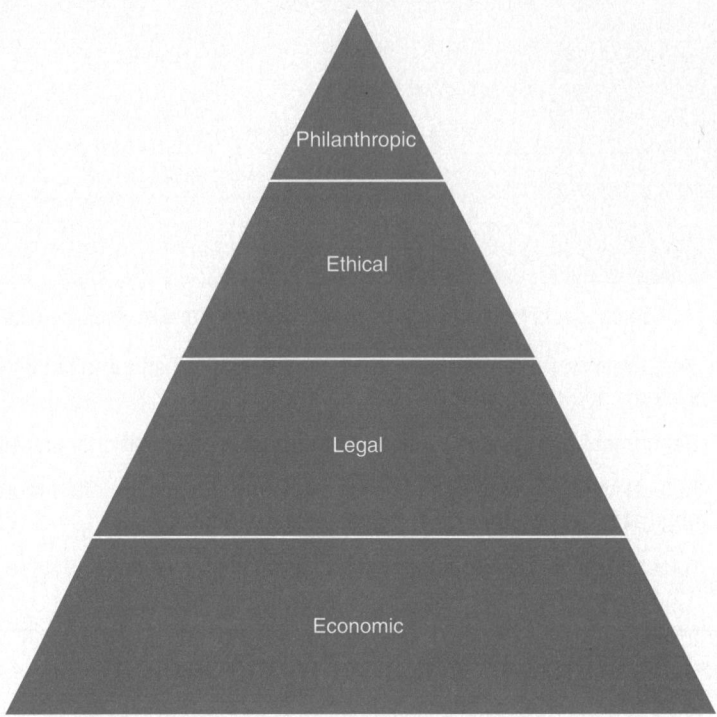

The pyramid suggests that there are four levels against which an organisation can measure itself.

13.1 Economic

At the very least an organisation has a responsibility to its stakeholders to be profitable so employees can continue to be employed and benefits can accrue to the local community. However, size can give an organisation undue influence over a sector.

13.2 Legal

It is expected that all organisations operate within the law, but where there are long distribution channels covering different countries this can prove problematical. Competition law and fair trade practices need to be considered. Often organisations will introduce their own polices on what is acceptable within the law.

13.3 Ethical

Ethics define what is right and wrong by establishing a set of guiding principles for people or organisations to work to.

For many organisations the concept of ethics has been successfully used to gain new business. Indeed, a number of organisations have built their entire business around ethical considerations, eg The Body Shop.

 The Chartered
Institute of Marketing

13.4 Philanthropic

An organisation can be the ultimate 'corporate citizen' where it works in partnership with the local community for mutual gain.

Some ethical concerns include:

- Misleading or false advertising where the product or price is misleading
- Shocking, tasteless or indecent material
- High pressure sales techniques to encourage purchase when it may not be in the consumers' best interests
- Payment of bribes to secure business or keep competitors out of the distribution channel
- Reward systems should be open and fair
- Privacy and respect for members of the channel

In the UK there has been an increasing trend for larger supermarket chains to purchase 'corner shops', or convenience stores. These shops would typically serve the needs of the local community by having long opening hours, but would charge a premium on the price for the goods sold.

Restrictions on opening out-of-town stores has meant that supermarkets have been looking for alternative locations and have been buying small local chains to increase their market share.

Local towns have been campaigning to retain their local stores and prevent the large supermarkets opening, because the residents claim the supermarkets are putting local shops out of business and people out of work.

THE REAL WORLD

Many retailers now adopt a highly visible stance in respect of their commitment to ethics and to sustainability generally, in particular through their outlets and throughout the supply chain. MINI has been high profile in its commitment to sustainability, across all elements of the marketing mix, but in particular to the sustainability of its outlets. Primark too, even though it is recognised as a 'low price' retailer has been high profile in its commitment to ethical trading throughout its various intermediaries in the supply chain.

14 Channel innovation

There are various definitions of what innovation is and innovation has already been discussed in the broad sense of product development. Here the focus are on innovation in the distribution channel.

Innovation is concerned with the introduction of new aspects or procedures in the channel so that costs, efficiencies and customer satisfaction are improved.

In particular, intermediaries can offer new products as a result of their position in the channel and their relationship with other members. This could lead to improved customer delivery times through the introduction of more effective ordering systems.

Through customer feedback, organisations may find that unacceptable level of goods are damaged upon receipt. New forms of packaging, or better procedures (training or the physical act of packaging) could reduce the complaints to a more acceptable (industry standard) level.

Increasingly the concept of just-in-time supply is being utilised. This often involves the introduction of sophisticated computerised ordering and product systems. Car manufacturers utilise this approach, eg as a completed car leaves the factory exit, new replacement components are being delivered to the entrance to be

incorporated into the next car. This requires the components manufacturer and the car manufacturer to work closely together to achieve these synergies.

Generating cost efficiencies is important. Competition in the market is usually intense and any additional margin that can be achieved can make a difference to sales.

While mass production techniques are important, technology now allows for high levels of customisation within the process. Many car manufacturers today offer the customer a wide range of choices in terms of colours, fabrics (for seats), wheel design and other extras.

Innovation can be linked to performance and growth through improvements in efficiency, productivity, quality, positioning, market share and customer satisfaction. While it is evident that all organisations are capable of innovation, not all do, either because they choose not to, or do not have the processes in place to facilitate innovation.

It is important to recognise and reward innovation which brings about improvements However, innovation comes about through research and competitor analysis and a balance needs to be struck between the costs of research and development and the potential benefits to be derived.

Increasingly we are seeing trends in the market where organisations are actively seeking to reduce the number of intermediaries (not levels, but the physical number) to develop collaborative relationships to support innovation and added value; just-in-time supply is a good example of this concept. Organisations will work together towards joint targets and effect solutions to problems that individually would have been difficult to solve.

All organisations, whatever their shape or size, face the constant challenge of innovation. To be effective the process needs to be managed cross functionally and typically interdisciplinary teams are formed to bring together a broad range of skills and knowledge.

15 New and emerging channels

The cost of setting up a new distribution channel is costly and time consuming. A manufacturer who opens a new channel to market risks upsetting existing channel members if it is not handled sensitively and in line with any agreements in place.

The concept of emerging channels is fundamentally different and can radically change the way in which products are distributed and sold.

The 'corner shop' once operated by individuals who served the needs of the local economy is being replaced by the main UK supermarkets.

Supermarkets also have petrol stations located near the store and we are seeing supermarkets move into house sales, car retailing and, with the change in legislation, into legal services. All of which change the nature of the distribution channel and the way we purchase.

Banks in the early 1990s generally believed that the internet would speed up the rate at which bank branches would close. The feeling was that customers would prefer to bank via the internet as it offered convenience and flexibility. In fact branches did not close down and the internet became only another channel for customers to access their money.

E-marketing has brought about disintermediation, ie eliminating channel members who no longer have a role to play. The internet had a major impact on the travel industry. It spawned the arrival of no-frills airlines that embraced technology and allowed customers to design their own travel itinerary which was a serious concern to travel agents. While this goes against the role of intermediaries, ie they are there to bring a range of products to the end user when they need it, the internet has brought a new type of intermediary who 'aggregates' products in one place and this in turn has brought about reintermediation ie the addition of a new channel member.

The role of the internet is to challenge conventional channels, which will need to adapt if they are to remain successful. Tesco, Asda and Sainsbury's are integrating the online shopping channel with the more conventional trip to the supermarket.

Consider the impact of Amazon and i-Tunes on the purchase and distribution of books and music.

While the extranet is a useful way for organisations to communicate with each other, it also a useful tool to manage distribution channels. Selected stakeholders will be given access to a specific area of the website where a range of key information can be accessed. Key management information can be located on the extranet allowing stakeholders access to a pool of data covering (for example) supply dates, volume discounts, and transaction levels.

Where there is no market sensitivity to data, catalogues known as e-catalogues can be posted on the website. Other uses of the web include:

- CMS – contract management systems that replace many of the paper-based systems previously used in distribution channels. Legal agreements can be issued through CMS along with performance management, ie how well the intermediary performs against targets.

- E-commerce, payment to and from intermediaries. This can cover automated invoicing or the movement of funds between the various intermediaries.

- EDI (Electronic Data Interchange) where standard documents used between the parties can be accessed.

While new channels do not have to be technology based, increasingly this is the case. The following offers a summary of the impact of emerging channels:

- **Quality of service**: the Royal Mail and other courier companies offer services which allow the customer to track exactly where the item is located.

- **Greater product ranges**: different channels can stock different product ranges.

- **Low costs**: through the elimination of intermediaries (see Chapter 6) that can be replaced by cheaper electronic channels.

- **Virtual channels** can be established through a 'virtual' group of intermediaries located around the globe.

- **Team working and partnerships** are improved. Electronic channels can allow existing members to access information that would have been difficult to obtain in a timely fashion.

THE REAL WORLD

Financial services channels

The changing face of channels in financial services

There is no doubt that technology has changed the face of the financial services landscape beyond recognition. Only a generation ago, consumer banking transactions across the globe were predominantly carried out in branches, which represented the only channel for customers. Many of these branches were heavily focused on back-office activities, carrying out much of their own transaction processing with relatively minimal resources focused on the customer interface.

It was not until the 1970s when the first ATMs were installed on a major scale, and even then their functionality was restricted to only making cash withdrawals. It took almost another twenty years before the first 'non-physical' banks entered the market, with First Direct being the first such bank in the UK. It had no branch network and customer access was by telephone only. It was around ten years later, with the advent of the internet, that it launched its first online service for consumer customers.

Nowadays, the flexibility that technology has brought to financial services is very much taken for granted. Many customers now enjoy a choice of channels including branches, ATMs, telephony, online and mobile. However, these changes have not been welcomed by everyone. Indeed, there is a view that the 'good old days' of branch banking created many more sales opportunities and offered customers a much better standard of service, although there is no doubt that operational benefits have far outweighed any potential drawbacks for the providers themselves. However a challenge for the providers is ensuring consistency (of brand and service) across all the channels they operate.

---

16 Criteria for selecting new channel partners

In this chapter we have discussed the numerous influences on channel strategy and the different approaches that can be adopted. In the next chapter we will be considering the roles of different intermediaries within different channel structures.

A key consideration for any organisation, having decided on its channel management strategy, are the criteria it should adopt to choose new channel partners. Typical criteria might include:

- Does the organisation meet the requirements of the chosen channel strategy?
- The experience of the organisation with the particular product / sector.
- The organisation's reputation.
- The 'reach' of the organisation, ie can sufficient customers access products via the organisation?
- Is there a 'fit' between the two organisations? Are they culturally-aligned and share common goals?
- Can acceptable pricing be agreed?
- Is it possible to agree terms and conditions?
- Can the organisation deliver to the required service standards?
- Does the organisation deal with competitors, which may lead to a potential conflict of interest?
- Can we do business with them, ie will it be possible to interact with them on a personal level?

▶ **Exam tip**

In June 2010, Daler-Rowney case, Task Two required students to:

'Explain Daler-Rowney's channel management strategy, giving consideration to the factors that have influenced its choice.'

The question comprised two elements, both of which should have been addressed fully.

Students should have provided an explanation of the current approach, which was set out in the case study. Simply repeating what was written in the case was insufficient to gain marks and explanation was needed and students were expected to provided their own views to justify the approaches adopted, which, broadly, were:

- Direct to educational establishments via direct sales force
- Direct to consumers/businesses via online channel
- Wholesale/retail distribution via intermediaries.

There are many factors that are likely to influence channel choice, for example market coverage (ie access to customers in the segment), costs, profit potential, control, expertise of the intermediary, brand alignment, strategic fit, access to overseas markets (if required), the intermediary's track record and reputation. Importantly, channel partner choice will also be influenced by whether or not the intermediary deals with any of the organisation's competitors. It goes without saying that these factors needed to be discussed in the context of Daler-Rowney and applying wherever possible the student's pre-prepared analysis.

CHAPTER ROUNDUP

- Channel management is an important element of the marketing mix (place).

- Channel management focuses on delivery of the organisation's products and services to the end customer.

- There are different channel structures which are used in different markets.

- Channel partners have important functions and can be critical to the end customer's overall 'experience'.

- Channel misalignment can have disastrous consequences for the organisation.

- Choosing the right distribution strategy is vital, ie exclusive, selective or intensive.

- There are many influences of channel strategy, eg the type of products, the chosen customer segment and the organisation's objectives.

- There are recognised options for entering overseas markets, eg exporting, joint ventures and direct investment.

- The effective management of relationships with channel partners is crucial.

- Cateora's 5Cs is a useful tool to managing and evaluating channel partners.

- Clear and regular communications are vital with all channel intermediaries.

- Competitor channel strategies should be closely monitored and analysed.

- Benchmarking is an effective way to track changes in competitor approaches and to identify 'gaps' in comparison with the organisation's own approach to channel management (and the impact on customers).

- Increasingly, ethical considerations are playing a vital role in channel management.

- Innovation has had a major impact on channels.

- Technology in particular has changed the face of how products and services are delivered to customers in some markets.

FURTHER READING

This paper discusses some the issues in channel management:

Wren, B.M. (2007). Channel structure and strategic choice in distribution channels. *Journal of Management Research*, Vol 7(2), pp78-86.

REFERENCES

Brassington, F. and Pettit, S.(2007) *Essentials of marketing.* 2nd edition. Harlow, Pearson Education.

Camp, P.E. (1989) *Benchmarking: The search for industry best practices that lead to superior performance.* New York, ASQC Quality Press.

Carroll, A.B. (1999) Corporate Social Responsibility: Evolution of a Definitional Construct. *Business and Society*, Vol. 38(3), pp.268-95.

Cateora, P.R. (1993) *International marketing.* 8th edition. Boston, Irwin.

Fill, C. (2006) *Marketing communications: engagement, strategies and practice.* 4th edition. Oxford, FT Prentice Hall.

Kotler, P. *et al* (1999) *Principles of marketing.* 2nd European edition. Harlow, Prentice Hall.

Palamountain, J. (1955) *The politics of distribution*. Boston, Harvard Business Press.

Paliwoda, S. (1993) *International marketing*. Oxford, Butterworth-Heinemann.

Stern, L.W. *et al* (1996), *Marketing channels.* 5th edition. New Jersey, Prentice-Hall.

QUICK QUIZ

1   What is the main function of a distribution channel?

2   What is an intermediary?

3   What are the three distribution strategies?

4   What type of distribution strategy does the store Harrods adopt?

5   What are Cateora's 5Cs?

6   What are the three types of vertical marketing system?

7   What are the three main distribution options for entering a new overseas market?

8   What is the role of an agent?

9   Describe some of the ways that channel members might contribute to the organisation's overall profit.

10   What is the role of benchmarking in channel management?

ACTIVITY DEBRIEFS

Activity 5.1

The answer to this activity is very much dependent on the organisation chosen and in particular if the organisation operates in the B2B or B2C market. Typical structures are shown in Figures 5.2 and 5.3. The rationale for the approach will depend on the market and the nature of the products/services delivered. Costs are also a key factor. The ability to, potentially, gain competitive advantage through the channel approach will also be a key consideration.

Activity 5.2

- Exclusive distribution is applied by organisations operating in niche markets. Associated with high value/premium brands. Often outlets are rare, reinforcing the feeling of exclusivity with customers.

- Selective distribution is applied by organisations which are operating in a larger market than those with exclusive approaches. However, the positioning of the brand is still relatively high quality.

- Intensive distribution is applied by organisations operating in the mass market. Its products are very widely available from many outlets.

Activity 5.3

There are a number of considerations, including:

- Strategic fit
- Product suitability
- Profit potential
- Speed of reaching customers
- Relationship, ie is it possible to build/maintain a relationship with the partner?

QUICK QUIZ ANSWERS

1   Distribution channels are used to deliver products and services to the end customer.

2   Channel intermediaries can comprise a multitude of organisations including wholesalers, retailers, logistics companies and agents. They are effectively involved, in some way or another in the movement/delivery of products/services through the supply chain and, ultimately, to the end customer.

3   Exclusive, selective and intensive.

4   Harrods has very few outlets and is recognised as being a very high quality and prestigious brand. It adopts an exclusive distribution strategy.

5   Coverage, character, continuity, control and cost.

6   Corporate VMS, contractual VMS and administered VMS.

7   Exporting, joint ventures and direct investment.

8   Generally agents are useful where it is not possible for an organisation to have their own physical presence/operation delivering a function within the channel structure.

9   Channel members may provide 'reach' to customers. They might offer potential competitive advantage. They can offer 'value add' by contributing to the organisation's overall customer value proposition. They can also help generate sales and therefore, ultimately' contribute to profit. Some channel members might offer/provide customer service.

10 Benchmarking enables the organisation to compare the cost, quality and performance of channel members, against themselves and against those used by the competition.

Channel intermediaries and stakeholders

Introduction

Having examined the different types of channel strategies, we will now consider the various intermediaries which are most commonly found within channel structures. In this chapter we will also consider the importance and role of the broader stakeholder community.

Topic list

Type of intermediaries (1)

The role of the intermediary (2)

Appointing new channel intermediaries (3)

Impact of intermediaries on profitability (4)

Stakeholders in channel management (5)

Stakeholders defined (6)

Stakeholder needs (7)

Managing stakeholders (8)

The nature of the stake (9)

Categorising stakeholders (10)

Dealing with conflict in the channel (11)

Communicating with stakeholders (12)

2.3	Assess the nature and scope of intermediaries and determine criteria for selecting intermediary partners and the likely return on investment (ROI) they can achieve
	■ Different types of intermediaries in distribution and the strengths and weaknesses of each
	■ Level of innovation and development demonstrated
	■ The roles and responsibilities of intermediaries in distribution
	■ Criteria for selecting intermediaries
	■ How intermediaries can influence profitability
	■ Impact of new and emerging channels
2.4	Determine the level and scope of controls required for effectively monitoring and managing distribution channels
	■ Setting objectives
	■ Monitoring performance of distribution channels
	■ Benchmarking of other sectors/organisations/countries
	■ Managing third party relationships in channel management, locally and internationally
2.5	Assess the requirements for managing the various stakeholders' needs within the distribution channel, in particular reviews, reporting, communications and conflict management
	■ Identification of the key stakeholders in channel management
	■ Determining stakeholders' needs in channel management
	■ The role of information in channel management
	■ The importance of communications in channel management, locally, internationally and globally
	■ Potential sources of conflict in local and international markets
	■ Reducing time to market
	■ Competitor conflicts
	■ Identifying, managing and resolving conflict

1 Type of intermediaries

> ▶ **Key term**
>
> **Channel intermediary:** an organisation which is part of the channel structure and which plays a role in the delivery of goods or services to the end customer.

An intermediary is an organisation or individual through which goods pass on their way from the manufacturing organisation to the consumer.

There are different types of intermediary. Each intermediary has a different role to fulfil which may also include taking legal ownership of the goods, adding some form of value (eg customer service), volume (ie storing goods) and/or then selling smaller quantities to other intermediaries or the end user. The types of intermediary and descriptions of their roles are shown in Table 6.1.

Table 6.1   Intermediaries and descriptions of their roles

Type of intermediary	Description
Wholesalers	Not usually consumer facing, but will typically deal with other intermediaries in the channel. Ownership of the product is a feature along with physical possession.
	Wholesalers will usually take in bulk and distribute to other intermediaries in smaller quantities. They can be categorised into:

Type of intermediary	Description

	■ **Merchant wholesalers**: independently owned businesses that take title to the goods and include full-service and limited service wholesalers (see below)
	
	■ **Full service wholesalers**: these wholesalers offer services such as maintaining stock levels. They will have a sales team and offer credit facilities. Additionally they will provide a delivery service. There are two types of full-service wholesaler: wholesale merchants and industrial distributors.
	
	   – Wholesale merchants: sell primarily to retailers and offer a full range of services
	
	   – Industrial distributors: sell to manufacturers rather than retailers and similarly offer credit and delivery services
	
	■ **Limited service wholesalers**: as the name implies they offer a reduced level of services and include: cash-and-carry and mail order wholesalers.
	
	   – Cash-and-carry: this group carries a small to medium range of goods typically fast moving consumer goods which are sold to small retailers mainly for cash
	
	   – Mail order: responsible for distributing catalogues through the post or courier

Retailers	Consumer-facing and will have purchased the products from the wholesaler (above) or direct from the manufacturer. Retailers take ownership and physical possession and sell direct to the consumer. Retailers vary in size, product and location. Examples of retailers include: supermarkets, department stores, convenience stores, speciality stores and factory outlets.
Distributors/dealers	Distributors have the right to sell the products in a defined geographical area and can add value to the product by making it available locally to the consumer. Dealers add value by offering their expertise as well as representing the manufacturer. They don't always take ownership of the product and typically represent the manufacturer, eg a car dealership
Franchisees	The most common franchise allows the franchisee (the person or business who has the contract) to sell a specific product or service in accordance with the terms agreed with the franchisor. In return for a payment (fixed fee, percentage of turnover or both) the franchisor shares much of the intellectual property rights of running the business.
Licensee	Similar to a franchise, but not as comprehensive. Typically the licensee is given the right to operate a business for a particular organisation within a given area.

Agents/brokers	This group of intermediaries will act on behalf of the organisation, but will not take ownership or legal title to the product. Their role is to generate wider distribution and make the product more accessible to the customer.
	
	■ **Brokers**: Their role is primarily to bring the buyer together with the seller. They do not hold any stock and get paid by the manufacturer when the sale has been completed. A typical example would be an insurance broker.
	
	■ **Agents**: There are four types of agent: manufacturers', selling, purchasing and commission merchants.
	
	   – Manufacturers' agent: sell similar lines from more than one manufacturer. A formal contract is agreed between the parties and these agents are often used when a manufacturer cannot afford its own sales force.
	
	   – Selling agent: A selling agent has the ability to sell a manufacturer's entire range.
	
	   – Purchasing agent: These agents will buy goods, receive them and inspect them for quality.
	
	   – Commission merchants: Here possession of the goods is obtained and takes a range of goods to a central point to be sold. Payment is by way of commission.

2 The role of the intermediary

The role of the intermediary is to simplify the distribution process, add value and reduce costs.

Webster (1979) suggests there are three groups of value-added service provided by intermediaries as seen in Figure 6.1:

- Facilitating
- Transactional
- Logistics

Figure 6.1 Three groups of value-added service provided by intermediaries (based on Webster, 1979)

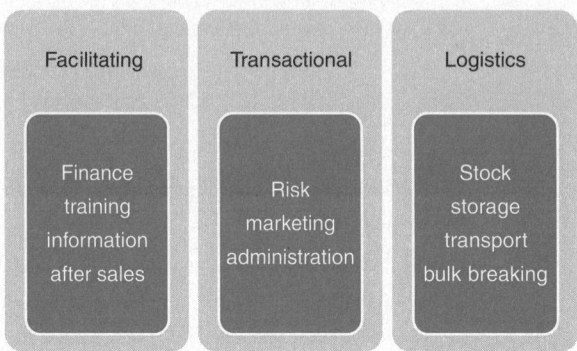

Intermediaries may perform one or more of these tasks. Beamish and Ashford (2008) have broken these elements down and Table 6.2 is based on their assessment.

Table 6.2 Intermediary tasks

Element	Description
Information	Collection and distribution of market research and intelligence data, such as sales data to help the planning process.
Management	Setting objectives and channel plans along with any risk that needs to be taken or managed.
Matching	Adjusting the offer to fit a buyer's needs, including grading, assembling and packaging.
Promotion	Setting promotional objectives and communicating through the different tools.
Price	Setting pricing policies and financing policies.
Distribution	Managing the transport, storing and stock control of goods.
Customer service	Providing channels for advice support and after sales service.
Relationships	Facilitating communication and maintaining relationships in the channel.

3 Appointing new channel intermediaries

The final stage of developing a new channel is to select those organisations that are going to undertake the various roles within the channel.

Channel members are appointed as part of a channel strategy, when a number of intermediaries may be appointed, or when circumstances require a new appointment. There are various reasons to appoint a new channel member including:

- Unsatisfactory performance of an existing member
- Intermediary ceases trading or declines to renew contact
- Conflicts of interest

The Chartered Institute of Marketing

- Expansion of the network requiring new intermediaries and skills
- Market expansion

Selection is important and should be made against clearly defined criteria. These were explored in the previous chapter.

4 Impact of intermediaries on profitability

It has already been stated that the role of the intermediary is to add value and reduce costs and an important consequence of this is to increase the manufacturer's overall profitability.

Intermediaries provide a range of services that the manufacturer may not have the skills or resources to undertake. A manufacturer may be skilled in manufacturing widgets but will not have the capability to ship the goods overseas.

Intermediaries can impact on profitability in the following ways:

- **Increased sales**: the intermediary can have its own sales team with an expert knowledge of the domestic and overseas markets

- As the intermediary will often take ownership of the goods, it will also **take responsibility for taking stock away from the manufacturer**, so if goods do not sell this will not impact on the manufacturer's profits

- **Packaging together** of groups of products to widen customer choice and appeal

- **Efficiency**: rather than dealing with possibly hundreds of retailers, distribution and hence control can be managed through a few (for example) wholesalers

- **Warehousing and transport costs can be shared** with other organisations, which may also eliminate the need for purpose-built facilities

- The value added by the intermediary may allow the price of the product to be **premium priced**.

THE REAL WORLD

For many manufacturing organisations the identification and appointment of new channel partners is a key decision, which might lead to overall success or failure of the business as a whole. For Procter & Gamble, for example, it is dependent on retail outlets owned and operated by other organisations enabling customers to access its products. Therefore the careful selection and management of these intermediaries within the channel structure are vital for the future of the organisation.

ACTIVITY 6.1

Identify ways in which intermediaries might have an adverse impact on the organisation's profitability.

5 Stakeholders in channel management

Channel members are also stakeholders (Johnson and Scholes, 2005).

We have seen that the distribution channel is a complex web of relationships and this chapter explores the concept of stakeholders in more detail, outlines the 'six' markets model and examines the concept of stakeholder analysis.

Organisations use intermediaries or distributors to get their products to the consumer and the various intermediaries will themselves have relationships with other suppliers' distributors, ie multiple stakeholders, and the importance of building relationships with these groups needs to be understood.

Such a diverse stakeholder group often presents organisational difficulties, ie how do you manage the relationships effectively when so many different divisions are involved in the process, so that there is co-ordinated effort and communication?

THE REAL WORLD

An organisation's stakeholders can have a significant influence on the marketing decisions it makes and the strategy it adopts. Even the choice of its customers can have a significant reaction, sometimes, from other stakeholders. This reaction can often lead to intentional loss of customers, where pressure has been exerted by stakeholders. The organisation will mostly take this decision due to the impact on its reputation and brand and the consequent potential impact on future revenues and profits.

Many organisations have experienced this in the past, for example when transacting with businesses which carry out testing on animals and, as a result, become targets of animal rights groups. Banks, in particular, are potentially exposed by the activities of customers, if these activities raise concerns for certain individuals and groups.

---

6 Stakeholders defined

> **Key term**
>
> **Stakeholder:** any individual, group, organisation or body which is might affect or be affected by an organisation's decisions and/or activities.

Stakeholders can comprise many different individuals, groups, organisations and bodies. To be classified as an organisation's stakeholder the individual, group, organisation or body must affect or be affected by an organisation's decisions and/or activities. Essentially, a stakeholder is anyone with an interest in the organisation and/or its activities.

Channel members are connected stakeholders, ie they have an economic or contractual relationship with the organisation.

Fill (2006) suggests that there are two main concerns when moving a product through the distribution channel:

- Management of the product (supply chain)
- Management of the intangible aspects of ownership and the communication between the different stakeholders

Our focus has been on the latter aspect and we will continue to examine this in more detail by determining the needs of the individual stakeholders within the channel.

We will see later in the chapter that stakeholders build up a complex set of relationships and that the various members of the channel can in fact be customers of each other and a series of networks can be established.

Organisations enter into partnerships because they see mutual benefit and an important element of maintaining these mutually beneficial relationships is the communication that takes place between the stakeholders.

It is necessary to understand the needs of stakeholders and this can be achieved through a stakeholder audit.

Having identified who the key stakeholders are through the process of mapping they are grouped together to identify the interdependencies between the stakeholders and establish any networks that may have been established.

The strength of the relationships can then be assessed along with the 'fit' of stakeholder with the organisation's objectives. This will then determine the nature of the communications that will need to take place.

The Chartered Institute of Marketing

The analysis will include:

- What are the needs, concerns and interests of the stakeholders?
- What power and influence do the stakeholders have on each other and the channel as a whole?
- Are there are any conflicts or potential conflicts in the channel?

7 Stakeholder needs

The exact needs of stakeholders will vary between organisations. Table 6.3 sets out the generic needs of stakeholders: suppliers and intermediaries.

Table 6.3   Supplier and intermediary needs

Suppliers	<ul><li>Will want to build long-term relationships, so that any costs invested in the channel will be recovered with an acceptable financial margin</li><li>Participative relationship which allows for innovation and efficiency in the systems and processes used</li><li>Clarity of information through well documented processes and SLAs so that errors are minimised</li><li>Clear process for tendering or applying for new business</li><li>Terms of payment clearly stated and payments made within the agreed time.</li><li>Clear CSR policy</li></ul>
Intermediaries	<ul><li>Clear CSR policy, particularly relating to sourcing of materials</li><li>Continuity of supply, eg components and parts</li><li>Transparent remuneration policy, especially with other members of the channel</li><li>Clear rules on competition</li><li>Clarity on roles and responsibilities within the channel</li></ul>

Other stakeholders include:

- Shareholders
- Customers
- Financial providers

The needs of these stakeholders are also considered in Table 6.4.

Table 6.4   Stakeholder needs

Financial providers	■ On-going relationship to capture new business opportunities
	■ Capable management team
	■ Regular financial and monthly accounts to ensure that any finance extended can be repaid in accordance with the loan agreement
Shareholders	■ Acceptable financial return recognising the level of risk associated with the investment
	■ Market for the buying and selling of shares (depending on the legal status of the organisation)
	■ Top class management team so that opportunities for business growth can be identified and implemented leading to improved financial returns
Customers	The saying 'The customer is King' is still important today. If the customers do not like the product, or the way it is sold they will look elsewhere to satisfy their needs.
	■ Acceptable product at an acceptable price (will be a range of options in terms of acceptable price depending on product and segment)
	■ Ease of purchase through a range of channels
	■ Enjoyable purchasing experience

ACTIVITY 6.2

Identify the different types of stakeholders to an organisation with which you are familiar and consider the needs of each stakeholder that you have identified.

8 Managing stakeholders

▶ **Key term**

Six markets framework: a tool for undertaking analysis of key stakeholder markets.

The six markets framework (Figure 6.2) highlights the key stakeholder markets (sometimes referred to as 'market domains') enabling an organisation to manage relationships more effectively. The model reflects the fact that not all stakeholders are equally as important and distinctions must be made.

The Chartered Institute of Marketing

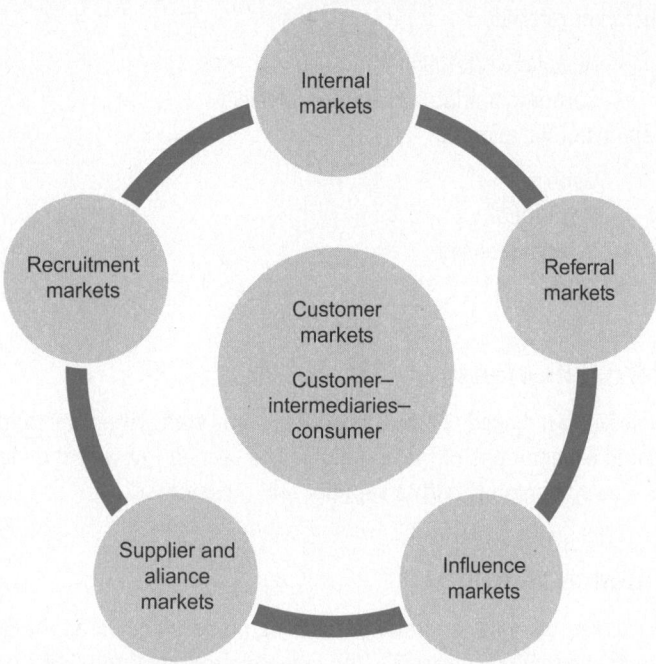

Christopher *et al* (2002) suggest that markets should be defined more broadly as being 'one in which the competing interests are made visible and therefore more likely to be managed'.

8.1 Customer markets

Relationship marketing has at its heart that an organisation must build lasting relationships with customers and the customer market is central to the six markets model.

The customer market reflects the distribution channel, which was discussed in Chapter 5.

But as a reminder, channels can be short, ie direct to the consumer. This is often used in financial services where a customer will make a purchase direct from a high street branch. B2B organisations include more complex examples, when wholesalers, distributors and retailers are included.

Organisations often develop informal referral groups, which as well as generating additional income also add value to the customer proposition.

8.2 Referral markets

Organisations work with their customers to move them through the ladder of loyalty so that they act as advocates actively marketing the organisation. However, non-customers such as third party introducers will also refer customers.

Customer recommendations are an important source of new business across all sectors and here business is directed to the supplier through sales leads.

Christopher *et al* (2002) break this category down into:

- Customer referrals
  - Advocacy referrals
  - Company initiates customer referrals
- Non-customer referrals
  - General
  - Reciprocal
  - Incentive-based
  - Staff

8.3 Internal markets

Internal markets are linked to two things: first, how staff within the company interact with each other to meet the goals and expectations of the company. The second involves the idea that every staff member is a potential customer – every person is both a supplier and a customer.

8.4 Influence markets

The B2B market has a more formal purchasing process known as the DMU (Decision Making Unit), also referred to as the buying centre. The individual members of the DMU can exert influences on the buying process and therefore each member needs to be carefully managed.

There are many external influences that impact on an organisation and these include:

- Government (local and central)
- Pressure groups
- Shareholders
- Press and media generally
- Trade unions

It can be a long list and it is generally recognised that the influence market includes the most diverse group of stakeholders.

8.5 Supplier and alliance markets

The supplier and alliance market refers to the partnerships an organisation builds with the supply chain in order to build efficient, cost effective value-adding activities.

Christopher *et al* (2002) suggest that supplier and alliance markets are viewed separately:

- **Supplier markets**: are suppliers who provide the organisation with the physical resources such as components, or the raw materials that go into the product. It is recognised the physical product can be augmented by services.

- **Alliance markets**: also suppliers but supply competencies and knowledge-based capabilities. Often this market develops because the organisation needed to outsource any activity previously undertaken in-house as part of the value chain. Collaboration, joint promotions, and strategic alliances are examples of alliance markets.

8.6 Recruitment markets

Increasingly people are becoming scarce resources and therefore organisations need to recruit, train and maintain the 'best' staff.

Organisations are not bound by geographical boundaries and will look to recruit staff from across the globe if necessary in order to ensure the continuity of the resource.

The recruitment can be categorised into:

- **The external labour market**: ie those people who have the skills to work for the organisation wherever they are located. Potential employees can interface directly with the organisation or through third parties (see below).

- **Third parties**: this group of people or organisations can facilitate access to the organisation or act as an access channel. This group includes:

    - Recruitment agencies
    - Executive search consultancies
    - Universities
    - Colleges
    - Staff

9 The nature of the stake

The nature of the relationship with individual stakeholders helps an organisation to:

- Recognise the role played by the stakeholder, its contribution to the channel, the implications of it not being there, and identify any potential conflicts which may arise through its relationship with other channel members or the extended enterprise.

- Keep the stakeholder motivated to ensure customer needs are met.

Channel members may have contractual, ie legal agreements to provide a specific role; failure to comply brings a range of penalties in law if the members have failed to carry out their responsibilities in the agreed manner, typically this would be seen in an Administered VMS.

However, there may be no legal agreement and through informal arrangements the member provides added-value services such as expertise, knowledge, resources or facilities.

Developing a distribution channel requires careful planning. The costs involved can be significant especially if a new facility, eg warehousing, is needed, or overseas selling becomes a feature. Consequently organisations will look to build long-term and lasting relationships with channel members as it is not in anyone's interests to start deconstructing the channel because of the additional (and unnecessary) costs and the additional work, which detract from the main purpose of sales and customer service.

10 Categorising stakeholders

> **Key term**
>
> **Mendelow's power/interest matrix:** a tool for categorising and analysing an organisation's stakeholders.

Some organisations can have many stakeholders, ie people or entities who/which have an interest in the organisation. These are commonly grouped as follows:

- Internal stakeholders – staff and management

- Connected stakeholders – customers, suppliers, financiers, brokers, intermediaries, shareholders

- External stakeholders – the community, the government, pressure groups

These various stakeholders have varying needs and can exert pressure on the organisation in order to influence its strategies and activities.

Mendelow (1991) developed the concept of stakeholder mapping based on stakeholder power/interest, enabling an organisation's management to identify and categorise the organisation's key stakeholders (see

Figure 6.3). The matrix enables the organisation to prioritise and allocate appropriate resources to stakeholder management. It also enables the organisation to develop appropriate communications and relationship management strategies for each stakeholder group.

Figure 6.3   Mendelow's stakeholder power/interest matrix

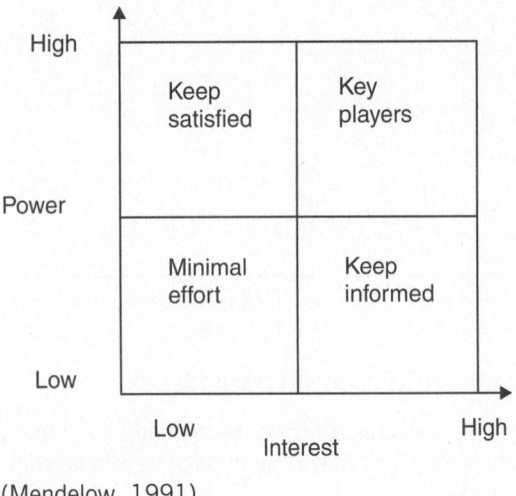

(Mendelow, 1991)

ACTIVITY 6.3

Using the stakeholders you identified in Activity 6.2, plot them on the Mendelow power/interest matrix and consider the approach you might adopt for each in terms of managing the relationship with them.

10.1 Stakeholder power

Having built a distribution channel we will see later that problems can arise and it is helpful to examine the 'power' that the various stakeholders can exert in the management of the channel.

Channels can take different forms and the stakeholders will need to agree roles and responsibilities. Stakeholders get their power from a range of sources. French and Raven (1960) defined a number of sources of power:

10.1.1 Legitimate power

Legitimate power arises from any legal agreement which may have been written to formalise the relationship between the parties.

An intermediary may have been appointed to undertake specific roles and therefore it can challenge anyone or any organisation that does not comply with the roles given to it.

Legitimate power also arises through a process of delegation where an organisation (or individual) allows their own power to be given to another party.

10.1.2 Expert power

An expert power intermediary may be appointed because of the skills or knowledge they possess. An international shipping company may be used to post products to customers, or because of the value added by the organisation.

The Chartered
Institute of Marketing

10.1.3 Reward power

This refers to the ability to reward other parties, perhaps with a bonus payment or additional business where performance targets have been achieved.

10.1.4 Referent power

Here power arises from the quality of the organisation because of its reputation in the market or the strength of its brand.

10.1.5 Coercive power

A dominant supplier in the distribution channel may withhold supply or work.

There may be other potential sources of power in stakeholder relationships including resource capability where one party is reliant on the other due to its superior skills and capacity. Dependency might also be another source of power. Here intermediaries actually cannot survive without each other and there is mutual dependency on each other.

Channels perform effectively when all the stakeholders are working together; otherwise the objectives initially set may be compromised and conflict between the members develops.

It must be clear where the balance of power lies. It does not necessarily need to rest with the manufacturer. However, having identified the channel leader, it must clearly guide the other channel members.

The different forms of power dependency raise another interesting area and that is 'conflict'.

11 Dealing with conflict in the channel

> ▶ **Key term**
>
> **Channel conflict:** the total breakdown, or deterioration, in the levels of co-operation between the channel, often caused by a disagreement between two or more intermediaries, conflict of interest or poor performance.

We have seen that co-operation between channel members delivers the best results.

No matter how good the planning process has been, conflict within the channel is likely to occur at some point and some form of conflict resolution mechanisms must be in place to deal with them. Conflict within the channel is effectively the total breakdown, or deterioration, in the levels of co-operation between the partners.

Conflict is a disagreement between two or more intermediaries or parties with different views or principles. It can arise from a huge variety of specific issues, or more general areas.

Brassington and Pettitt (2006) suggest examples that include exclusivity, payment terms, profit margins, appointment of new channel members, lack of information or co-operation.

Brassington and Pettitt (2006) also suggest there are broadly two different types of conflict; manifest and underlying conflict, which can then be grouped into five areas.

- **Manifest**: open conflict between the channel members which may potentially prevent achievement of the channel objectives/goals. Clear procedures need to be in place to address the problem.

- **Underlying**: while not overt, underlying conflict can easily develop into manifest conflict. It is important to identify the conflict at an early opportunity and take action in order to prevent the cessation of co-operation between channel members

Table 6.5, based on Brassington and Pettitt (2006), outlines the five areas for underlying conflicts.

Conflict in the channel, whether it is manifest or underlying, causes tension within the channel. It must be addressed if the organisations involved are to achieve their stated objectives. Some channels, as we have seen,

are simply a group of organisations that come together without any form of legal agreement and will exert a range of influences on channel members.

Table 6.5   Underlying conflict areas

Areas of conflict	Summary
Incompatible goals	Members of the channel disagree on a range of issues, including strategy, new ways of doing things, or financial returns. ■ A manufacturer may want to widen the channel, by opening up new markets. Existing members may object because additional investment may be necessary or it conflicts with their other business. ■ A retailer who is failing to achieve target margins, may want to reduce the amount of stock held to reduce costs and improve margins
Role conflict	Members of the channel cannot agree on the role each should take. ■ The manufacturer believes the retailer should take responsibility for managing the promotional aspects at point of sale. However, the retailer may not agree, believing the manufacturer has more experience.
Domain differences	This concerns who should make the marketing decisions
Perceptions of reality	Different channel members may interpret issues in different ways ■ An intermediary may perceive the use of technology by the buying organisation as a threat, whereas in reality it might streamline order processing and improve efficiency.
Expectations	Changed circumstances may bring about a change in the way channel members want to do things in the future. ■ A downturn in the British economy causes a manufacturer to consider its options. It decides to reduce production by 50% for six months and maintain margins. Channel members may prefer to see price and margin reductions, but try to expand the market.

Some members will have significant influence over members; this can be termed power dependency.

Power dependency can manifest itself in a number of ways;

■ **Reward power**: where one channel member has the ability to reward another member
■ **Coercive power**: rather than rewarding a channel member, a form of penalty could be imposed
■ **Expert power**: where the member is seen as having some specialist knowledge not easily replaceable

While conflict is generally not to be encouraged, if managed correctly it can improve a distribution channel. A member who runs a distribution depot may express concern at the length of time goods have to remain in storage before being transported to the retail stores. Rather than demand extra money, a better solution would be to re-engineer the process to make it more effective which is to the benefit of the entire channel.

At the heart of any relationship is the concept of trust. In the context of channel management, trust is the belief that another company will perform actions that will result in positive outcomes for the other channel partners. In addition it is also the belief that others in the channel will not take any unexpected actions that would result in negative outcomes for other channel partners.

When trust is lost within the channel it is much harder to build back relationships as the stakeholders are less likely to share information.

Communication and information exchange between channel members builds trust, promotes supportive relationships and minimises conflict.

It has been suggested by Leuthesser (1997) that information can be exchanged between channel members in three different ways:

- Initiating behaviour
- Signalling behaviour
- Disclosing

Initiating behaviour involves a better understanding of the needs of the stakeholders so that they can add greater value to the process, and also ensures that co-operation improves the position of the parties within the channel.

Signalling behaviour involves the giving of additional information to the stakeholders in advance about future changes that may be about to take place.

Finally, disclosing behaviour occurs where one stakeholder gives information that may affect the other's position.

Trust offers the opportunity to engage in mutually beneficial behaviour and encourage openness.

Regaining trust reduces the effects of any damage caused by previous conflict and helps to build back relationships quickly.

Transparency also helps address conflict by developing a mutual understanding of the various parties' needs, possibly through the exchange of information which supports the concepts of trust and commitment.

Building commitment, which is the desire of one or more stakeholders to continue in a relationship, also contributes to overcoming conflict.

Conflict is clearly best avoided but once identified needs to be managed effectively and some guiding principles have been given above.

In practice, organisations will need to have in place a comprehensive set of procedures, eg service level agreements, regular meetings, key account management or research to identify potential issues that can then be addressed through cross organisational visits and training. In addition supporting communication through internet or extranet access, emails and briefings will help to reduce the conflict.

12 Communicating with stakeholders

The responsibility for communication must rest with the channel leader or a nominated party. The role of communication is to improve the overall performance of the channel network.

The communication consists of two components:

- **Data flows**: the operational, ie day-to-day, information that flows across the channel.
- **Marketing communications**: the use of the promotional mix designed to influence the channel to take a particular course of action. Other purposes include motivation, goodwill and understanding.

The data flows between organisations can extend beyond operational and cover market and strategic data flows.

Communication needs to be consistent and co-ordinated to ensure the shared values and attitudes of the various stakeholders are maintained.

UK high speed rail link causes concerns

At the beginning of 2012 the UK government gave the go-ahead to a new high speed rail link between London and Birmingham, designed to significantly reduce the journey time between the two major cities. It also hoped that by improving the connection, traffic volumes between the destinations will also be reduced.

While the decision has been welcomed by many, including businesses, some commuters and those who are looking forward to bidding for contracts to build the new link, many other stakeholders are furious about the decision and the government faces a back-lash from many of these over the months to come.

Many residents and communities as a whole which will be impacted are furious about the impact on their quality of life and the negative effect on property values. For some the impact will be even greater as they will be forced to sell their homes under compulsory purchase orders.

While much of the line will be underground, many environmental groups are also furious with the decision because of the impact on the countryside and wildlife. A number of Local Authorities are also proposing to challenge the decision because of the impact on their residents. In addition, many of the population, even though not directly affected, are furious about the government's decision to spend what initial estimates place at £33 billion on building what is perceived to be just 'another line', especially as the journey time from London Euston to Birmingham New Street station is already less than 90 minutes.

▸ **Exam tip**

There have been some examples of questions in the examination which have involved the consideration of stakeholders.

June 2011: Waitrose case study. Task Two:

'Describe how Waitrose has developed its distribution alliances and channels and analyse how this has enabled the organisation to meet the needs of its major stakeholders.'

December 2011: MINI case study. Task Two:

'Examine how MINI applies the marketing mix to demonstrate to stakeholders its commitment to sustainability.'

To answer both of these questions correctly the student first needs to have undertaken analysis of the organisation's key stakeholders. In the first question (Waitrose case study) students should also have analysed the likely needs of these key stakeholders.

While the first question relates to channel management and the second question relates to the marketing mix, both had to be answered in the context of the organisation's stakeholders. The second question too required emphasis on MINI's commitment to sustainability.

Clearly, those students who performed best on these questions were those who had included consideration of stakeholders as part of their pre-prepared analysis ahead of the examination, and then applied this properly within their answer.

- Intermediaries are found within most channel structures.

- There are several different types of intermediary and each has a different role/function.

- Intermediaries can have a significant impact on the organisation's profits and on the overall customer experience.

- Careful selection and management of intermediaries is vital.

- Appointing the wrong intermediary can result in business failure.

- All organisations have stakeholders

- Undertaking thorough analysis of stakeholders and their needs is important.

- The six markets framework and Mendelow's power interest matrix are useful tools for analysing stakeholders.

- There are a number of recognised sources of power in relationships.

- Conflict can often arise and will require careful management.

- Effective communication within the channel structure is essential.

FURTHER READING

This paper presents suggestions for categorising, managing and influencing stakeholders:

Walker, D. H. T. *et al* (2008) Influence, stakeholder mapping and visualization. *Construction Management & Economics*, 26(6), pp645–658.

REFERENCES

Beamish, K. and Ashford, R. (2008) *Marketing planning*. Oxford, Butterworth-Heinemann.

Brassington, F. and Pettitt, S. (2006) *Principles of marketing*. 4th edition. Harlow, FT Prentice Hall.

Christopher, M. *et al* (2002) *Relationship marketing: creating stakeholder value*. Oxford, Butterworth-Heinemann.

Fill, C. (2006) *Marketing communications: engagement, strategies and practice.* 4th edition. Harlow, FT Prentice Hall.

French, J. P. R. Jr. and Raven, B. (1960). The bases of social power. *In:* Cartwright, D. and Zander, A. (eds.) (1968), *Group dynamics*. New York, Harper and Row.

Johnson, G. and Scholes, K. (2005) *Exploring corporate strategy*. Harlow, FT Prentice Hall.

Leuthesser, L. (1997) Supplier relational behaviour: an empirical assessment. *Industrial Marketing Management*, 26(3), pp245-254.

Mendelow, A. (1991) *Stakeholder mapping*. Proceedings of the 2nd International Conference on Information Systems. Cambridge, MA

Webster, F. (1979) *Industrial marketing strategy*. USA, John Wiley & Sons.

1   Describe the role of wholesalers.

2   Who is a licensee?

3   What is an intermediary?

4   How might intermediaries help to generate additional sales and profits for the organisation?

5   Stakeholders can be broken down into three categories. What are they?

6   Give an example of connected stakeholders.

7   The six markets framework, for considering an organisation's stakeholders, comprises which different elements?

8   Which matrix is useful to consider the different levels of power and interest of stakeholders?

9   State different potential sources of power.

10   Why might conflict arise in the channel structure?

ACTIVITY DEBRIEFS

Activity 6.1

There are potentially many ways that an intermediary might have an adverse impact on profitability. For example, any negative PR it generates, even if through its own activities, can have an impact on its channel partners. It may fail to provide adequate customer service. It may not promote the goods/service effectively and/or may fail to portray the required (brand) values of its partners

Activity 6.2

The answer to this activity is very much dependent on the organisation chosen. A useful start point is to consider the organisation's stakeholders from different perspectives:

- Internal stakeholders – staff and management.

- Connected stakeholders – customers, suppliers, banks, brokers, channel and other intermediaries and shareholders.

- External stakeholders – the community, the government and pressure groups.

These are only examples and other types might also apply, depending on the business/market.

The activity also required consideration of stakeholder needs. These too will vary but typically, for example, staff needs are for continuity of employment and interesting and fulfilling jobs. Shareholders will expect positive returns and capital growth.

Activity 6.3

Using the stakeholders identified in Activity 6.2 above, plot them on the matrix. Different management approaches should be adopted for each, for example for the key players regular one-to-one dialogue should take place.

The Chartered
Institute of Marketing

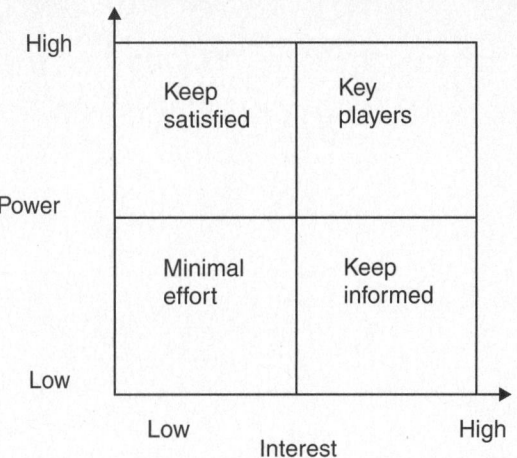

QUICK QUIZ ANSWERS

1   Wholesalers typically deal with other intermediaries in the channel. Often used to by goods in bulk and then to distribute to other intermediaries (possibly retailers) in smaller quantities.

2   A licensee is someone (or an organisation) who has the right (under license) to operate a business with the permission of another party (the licensor), subject to the terms agreed.

3   An intermediary is an organisation which is part of the channel structure and which plays a role in the delivery of goods or services to the end customer.

4   A primary role of many intermediaries is to actually sell the goods/services to end customers. In addition, many provide service to the end customer. Some intermediaries are responsible for packaging and logistics which are key to profitability.

5   Internal, external and connected stakeholders.

6   Connected stakeholders might include customers, suppliers, banks, brokers, channel and other intermediaries and shareholders.

7   Internal markets, referral markets, influence markets, supplier and alliance markets, recruitment markets and customer markets.

8   Mendelow's power interest matrix.

9   Legitimate, expert, resource, referent, coercive, reward, resource, dependency.

10 Divergence of strategy, unrealistic goals, underperformance, personality clash, changing market conditions.

CHAPTER 7

Contractual requirements and service level agreements (SLAs)

Introduction

This final chapter on channel management looks at two specific issues: contractual requirements and service level agreements (SLAs).

Organisations need to be reassured that the investments made in developing customer-focused channels will be rewarded through satisfied customers and the prospect of an acceptable return on their money.

While many organisations may have worked together for many years and 'trust' has been the foundation of the relationship, increasingly organisations are formalising their relationships through contracts and service level agreements. This ensures that when things do go wrong each of the parties to the agreement can adopt a specific course of action to correct the situation. Of course if the contracts are well written the consequences will have been anticipated and action taken proactively to address.

Topic list

The legal framework   1

Transacting with EU public sector bodies   2

Contractual requirements   3

Service level agreements (SLAs)   4

Other obligations   5

Typical service level agreements   6

SLA costs and benefits   7

Measuring the effectiveness of intermediaries   8

Setting targets for intermediaries   9

Monitoring performance   10

2.4	Determine the level and scope of controls required for effectively monitoring and managing distribution channels
	■ Setting objectives
	■ Monitoring performance of distribution channels
	■ Benchmarking of other sectors/organisations/countries
	■ Managing third party relationships in channel management, locally and internationally
2.6	Determine the contractual requirements and service level agreements for engaging intermediary partners within the distribution channel
	■ Types of contracts and typical terms
	■ Implications of contracting with overseas
	■ Role of service level agreements
	■ Determining service levels based upon efficiency expectations
	■ Establishing and monitoring key performance indicators
	■ On-going management and review of service level agreements

1 The legal framework

When organisations come together to do business they do so for mutual benefit. The guiding principles and rationale for the mutual exchange should have been enshrined in the organisation's strategic planning process. However, organisations that trade overseas are also subject to national and local government influences in the countries in which they operate and will have to adhere to the legislative and competitive framework that applies. This will cover aspects such as contract law, protection for consumers, finance, competition and trading practice.

In the UK, parliament is responsible for passing legislation, but increasingly implementation is the responsibility of other bodies such as the Office of Fair Trading (OFT). Within Europe there is an approach to standardise legalisation across member states and for some organisations this will be welcome news.

Legislation is most profound in the area of competition and varies according to the local laws, customs and practices within different countries. In the international economy there is no one legal system and the organisation that uses different channels in different countries will in effect be responsible for adhering to the laws of each of the countries in which it operates.

Within Europe, there is some legislation that prevents distributors selling outside their allocated territory in response to unsolicited enquiries.

Another consideration to note is the concept of product quality standards. Globalisation is pushing standards higher and often smaller players in the market find they cannot meet the minimum standards and therefore have no choice other than to leave the market, which is then left to the bigger players to dominate.

Common law which has guided legal systems in most countries of the world, requires disputes to be solved on the basis of tradition, common practice and the interpretation of existing statutes.

Civil law on the other hand, has at its basis that all foreseeable circumstances are identified and codes of law are then written for the various legal sectors such as commercial, civil or common applications. This includes issues such as copying, the use of brand names, and impact on the nature and profitability of international trade.

The Chartered Institute of Marketing

Different industry standards may require that a product is modified for the local market, which in reality can mean a different product for each market in extreme circumstances. Products must also be sold in the unit of measurement applicable to the market, so a pint, or litre. But different countries have different sized pints!

2 Transacting with EU public sector bodies

Transactions with public sector bodies within the EU are subject to strict regulation. Public sector organisations must spend their budgets, externally, strictly in accordance with the EU Public Procurement Directives and according to national legislation. In the UK this is the Public Contracts Regulations 2006 (Amended).

EU buyer and supplier relationships must be carried out on the basis of key European principles of equal treatment, non-discrimination and transparency. This may give rise to certain issues and challenges for marketing organisations when dealing with EU public sector organisations.

3 Contractual requirements

A range of contractual issues are identified below.

3.1 Restricted sales area

A producer will often grant a specific geographical area (postcode area, town, or region) to an intermediary such as an agent or distributor. This is favoured by the parties as it is clear who has responsibility for sales, or business development. The intermediary can identify the sale potential within the designated area and confirm its viability. The legality of granting such a territory has been challenged in court and apparently conflicting judgements made. While clarity is sought, organisations must continue to be cautious in the approach.

3.2 Tying contract

In return for the rights to sell a particular product, producers may insist that intermediaries must purchase other items as well. Often this is done to encourage sales of weaker items, however, in some situations a manufacturer will insist on a range of products being supplied. A good example of this is in a franchise, where the franchisee is required to purchase a range of ancillary products from the franchisor generally for reasons of consistency.

3.3 Exclusive deal

A producer may insist that an intermediary does not stock competitor products, ie offers an exclusive deal only. This affords the producer significant protection, but it will generally be permissible if similar products are available.

3.4 Refusal to deal

Producers, as we have seen earlier, go to considerable trouble to select the right distributor for their products. Equally they may choose not to allow certain intermediaries to distribute their products for a variety of reasons such as image or cost.

In 2001, Levi, the jeans manufacturer, became involved in a high profile court case because it refused to supply Tesco with its jeans. Tesco was sourcing the jeans through an alternative channel and wanted to sell the jeans for around £10, which was considerably less than other retailers. Tesco argued that value for money

offers made Tesco a success and Levi argued that selling the jeans so cheaply devalued the quality of the Levi brand. Tesco lost the case.

3.5 The specification

A specification is a clear statement or description of what the buyer wants the supplier to perform, including where it is to be carried out and/or delivered, when and to what quality or other standard. It is an essential component of contractual relationships.

ACTIVITY 7.1

Prepare an outline specification setting out your requirements for an intermediary within a channel structure of an organisation with which you are familiar.

4 Service level agreements (SLAs)

While the concept of product guarantees or warranties is nothing new, the idea of offering customers some form of guaranteed level of service is a lot less established, but growing steadily.

It is also worth making the point that a guaranteed level of service does not just apply to service organisations. It has been demonstrated that tangible products can also have an intangible dimension to them and therefore the concept of service guarantees can apply across a wide range of organisations.

A service level agreement (SLA) sets outs the minimum level of service a third party can expect to receive measured against set dimensions.

The SLA has three main objectives, which are to:

- Act as a point of differentiation
- Improve quality
- Improve customer service

Organisations, particularly those offering some form of service, are generally considered to be similar (eg financial service providers), so establishing some form of differentiation can be seen as a competitive advantage.

The SLA is usually written or published on the organisation's website and should:

- Clearly establish the organisation's needs
- Simplify complex issues so that they are clearly understood by both parties
- Reduce areas of conflict by identifying them at the outset of the relationship
- Encourage dialogue in the event of disputes to work towards an acceptable solution
- Encourage realistic expectations

The Chartered Institute of Marketing

It is not uncommon for organisations to quote SLAs within their marketing campaigns. For example a train operator might quote that '98% of our trains ran on time last year'. As service provider might state that 'all customer queries are responded to within 24 hours'. A burglar alarm company might commit to 'attend the scene within one hour'.

5 Other obligations

5.1 Terms and conditions

▶ **Key term**

Terms and conditions: a vital part of the contract between buyer and seller, which sets out the legal basis of the relationship between all parties to the contract.

The terms and conditions by which the service is made available are a vital part of the contract between the buyer and seller. The terms and conditions (often simply referred to as Ts&Cs) comprise the basis of the legal relationship between the parties, and there may be several parties to the contract (especially within more complex channel structures). The terms and conditions will state clearly what will happen if the stipulated terms and conditions are not met. In this event, the 'injured' party, ie the one which has suffered a loss, can take legal action through the courts against the other for compensation.

Terms and conditions are part of everyday business life and should always be completed before commencing work with a new channel partner. Terms and conditions do not only apply to relationships between channel intermediaries but also exist between the organisation and its customers. For example when leasing or contract hiring a car the dealer will insist that the customer signs its terms and conditions. This will set out when payments are due (often this will be set out in a credit agreement) and will also specify conditions of maintenance, use of the vehicle (eg the vehicle can only be used for social, domestic and pleasure purposes), annual mileage restriction and what the arrangement s will be in the event that the vehicle is damaged on return.

5.2 Trade or professional body membership

Organisations often (or must) belong to trade or professional bodies which set out minimum standards of service the organisation must adhere to in providing the service. For example, where a solicitor has agreed a fee for carrying out work but on completion of the work charges twice as much, in the UK, the customer can complain to the Law Society.

5.3 Service guarantees

Organisations often offer specific guarantees for performance levels.

5.4 Customer charters

Some organisations sign up to industry standards or voluntary 'codes'. Others simply make their own commitment to customers and to other stakeholders generally. Often the charter is a combination of statements and SLAs. An example of a customer charter is used in the final 'Real World' case at the end of this chapter.

5.5 Bench mark accreditations

ISO9001 is the internationally recognised Quality Standard. It defines the elements required by a company to systematically deliver quality products, services or advice. It's an indication of reliability, consistency and commitment to quality supply verified by independent certification.

While ISO certification does not guarantee perfection or indeed high quality, when things go wrong, it allows a systematic review of procedures and where fault is found allows for correction and improvement measures to be initiated.

---

6 Typical service level agreements

SLAs can be used internally within an organisation as well as externally. However, the remedies for breaching an internal agreement will need to be carefully considered given the relationship that is likely to exist.

Each SLA will be individual to the parties involved, however, it is important that there is some standardisation of clauses within the agreement. SLAs must be agreed prior to the commencement of the service and of course while serving the needs of all parties it is primarily provided to offer end user (customer) satisfaction.

Typical aspects that need to be included are:

6.1 Nature of services to be provided

The SLA should clearly and simply set out the services that the organisation (service provider) will deliver. If this is not clear, it will be difficult for the customer to later claim certain services were not delivered in accordance with the agreement.

6.2 Performance measures

Both parties need to be clear on what exactly the measure of service quality will be. Benchmarks and any target metrics should be stated here, along with any improvement initiatives that may prove necessary. It is essential that the performance is capable of being measured.

6.3 Issues management

It is not unusual for things to go wrong within a relationship, so it is critical to have a documented procedure to cover the eventuality. Generally when a 'failure' takes place a process to recover from the failure is initiated. This process will document any escalation procedures ie make senior management aware within six hours. It may also provide for key stakeholders to be kept informed of the situation in specific timeframes. Where agreement cannot be reached in certain areas, independent arbitration may be provided for.

6.4 Duties and responsibilities

Both parties to the agreement need to define exactly what their duties and any associated responsibility are. This could include the need to ensure staff receive training every six months, or maintaining a certain number of staff at any one time.

 The Chartered Institute of Marketing

6.5 Cost associated with the SLA

If there are any costs involved in establishing the SLA they must be stated along with the party that will be responsible for paying them. Where a specific or new SLA is being implemented, certain new procedures may need to be established, eg a database or new reporting process. It needs to be clear who is responsible for the costs. Once the SLA is established the client may ask for more detailed reporting of information, or on a more regular basis. Again, allocation of costs needs to be clear.

6.6 Termination

At some point one or all of the parties may want to terminate the relationship, so it is necessary for the methods for termination to be clearly set out.

A SLA can be terminated because a specific event occurs, eg the bankruptcy or death of one or more of the parties. Equally it can be terminated by mutual agreement. Usually there is a set period allowed to wind down the agreement.

Depending on the reasons for termination a compensation payment may be payable.

SLAs will have minimum and/or maximum terms specified, or alternatively the SLA will stipulate a specific time period with an interim review, eg the SLA will run for five years, with interim reviews at 12 months and 36 months. Then interim reviews may allow for termination if specific terms haven't been met.

ACTIVITY 7.2

Write three SLA performance standards for three different organisations in different sectors.

---

7 SLA costs and benefits

An SLA has considerably more appeal to the end user if there is some financial benefits attached in the event the agreement is breached. Clearly, the cost and the level at which failure is deemed to occur can have a significant financial impact on the organisation delivering the service, but another consideration is the level of proactivity involved.

For example, to demonstrate its commitment to customer service a financial services organisation could offer a customer a £10 credit to their account automatically if an instruction is not carried out within a specified time limit. This is much more proactive than, say, making the same offer to all customers telling them to 'contact us for a credit of £10 at xxxxxx if we have not carried out your instruction within xx days'.

However, the costs associated with organisations delivering against a SLA are complex. It is expected that an organisation that consistently meets or exceeds its SLA will benefit from increased retention levels. Therefore one line of argument suggests a distributor will stay longer with the organisation and continue generating additional income. Consequently the organisation will have less reliance on recruiting new distributors to generate revenue. This also has the added benefit of 'price sensitivity' as distributors who stay with the channel tend to be less price-sensitive and less likely to defect to the competition.

So far this is all good news and it follows that employees may become more motivated, suppliers will want to do business and any shareholders should benefit from a more favourable market position.

If SLAs are being breached on a regular basis, then this could suggest an inherent problem within the organisation that needs to be addressed, or that the organisation was being too optimistic in its targets. Either

way, the organisation will now have to incur costs either by improving its internal systems and/or compensating customers for the service provided.

Organisations will need to invest in internal systems and staff if they are going to meet (or exceed) customer expectations and depending on the scale of the work involved, may have a significant cost impact, which will needs to be recovered through the income to be derived from enhanced customer satisfaction.

Figure 7.1 shows an example draft SLA.

Figure 7.1   Draft service level agreement

Draft service level agreement

This service level agreement forms the basis of a joint venture between organisation X and organisation Y relating to the provision of a telephone service to organisation Y and its customers. The agreement sets out the roles and responsibilities of the parties in relation to the provision of the service.

1. Aims

The SLA sets out the service to be provided by X and the minimum service standards.

2. Duration

This agreement will commence on 1st June 2012 and will last for five years. Annual reviews will be undertaken and unsatisfactory performance can initiate termination procedures.

3. Service specification

The telephone service will be operated between the hours of 9am-5pm on weekdays and 9am-12pm on a Saturday.

There will be no service available on public holidays. Outside of the service hours an answer phone messaging service is available. Calls will be returned within 24 hours.

All calls received to be answered within a maximum of 30 seconds.

Organisation X will provide the technical infrastructure, premises and staff.

A backup IT system is in place which will be activated within 15 minutes if necessary.

4. Monitoring and review

Monthly performance reports will be produced in the format agreed. Additional reporting can be provided at the standard rate of £x per day.

Any failings will be noted and an Action Plan for remedy initiated.

5. Disagreements

Any disagreement must be recorded in the prescribed manner and dealt initially by the Key Account Manager (KAM) or a nominated member of the team.

If the issue cannot be resolved to the satisfaction of both parties, the matter must be referred to the Group Service Manager, who will escalate within the organisation to a nominated Director.

8 Measuring the effectiveness of intermediaries

Channel members will have been carefully selected for the value they bring to the overall channel and in accordance with specific criteria.

At regular and pre-agreed dates, the performance of channel members must be evaluated against the standards or targets set to ensure continued efficiency.

The performance criteria to be applied will have been mutually agreed and can form part of the SLA.

Typical criteria for measuring the effectiveness of intermediaries include:

- Sales: target levels of sales to be achieved in a given period
- Stock levels: minimum levels of stock which must be maintained
- Delivery times: maximum time between order and delivery
- Returns policy: maximum period in which faulty goods can be returned
- Training programmes: minimum number of staff to be trained in a set period
- Customer service: maximum time a telephone call can go unanswered, complaint handling times
- Customer retention rates.

9 Setting targets for intermediaries

Performance management of intermediaries is vital, due to the significant impact that they can have in the event of failing to deliver to the correct standard. All targets must conform to the conventional SMART criteria (specific, measurable, achievable, realistic and time bound). There are a number of considerations when setting effective targets.

9.1 Quantitative and qualitative measures

Quantitative measures are more objective and tend to be numerically focused. For instance the number of complaints, the number of late deliveries, how many rejected items there are, how many sales are generated.

Qualitative measure are more subjective and focus more on views and opinions. For example how end customers feel about the service, what other intermediaries think about them, how service has been improved, why customers are unsatisfied.

It is often useful to set both quantitative and qualitative targets in order to get a detailed view of performance. However, qualitative data may be expensive to obtain especially from customers, ie market research will need to be conducted.

9.2 Key Performance Indicators (KPIs)

▶ **Key term**

Key Performance Indicator (KPI): used in performance management and measurement. KPIs are focused on significant goals and are useful in ensuring that the organisation remains on course to achieve its key objectives.

KPIs are used to determine whether or not an organisation is moving in the right direction towards the attainment of its strategic goals. When devising KPIs it is absolutely vital that it is clearly understood what is important to the organisation. Typical KPIs might include new customer acquisition, customer retention, income growth, and cost savings.

9.3 Service standards

Most commonly service standards are communicated to intermediaries through service level agreement, which has already been explained. The standards applied must be sufficient to meet customer expectations and must have been clearly communicated to the intermediary, so they understand what is required.

9.4 Balanced Business Scorecard (BBS)

Devised by Kaplan and Norton (1992), the BBS is a commonly used tool in performance management. Typically focusing on four quadrants (often financial, customers, processes and innovation), but there could be more, it enables the organisation to identify a number of key areas of importance and to base performance targets on these.

ACTIVITY 7.3

Devise a BBS using four quadrants (financial measures, customer measures, process measures and innovation measures) for an intermediary within a channel structure.

9.5 Other targets

For lower value contracts KPIs, SLAs and BBS may not be necessary and lower level targets might be set to determine performance, eg delivery date and time. Irrespective of the value, however, both parties should have a very clear understating of their responsibilities under the contract. Failing to deliver against the expectation of the other party is a major source of conflict in the channel structure and so establishing the ground rules early and setting/managing expectations are vital to ensure there is no potential for misinterpretation.

10 Monitoring performance

Performance against SLAs and other targets can be monitored in a number of ways, including:

- Complaints tracking
- Observation
- Mystery shopping
- Spot checks
- Sample checking
- Customer research/feedback
- Self-assessment by the service provider

The Chartered Institute of Marketing

NatWest Bank Customer Charter

The financial world has been in turmoil for the last few years. To demonstrate its commitment to customers and the broader community NatWest launched this Customer Charter. NatWest is part of the RBS Group. Towards the end of 2009 the UK Government increased its stake in RBS to more than 80% in a move to stabilise the group as a result of the banking crisis.

NatWest Customer Charter

1. We will extend our opening hours in our busiest branches.
    During 2011 more than 650 branches will be open on Saturdays, while our 160 busiest branches will continue to open either early in the morning, or late in the evening. We will regularly review customer demand for longer opening hours.

2. We will serve the majority of customers within 5 minutes in our branches.
    This year we will serve 80% of customers within 5 minutes in our busiest branches.

3. We will provide you with friendly, helpful service whenever you deal with us.
    We are aiming for 9 out of 10 customers to rate our service as friendly and helpful.

4. We will help you to make the right choices for you and your money, providing a clear product range with simply explained features and charges.
    In line with customer feedback, all of our branch literature, standard letters and key web pages will be rewritten to make them simpler and easier to understand.

5. We will provide a 24/7 telephone banking service from our UK based call centres.
    All of our call centres will continue to be based in the UK and you will always have the option to speak to a real person.

6. We will work with you to keep you safe when you bank online and on your mobile device with us.
    We will provide free market-leading enhanced security software for all online banking users.

7. If you become a victim of fraud when banking with us online, or on your mobile phone, we promise to refund any money taken from your account in full, in accordance with our security promise published online.
    We will help you quickly if your debit card is lost or stolen and you need access to cash.
    We will despatch all lost and stolen replacement debit cards the next working day by first class post. We will also offer a free emergency cash service through our ATMs to customers whose debit card is lost or stolen.

8. We will continue to be a responsible lender and are committed to finding new ways to help
    We will send text messages when you register for our Act Now Alerts, helping you take action to avoid current account charges. We will not provide credit limit increases if we know you are struggling to meet payments on your credit card. We will support first time buyers by always having mortgages available for up to 90% of the property value.

9. We pledge to stay open for business if we are the last bank in town and will consider a range of options to ensure a local banking service is available
    We will continue to provide a local banking service wherever we are the last bank in town and will continue to serve more than 45 communities with our mobile banks.

10. We will provide young people with financial education through our independently accredited MoneySense programme
    In 2011 we will deliver 19,000 MoneySense lessons in schools.

11. We will actively support the local communities in which we live and work
    We are launching CommunityForce, a new initiative to support local communities, by donating time, expertise and £1.9m in funding. We will also offer all our employees a day of paid leave for local voluntary work and provide 7,000 days of community volunteering in 2011.

12. We will resolve customer complaints fairly, consistently, and promptly
    75% of customers will be satisfied with the way their complaints have been handled.

13. Twice a year we will publish the most common complaints
    And we will strive to address the causes.

14   We will actively seek your thoughts and suggestions on how we can become more helpful
      We will continue our Customer Listening Programme to ensure our staff, including executives, hear first hand about the needs and frustrations of our customers.

(Source: www.natwest.com. Reproduced with permission.)

> **Exam tip**

At this level of qualification, rather than just focus on the detail and the terminology, students should ensure that they understand the issues facing marketers, in the context of contractual requirements and service level agreements, in channel management. We have already established the potential risks in relying on intermediaries and contract and performance management both are vital in helping the organisation to minimise such risks.

Given that this is a case study based examination, students should focus on how to performance manage intermediaries and the factors that will lead to different approaches being adopted. It goes without saying that in the examination answers must relate to the case material.

The whole area of channel management is generally one in which students perform less well in the examination. Students should spend some time considering this important element of the marketing mix during their analysis of the case as they need to feel confident that they could answer a contract or performance related channel management question in the examination.

The Chartered
Institute of Marketing

CHAPTER ROUNDUP

- The international legal framework for contracts is complex and inconsistent.

- There are specific regulations for transacting with EU public sector bodies.

- Contract requirements are commonplace and wide ranging in channel management.

- SLAs are commonly used in performance management and set direction for the standards required in respect of service.

- SLAs can be used externally (with suppliers) and for other business units within the same organisation.

- Terms and conditions are essential in business relationships as they set out the legal obligations of all parties.

- International standards are available in many areas and can add consistency and clarification in some aspects of the relationships between contracted parties.

- Measuring and monitoring the effectiveness of intermediaries is essential as their failure can be catastrophic for the organisation.

- It is important to set the right measures/targets for intermediaries.

- Consider using both quantitative and qualitative measures.

- KPIs are useful to ensure direction and focus remains on key business goals.

- A BBS is useful to ensure a focus across a range of performance areas, commonly featuring these dimensions – financial, customer, process and innovation (but can be adapted to suit the organisation's requirements).

FURTHER READING

If you are unfamiliar with the Balanced Business Scorecard you might like to read the following article:

Kaplan, R. S. and Norton, D. P. (1992) The balanced scorecard: measures that drive performance. *Harvard Business Review,* Jan – Feb pp71–80.

REFERENCES

Kaplan, R. S. and Norton, D. P. (1992) The balanced scorecard: measures that drive performance. *Harvard Business Review,* Jan – Feb pp71–80.

NatWest. (2010). NatWest customer charter. NatWest, http://www.natwest.com/ [Accessed on 9 February 2012]

1   What is a tying contract?

2   What is a specification used for?

3   Why is an SLA useful?

4   What is the purpose of having a terms and conditions document signed by all parties to the contract?

5   Why are international standards (eg ISO9001) useful?

6   Give an example of a quantitative performance measure for an intermediary.

7   Give an example of a qualitative performance measure for an intermediary.

8   What are KPIs used for?

9   What is a BBS?

10 Suggest five ways that performance against SLAs can be monitored.

ACTIVITY DEBRIEFS

Activity 7.1

The answer will depend on the role and type of intermediary. Typically, a specification will include a detailed description of what the service provider is expected to deliver. This will include a description of the goods/service themselves, volumes, sizes, quantities, frequencies, packaging, quality and any other appropriate standards.

Activity 7.2

The answer will depend on the examples chosen. For example, for an airline they might operate to these customer SLAs:

- Online check-in available from 24 hours before take-off.
- 95% of flights leave and arrive on time.
- Complaints dealt with within 48 hours.

Activity 7.3

Financial: Generation of XX sales/income; reduce costs by X%.
Customer: 95% customer satisfaction; 30 new customers per month.
Process: 100% relevant paperwork submitted on time; 100% invoicing accuracy.
Innovation: Generation of one improvement idea per month; four new/enhanced product ideas per annum.

The Chartered Institute of Marketing

1   An agreement in which a producer requires a buyer (usually a retailer) to purchase one or more other products as a condition.

2   To set out precisely what services/goods are to be delivered, when, how often, using what type of packaging and to what standard.

3   To be precise to all parties as to the standard of performance required. The SLA also facilitates performance management and measurement. In addition it provided focus for the supplier on key areas of service.

4   The document sets out fully the basis of the legal relationship between all parties. There should therefore be no ambiguity between the parties as to the basis of the relationship.

5   International standards are consistent and widely recognised and so are useful to avoid disputes in contracts, especially when dealing with overseas partners.

6   To make ten deliveries a month; to receive no more than three complaints from customers per month; to have fewer than 2% rejected items.

7   To improve customer satisfaction by 5%; to improve our overall offering to customers by 8%; to improve our positioning against competitors.

8   KPIs focus on more significant and broader deliverables and are useful in performance management and measurement to guide the organisation towards its overarching objectives.

9   A BBS enables a balanced view, in terms of performance management and measurement across a number of key areas, frequently financial, customer, innovation and process.

10   Observations, mystery shopping, customer feedback, complaints, spot checks, sample checking, self-assessment by the service provider.

Section 2:

Senior Examiner's comments

By the time students have completed Section 2 they should have a thorough understanding of:

- The development of channel management strategy and objectives

- The range of channels available to organisations operating in different markets and sectors

- The factors that influence channel choice

- The role and importance of stakeholders in channel management; and

- Undertaking control and performance management of channel partners and intermediaries.

For students to succeed, they must be able to apply what they have learnt to various types of organisations. In particular, students must be able to demonstrate that they can relate the application of the various theoretical aspects of channel management to both domestic businesses and to organisations which operate internationally.

Students should examine channel management in action by identifying their own examples, for instance from reading case studies. Technology has had a major impact on channel management and, in many industries, continues to change the ways in which organisations interact with their customers. Financial services are an example of this, where today a significant number of customers, both consumers and businesses, only have a 'virtual' relationship with their chosen providers.

Students should also consider the contribution of channel management strategy and its application towards the achievement of critical organisational and marketing objectives, for example improving profitability, growing market share and increasing levels of customer satisfaction.

Section 3:

Managing marketing communications

We now turn our attention to the third section of the syllabus: managing marketing communications. It is worth remembering that the syllabus requires students to consider the topic from an international as well as a UK perspective.

We will examine the relationship between marketing communications and the organisation's overarching business goals. We shall also consider marketing communications in different organisational contexts.

In this section we will focus on different marketing communications strategies and the impact these will have on the development of the communications mix and on the communications plan as a whole. The section will be concluded with an evaluation of the manner for selecting marketing communication agencies where the work is not undertaken in-house and the processes necessary to monitor the output produced.

In the final chapter, in this section, we will consider the role of agencies and how relationships with them should be managed.

CHAPTER 8

Managing marketing communications

Introduction

First, in this chapter, we will consider the relevance of marketing communications within the organisation and how marketing communications objectives must align to the organisation's corporate goals. We will look briefly at the marketing communications plan, which will be examined in detail in Chapter 10, and will consider different strategies for marketing communications. The chapter will conclude by examining marketing communications in different contexts, including internal communications activities.

Topic list

The role of marketing communications	1
Alignment with corporate objectives	2
Introduction to marketing communications plans	3
Marketing communications in building relationships	4
Communications in different contexts	5
Marketing communications and competitive advantage	6
Relationship marketing and marketing communications	7
Legal issues	8
Internal marketing	9
The importance of internal communications	10
Internal communication methods	11
External communications audiences	12

3.1	Determine marketing communications strategy and objectives to align with and deliver the organisation's marketing strategy and plans
	■ The role of marketing communications
	■ Legal aspects of marketing communications
	■ Global/international aspects of marketing communications
	■ Aligning communications strategy to corporate and marketing strategy
	■ Utilising communications strategies to achieve competitive advantage
	■ Strategic aims of marketing communications
	■ The role of communications in achieving competitive advantage
	■ The contribution of marketing communications in relationship marketing for all stakeholders
3.2	Prioritise the internal and external marketing segments to be targeted for marketing communications in different organisational contexts and sectors
	■ Role of internal communications
	■ Identifying key internal audiences
	■ Internal communications methods, Intranet; notice boards; seminars; briefings, newsletters; portals; SMS
	■ Identifying key external audiences
	■ Role of marketing communications in different organisational contexts and sectors
	■ Internal marketing as a key tool to aid and deliver service excellence
3.4	Develop and manage a co-ordinated marketing communications plan, in the context of the strategic marketing plan, in order to establish and build relationships appropriate to the needs of customers, stakeholders and prospects in different organisational contexts and sectors
	■ Developing a communications plan
	■ Communications planning frameworks
	■ The role of communications in building customer relationships and value
	■ Role of communications in gaining new prospects
	■ Communications planning and execution in different organisational contexts and sectors, (B2B, B2C, third tier, not-for-profit, international/global)

1 The role of marketing communications

> ▶ **Key term**
>
> **Marketing communications:** another term for 'promotion' which is an element of the marketing mix. Marketing communications involves a range of activities with the purpose of conveying marketing messages to target audiences.

Doyle (2000, p295) suggests 'It is not enough for a firm to produce a good product; it also has to communicate its values effectively to potential customers. Today, the number of products competing for the customer's attention is so great that gaining share of mind is a major problem. The business has to invest in communications to make people aware of the product, to communicate the value of its functional and emotional attributes, to persuade them of its advantages over competitive products, and to reassure customers once they have bought it.'

Fill (2006, p2) says 'Marketing communications is a management process through which an organisation engages with its various audiences'. He continues, 'By understanding an audience's communication environment, organisations seek to develop and present messages for its identified stakeholder groups, before evaluating and acting upon the responses. By conveying messages that are of significant value, audiences are encouraged to offer attitudinal and behavioural responses'.

The Chartered Institute of Marketing

Pickton and Broderick (2005, p4) provide the following definition: 'All the promotional elements of the marketing mix which involve the communications between an organisation and its target audiences on all matters that affect marketing performance'.

Whatever definition is chosen, the role of marketing communications is to establish a dialogue with the audience to promote the organisation and the products it offers. The organisation can choose to communicate directly with its audiences or through distribution channels.

1.1 DRIP

> ▸ **Key term**
>
> **DRIP:** stands for Differentiate, Remind, Inform and Persuade. These are frequently quoted as a definition of the role of marketing communications.

Fill (2002, p48) defines the role of marketing communications as either to:

- **Differentiate**: to make a product or brand appear to be different to that of a competitor.
- **Remind**: to reassure the target audience as to the benefits of making a purchase.
- **Inform**: to provide new information to a target audience, for example about a new product.
- **Persuade**: to encourage a target audience towards an action or to change an opinion.

Marketing communications is essential to achieve positioning and to portray brand value to the target audience. It can also be used to build loyalty and to support customer retention, as well as supporting new business acquisition activities.

ACTIVITY 8.1

Identify three different marketing communications activities, eg advertisements, and for each consider how it performs against DRIP, as outlined above.

2 Alignment with corporate objectives

As organisations do not operate in a vacuum, the communication objectives cannot be developed in isolation of the wider business and planning process conducted by the organisations. The marketing communications plan (see below) is set against the background of other planning tools and forms a hierarchy of interconnected activities which collectively link the process together.

The communications objectives are directly derived from the marketing objectives that in turn come from the corporate objectives, themselves coming from the organisation's mission statement.

A typical hierarchy could look like that shown in Figure 8.1.

Figure 8.1   Hierarchy of objectives

- Organisation mission statement
- Corporate objectives
- Functional objectives (which will include marketing objectives)
- Marketing communication objectives

3 Introduction to marketing communications plans

▶ **Key term**

Marketing communications plan: a structured and considered framework for analysing an organisation's current situation, identifying and analysing target audiences and designing specific messages for them delivered through execution of an appropriately tailored communications mix. An effective plan should also include budget considerations and proposals for measurement.

In order to ensure all parts of the organisation are focused on effective communications, a clear marketing communications plan is necessary. This will be explored in more detail in the next chapter.

Generally organisations communicate with more than one audience and each audience may need a different message. It is vital, therefore, that the marketing communications plan clearly identifies each audience and that the organisation develops a different (but appropriate) message and communications mix for each group it is targeting. Within the plan there must also be consideration of how its success, or otherwise, will be measured.

A typical marketing communications planning framework is shown in 8.2. While the plan is presented sequentially, in practice many of the activities can take place at the same time.

Figure 8.2 Framework for a marketing communications plan

1	Situation/context analysis
2	Set communications objectives
3	Target market profile
4	Marketing communications strategy (push/pull/profile)
5	Segmentation, targeting and positioning
6	Develop the communications message
7	Develop an integrated communications mix
8	Schedule media
9	Set promotional budget
10	Allocate resources
11	Execute and monitor
12	Evaluate effectiveness

3.1 Situation/context

The context in which the marketing communications activities are to be undertaken must be fully evaluated and will, effectively, comprise detailed analysis of the organisation itself, the competitive environment, market analysis and customer analysis. A number of different analytical tools might be useful at this stage, for example:

- PESTEL analysis
- SWOT analysis
- Porter's five forces model

This preparatory work is vital to ensure that the planned marketing communications activities will be relevant to the changing landscape faced by the organisation.

Market research might also be required at this stage. This is particularly important when a number of different audiences are involved. Research helps organisations to understand the context in which the organisation must communicate and helps it position the messages correctly in the minds of the audience, encouraging them to take action. Fill (2006) suggests the research should provide information on the needs of the audience, their perception, attitudes, and their decision-making characteristics.

3.2 Marketing communications objectives

It can be seen from Figure 8.1 that the marketing communications objectives must link into the organisation's marketing objectives. It is vital that any objectives satisfy the conventional SMART criteria (ie specific,

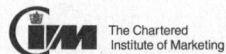

measurable, achievable, realistic and time bound). The precise objectives chosen will of course vary depending on the purpose of the campaign and its desired outcome.

Typical marketing communications objectives might focus on:

- Changing perception
- Creating/building awareness
- Achieving positioning (or re-positioning)
- Influencing the target audience
- Generating sales (volumes and/or revenues)
- Improving customer retention
- Improving customer satisfaction
- Supporting the launch of a new product

The importance of setting the right objectives cannot be over-emphasised. The objective will determine the make-up of the communications mix and the strategy(ies) adopted.

3.3 Marketing communications strategies

> ▶ **Key term**
>
> **Marketing communications strategy:** push, pull and profile strategies.

The nature, location and types of customers make a significant difference to the tools that can or will be used in order to achieve the DRIP objectives (as mentioned earlier). The organisation must first consider what marketing communications strategy is the most appropriate for it to adopt. There are three marketing communications strategies, which can be executed either individually or simultaneously:

3.3.1 Push strategy

This involves 'pushing' the product into distribution channels, for example through personal selling, incentives and trade advertising. With a push strategy the manufacturer 'pushes' the product through the distribution channel to those members who will add value to the product. Information is pushed down, by the manufacturer, to channel intermediaries.

3.3.2 Pull strategy

This involves 'pulling' the product through by encouraging end customer demand through advertising, sales promotions and in-store merchandising. In a pull strategy, communications are directed at the end-user rather than through the distribution channel. The intention being that the increased levels of awareness will encourage the consumer to demand the product(s) from suppliers in the distribution channel (if there is one), thereby 'pulling' the product through and satisfying demand.

3.3.3 Profile strategy

This involves communicating with the target audience and other key stakeholders to build and maintain the organisation's profile, or the profile of a new product/brand.

ACTIVITY 8.2

Identify examples of where organisations are adopting a pull and profile marketing communications strategy.

3.4 The marketing communications message

This is a vital element of any marketing communications campaign and must be considered carefully. It must have some relevance and appeal to the intended audience otherwise they will not notice the activity. It is important also that the message reflects the values of the organisation and/or the brand.

The effectiveness of the message content and design can be determined by assessing the levels of consumer recognition and recall. These are two key measures of marketing communications, especially advertising activity. Recognition relates to awareness, eg a market researcher may ask a member of the public 'Are you aware of this advertisement?'. Recall is more to do with whether or not the consumer can remember the advertisement. Importantly, in the context of the message, it is important that the consumer, having seen the advertisement, say, feels inclined to take some further action, which has been prompted by the marketing communications activity.

3.5 Integrated marketing communications activities

Often organisations forget that to support the marketing communications plan, additional resource is needed. Finance is an important resource which must be used effectively and produce an acceptable return on the investment. The use of SMART objectives will help this process. The choice of promotion must be in keeping with the budgets and objectives set. It would be ludicrous for a small family run business to run a TV campaign at a cost of £1 million plus, where the return could not be justified. Where additional resource is needed this must also be factored into the plan. There may be cost implications, but equally where the resource is skilled staff, or new equipment, the time delay from advertising for the new staff, or placing the purchase order to delivery of the new equipment must be factored in to the plan.

Control is often managed through the use of Gantt charts which plot activities against a timeframe. It is a useful method of control as it highlights the 'knock-on' effects of delays. For example, the appointment of a new Communications Manager may be delayed by five days but the knock-on effect is to delay the overall activity by 15 days due to other resources being otherwise engaged.

Once the plan becomes operational then the control methods will depend on what the specific objectives were. If for example raised awareness levels for the organisation were being measured, it may be necessary to monitor them on a daily basis.

Having invested in the marketing communications process, it is necessary to get feedback on the key components of the process, so that those aspects that worked well can be used in future campaigns, equally things that didn't work well can be changed.

THE REAL WORLD

Integrated marketing communications activities are vital for larger organisations but can be difficult to execute effectively. It is not uncommon, for example, for major campaigns to involve TV advertisement at the same time as outdoor advertisements, cinema advertising, PR, sponsorships, direct marketing and online. A key challenge for the marketer is to ensure consistency (look, feel, brand, messaging etc) across the various communications mix elements.

4 Marketing communications in building relationships

Organisations are increasingly looking to build ongoing relations with customers so that their lifetime value is enhanced through maintaining a customer for longer than expected, or purchasing additional products.

Not all customers are equally profitable and therefore organisations need to communicate with customers and potential customers in a way that reflects their current or potential worth to the organisation.

The Chartered Institute of Marketing

Each interaction with the customer is an opportunity to reinforce and must reflect quality and value. Porter's value chain (Porter, 1985) demonstrates how organisations internally seek to take a concept or product and add value by undertaking a series of activities. For example a large diamond extracted from the earth has considerably more value when it has been cut into smaller pieces and polished. The concept relies on the fact that each activity generates more value than the cost of undertaking it. Where this is not the case the activity should be monitored for effectiveness.

The value that a brand or organisation offers is determined by the consumer and is based on a number of criteria such as price or quality, or 'softer' issues such as confidence or status. Also factors such as availability of supply, or replacement parts can determine value. However, trust is at the heart of any relationship.

Transactional marketing focuses on the current product and price and relies on mass communication to get the message across. Relationship marketing on the other hand relies on targeted communication to emphasise the importance of the relationship between the parties and build interaction and dialogue.

4.1 Customer loyalty

> **▶ Key term**
>
> **The Loyalty ladder** is used to understand customer loyalty. The ladder suggests that customer relationships progress through a number of recognised levels from prospect, purchaser, client, supporter, advocate and partner.

Several writers have used a ladder concept to depict ascending levels of customer loyalty. One of the best known versions is the relationship marketing ladder of loyalty (see Figure 8.3) developed by Christopher *et al* (2008, p48):

Figure 8.3   Ladder of loyalty

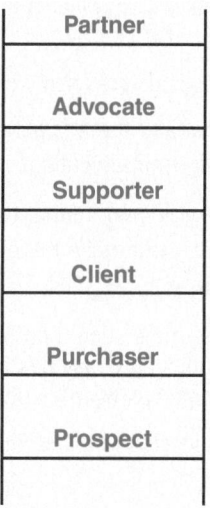

- Prospect: someone (or a business) who (which) is believed to be a potential customer, ie could potentially be persuaded to do business with the organisation.

- Purchaser: someone (or a business) who (which) has done business once with the organisation.

- Client: someone (or a business) who (which) has done business with the organisation on a repeat basis, but may be negative or neutral towards the organisation.

- Supporter: someone (or a business) who (which) likes dealing with the organisation but only supports it passively.

- Advocate: someone (or a business) who (which) actively recommends the organisation, ie effectively does some marketing on behalf of the organisation.

- Partner: someone (or a business) who (which) has a strong independent relationship with the organisation.

This is a useful tool for marketers to attempt to understand the positioning, in relationship terms, of the target audience.

5 Communications in different contexts

5.1 Business to business market (B2B)

B2B markets consist of commercial organisations, not-for-profit, schools, churches, charities, in fact anything which is not considered personal. The market has fewer, but larger, buyers with a more formalised buying process and more rational purchasing behaviour. The commercial side of the B2B market can be broken down into four categories:

- **Retail**: goods are sold to the consumers
- **Resale**: goods are sold into the distribution channels where the distributor adds value through packaging, distribution, quantity or storage
- **Assembly**: raw materials or components are sold which are then combined to produce a finished product
- **Own consumption**: the goods are used within the business, ie are not on-sold

Organisational buying behaviour and the actual buying process differs from the B2C market and therefore there is a difference in the marketing communications mix.

Organisational buying behaviour is more formal than in the consumer market. A group of individuals known as the Decision Making Unit (DMU) will make the purchasing decision and that decision itself contains additional risk depending on whether it is a:

- **New buy**: this is the first time such a purchase has been made
- **Modified rebuy**: a previous purchase has been made, this time a change has been made
- **Straight rebuy**: no change has been made to the previous order

A new buy carries the highest level of risk and Fill (2006) identifies seven types of organisational risk:

- Technical
- Financial
- Delivery
- Service
- Personal
- Relationship
- Professional

Effective communication is intended to satisfy the expectations of the buyer and reduce the levels of associated risk.

The promotional mix between B2B and B2C differs between the two markets. B2B relies heavily on personal selling due to the perceived complexity of products and profit margins involved. A brief summary of the different forms of marketing communications is set out in Table 8.1 as they relate to the B2B market.

Communication form	Description
Personal selling	Allows complex products to be explained so that the purchaser is clear on the various product options.
Trade advertising	Most industries and markets have a specific journal or newspaper that can be used to target the sector.
Direct marketing	Direct mail in the B2B sector needs to be highly targeted which requires considerable research. Outbound telesales is often used in routine purchases and a relationship can be built through this approach. It is also used to support the sales team by making courtesy calls again to build the relationship and keep the dialogue open.
Sales promotion	Tactical way to generate increased sales by offering additional incentives on selected product lines for a short period of time.
Exhibitions	Often used to focus on an organisation's new product range where potential buyers come specifically to see the season's new product range(s).
PR	We will see later that PR is outside of the control of an organisation, however, it is an important tool and needs to be managed effectively so that the organisation is always at front of mind with customers.
Internet/online	This is an increasingly important medium. The web acts as showcase for the organisation and, while impersonal, offers cost savings and improved efficiencies especially when linked with e-commerce. Social media is becoming increasingly popular in both B2B and B2C marketing.

5.2 Global and international aspects of marketing communications

Increased international travel, coupled with the dramatic growth in the internet, could increasingly lead to the belief that all markets can be similarly treated and communicated with.

International, global and multinational organisations adopt different frameworks for their marketing mix:

- **International**: countries beyond the home market receive the same marketing mix(es) as the home country and home market

- **Multinational**: individually designed marketing mix(es) for each country

- **Global**: one single marketing mix

It can be appreciated that organisations will encounter a number of variables (controllable and non controllable) when communication is being undertaken outside of the home market. Fill (2006) divides the variables into two:

- Culture
- Media

5.3 Culture

Culture consists of the values and attitude of people and organisations that determine the way they communicate to other individuals and organisations. Culture is developed through learning and it recognises that not all of the markets or the people within the market will respond or behave in a similar way. Corporate culture is often regarded as 'the way we do things here' and it is important to appreciate the different kinds of culture, such as:

- **Symbols**: in some countries symbols are important, particularly where the levels of education may not be high

- **Religion**: in many countries a particular religion has an effect on what is purchased and how it is purchased
- **Values**: the things or beliefs that people or organisations place on particular things

5.4 Media

Different countries have different media channels available and while 98% of the UK population may have a TV, such high penetration is not universal. The range and type of media available across the globe is variable and must be carefully considered prior to a campaign being initiated. In addition, some countries may also have multiple languages spoken each with its own set of media channels.

The advent of satellite/cable TV and of course the internet have significantly opened up communication channels. However, not all countries have the same levels of access to technology.

5.5 Standardisation or adaptation of marketing communications?

The choice for organisations to standardise or adapt their marketing communications is the subject of ongoing debate and is likely to remain so. Table 8.2 shows the various arguments both for and against.

Table 8.2 Standardisation versus adaptation

Adaptation	
	■ A central theme can be tailored to the needs of the local market making it more tailored and relevant. It can also be modified to show greater understanding of the individual market as the message can be developed by 'local people for local people'.
	■ Adapting the communication recognises that local needs do vary and a generic message may not always be appropriate. Needs, wants, purchasing habits, behaviours, and so on vary across markets.
	■ Educational levels vary and 'sophisticated' messages may not always be appropriate. Similarly, as we have seen with the concept of culture, messages can be interpreted differently.
	■ Legal issues and constraints will vary across national boundaries and sometimes within countries, so what may be acceptable in one market may not be acceptable in another and similarly different codes of practice with legal or voluntary controls may be in place.
Standardisation	
	■ As highlighted earlier, satellite television has broken down many barriers which separated markets, including culture. Consequently many earlier arguments for adaptation are being eroded, eg Disney has appeal in most countries and the message can be standardised.
	■ Locally-developed campaigns have historically been perceived as being of poor quality which standardisation addressed.
	■ Standardisation allows for a consistent and strong brand to be developed across all markets.
	■ Organisations may prefer to control campaigns in each and every market centrally because they want to maintain control.
	■ Costs are reduced as a result of standardisation; few advertising agencies, and greater production volumes all contribute to efficiency.
	■ Consistency: the message can be tightly controlled leading to greater brand consistency across the various markets.

6 Marketing communications and competitive advantage

We have seen earlier that the role of marketing communications is to differentiate, remind, inform and persuade (DRIP) but how can it secure competitive advantage for an organisation?

The Chartered Institute of Marketing

We need to remind ourselves that customers do not buy products, it is the benefit the product offers that is bought. The frequently quoted example is the customer who wants a 1 inch hole in the wall, but has to buy a 1 inch drill bit to get the hole. But someone may invent a better way to obtain the hole and then the customer may evaluate that product rather than the drill bit.

The role of marketing communications is to provide the organisation with a competitive advantage by clearly labelling what the product does and positioning it relative to the competition, so the customer is able to differentiate the offering from the competition and can make a clear choice about which one best meets their needs.

This requires a compelling message to be created and maintained in the mind of the target audience so that when they are ready to purchase or repeat purchase they will consider your organisation. They understand the positioning and believe the product best meets their needs. However, many academics suggest that the frequency of communication generates competitive advantage because of the customer's ongoing exposure to key messages.

7 Relationship marketing and marketing communications

Communication is an important element in an organisation's efforts to build relations with its stakeholders.

An organisation's stakeholders can be varied in nature and consist of large numbers. They include:

- All the various publics (people and individuals) who have an interest in the organisation
- Distribution channels and the various members
- Customers ie the people or organisations who purchase the product(s) on offer

Organisations want to build long and profitable relationships and will therefore want to move beyond 'one-off' transactions in order to achieve long and mutual satisfying relationships which add value for all parties.

Communication is an important part of the 'added value' process that is achieved through:

- Effective and two-way dialogue; stakeholder needs are established and a dialogue is maintained so that each stakeholder, or stakeholder group, is understood and can be effectively targeted with messages.

- Regular communication which provides timely and relevant information across a range of communication media and at different frequencies depending on identified need.

8 Legal issues

Marketing professionals are expected to carry out their role in a decent, honest, truthful and legal manner and legislation is in place to ensure:

- Consumer protection
- The image of the industry is maintained at a high level
- Credibility of the messages being communicated
- Decency, ie no one is likely to be offended by the messages or imagery being communicated
- Vulnerable groups are protected

In the UK, marketers are regulated by a comprehensive range of legislation which is intended to protect the public and in the EU centralised or harmonised legislation is also having an impact. Organisations that operate globally need to recognise and understand the legalisation applicable in each country in which they operate.

8.1 UK legislation

Legislation in the UK includes the following:

- **The Data Protection Act 1984**: certain organisations must be registered with the data protection registrar if they hold data on individuals and there are conditions about how the data is to be maintained.

- **The Control of Misleading Advertising Advertisements Regulations 1988**: where complaints regarding marketing communications will be considered.

- **The Sale of Goods Act 1979**: requires that goods must match their description.

- **The Trades Description Act 1968**: organisations must not make false or misleading statements about the products (including services) being marketed.

- **The Office of Fair Trading (OFT)** aims to ensure that competition and consumer protection laws are followed. However, there are a number of voluntary bodies in the UK whose members agree to comply with the various codes of practice.

- **The Advertising Standards Authority (ASA)** oversees the British Code of Advertising, Sales Promotion and Direct Marketing which should be:

    - Legal, decent, honest and truthful
    - Responsible to consumers and society
    - In line with the principles of fair competition

The ASA can only request an advertiser to change their advertising which is found to be in breach of its guidelines.

If a complaint is made by the public it is the ASA who will investigate it and if it believes the advertiser has breached its code, it will be asked to withdraw the advertisement. If the advertiser chooses to ignore the ASA warning, then a media warning will be distributed to all members of the Committee of Advertising Practice (CAP) which deals with advertisers, rather than the public. The intention is to prevent organisations such as media owners carrying the offending material. Agencies which continue to breach the guidelines will find their membership of the trade bodies terminated and find it difficult to attract new business.

However, it is often not a clear cut decision. Some organisations set out to be deliberately provocative in their marketing communications activities. Benetton, for example, has frequently pushed the boundaries by running campaigns with graphic images which many members of the public have found upsetting. FCUK (acronym for French Connection UK) is another brand which has been portrayed against a backdrop of advertising campaigns, some of which have offended some segments of the population.

Other organisations, including charities and the UK government, run campaigns that are intended to shock people and change behaviour. Yet this can also cause offence.

In many instances it is simply necessary for an organisation to be clear that it is not breaking the law, ie its materials and communications are legal. This will require the organisation to ensure that its communications are 'signed off' by its in-house legal team, or external lawyers as appropriate. The legal team would routinely be expected to advise on:

- Brochures
- Editorials
- Annual reports
- Accounts
- Recruitment brochures
- Product literature

8.2 Outside the UK

The European Advertising Standards Alliance (EASA) is the single authoritative voice on advertising self-regulation issues for Europe and promotes high ethical standards in commercial communications by means of effective self-regulation, while being mindful of national differences of culture, legal and commercial practice.

As a non-profit organisation based in Brussels, it brings together national advertising self-regulatory organisations (SROs) and organisations representing the advertising industry in Europe. EASA has three goals:

- The promotion of self regulation
- Support for existing self-regulatory systems
- Ensure cross border complaints are dealt with effectively

The International Chamber of Commerce was the first organisation to publish its International Code of Advertising Practice and all the codes operative today are based on this code. However, across Europe there are many advertising restrictions that vary from country to country and across media, and each country has its own regulatory bodies. Consequently acceptability in one country does not guarantee acceptance in another.

---

9 Internal marketing

Internal marketing refers to the promotion of a marketing orientation throughout an organisation. It aims to create awareness among all employees including those who do not have direct customer contact. For many organisations, achieving marketing orientation can involve major changes in working practices and culture.

Internal marketing also includes:

- Creation of customer awareness
- Quality management programmes
- Change programmes

Peck *et al* (1999) suggest that internal marketing is concerned with creating, developing and maintaining an internal service culture. Internal marketing is important, not just in service industries, but across all sectors.

Research has shown a strong correlation between satisfied employees and operational performance. Customers do not just purchase a tangible product, the intangible aspects such as culture and attitude affect customer satisfaction which can be more important to consumers in many situations. Therefore to achieve the stated aims and objectives of the marketing plan, an integrated approach is necessary in order to bring together the skills of the various employee groups. Organisations are increasingly competing on the grounds of service excellence and improved service quality relies on the effectiveness of the people who are charged with delivering the service.

Employees can be regarded as a discrete group of customers who need to be segmented into different audiences, so that targeted communications campaigns can be developed. Staff, because of the nature of their work, are often responsible for a very small part of an organisation's output, so it is necessary to mirror customer campaigns internally, so that they see the tone and values set out by the organisation.

Equally, for many customers the only interaction they may have with the brand is with individual members of staff and therefore their attitude may impact on the customer's view of the brand. A helpful and enthusiastic member of staff will have a positive impact on the organisation and many organisations have deployed the concept of 'brand ambassadors' as a result of their internal marketing programmes.

Marketing, in addition to being a management function and ethos which permeates the entire organisation, needs to ensure effective co-ordination of its activities internally. Therefore systems and processes covering resources (financial, people and equipment) need to be put in place to ensure products are delivered to customers within agreed timescales to the quality standards set by the organisation. This requires effective co-ordination of activities so that all staff are working towards the same goals.

Internal marketing has two main aspects:

- All employees and departments have an internal and external customer
- Staff must work together in a way that is aligned to the organisation's mission

And the overall objective of internal marketing is to improve the quality of service offered to customers.

Internal marketing is shaped by the prevailing culture of the organisation as it is this culture which provides the context within which internal marketing takes place.

An internal marketing plan (derived from the overall marketing plan) is necessary to ensure the achievement of organisation goals. The key components of an internal plan could include:

- Organisation aims and objectives
- Marketing strategy
- Segmentation, targeting and positioning (STP)
- Marketing programmes (see below)
- Implementation
- Monitoring and control

10 The importance of internal communications

Internal communications are important for a number of reasons:

- Staff need to be kept informed about plans, objectives and other developments.
- Customer-facing staff must be kept informed about new products and relevant policy changes.
- Clear communication is important for motivation and morale.
- Support staff engagement.
- Encourage information sharing and cross-functional collaboration.
- Promote customer/marketing orientation.

It is especially important in larger organisations, especially where staff are working in different locations, where consistency of message is paramount to ensure that all workers are fully aligned to the direction etc of the business.

11 Internal communication methods

Marketing communications is concerned with the way various stakeholders interact with each other and internal communications relates to the way stakeholders within an organisation communicate with each other and receive marketing attention. It draws a boundary between internal and external stakeholders.

Internal stakeholders are employees and management who are interested in different issues, however, it is generally accepted that employees should be the key focus of internal communication.

Many organisations refer to the concept of 'treating employees as customers'. Indeed in many cases this may literally be true if they are also, for example, shareholders or customers. An employee of a bank may take an annual bonus in the form of shares and also maintain a current account.

The internal marketing mix consists of:

- **Product**: usually relates to the changing nature of a job role

- **Price**: the balance of psychological costs and the benefits of adopting a new orientation

- **Place**: where the activity takes place

- **Promotion**: external promotional methods can be adopted internally to demonstrate to staff the image portrayed in the market. Internal advertising campaigns can be undertaken reflecting external advertising. This is to be tailored to the different audiences but should be throughout the organisation.

The Chartered Institute of Marketing

- **People**: this relates to those involved in producing and delivering communication, training media and meetings. The management of service levels reflects customer expectations

- **Processes**: the communication and media process by which the product is brought to the customers' attention

- **Physical evidence**: training, briefings, documentation and, to an extent, place.

Internal communication is needed to reflect the messages given to other stakeholder groups, so that not only is there consistency in the message, but the values, attitudes and the general ethos of the organisation are clearly visible to all staff, so that they know what is expected of them in certain circumstances. This has been referred to as 'living the brand'. This is particularly important in organisations where staff deal solely with internal customers.

There are a number of important roles for internal marketing communications, as shown in Table 8.3.

Table 8.3   Roles for internal marketing communications

Role	Explanation
General communications	Differentiate: to differentiate the type and nature of communication across different employees or groups of employees. Remind: to remind staff of key values Inform: to provide staff with information Persuade: use persuasive language or imagery to convey consistent messages
Transactional	Directing new initiatives or co-ordinating actions or using resources effectively
Affiliation / cultural	Generating a sense of identity with the organisation as well as promoting and co-ordinating activities with external groups or individuals

Hooley *et al* (2008) identify other roles, which are:

- **Team building**: ensuring that barriers between different divisions are broken down so that all staff are working towards providing customers with service excellence and reducing the potential for conflict

- **Goal setting**: so that the focus is on achieving corporate goals which are clearly stated and measurable

- **Involvement**: a channel needs to be created so that problems and issues can be resolved in a constructive manner

- **Change management**: making changes to current structures and process and responding rapidly (internally) to external changes

It must be recognised that organisational structures are evolving and increasingly project teams are being used to launch new products into the market. Project teams can incorporate:

- Staff seconded from other divisions of the organisation
- Temporary staff who are employed just for the life of the project
- External consultants
- Customers

While this has the effect of blurring the boundaries between different stakeholders, it also affects the form that communication takes. Therefore, an organisation must clearly identify the different range of internal audiences so that messages can be effectively tailored to the needs of the audience.

The communication of clear and consistent messages ensures brand consistency. Large organisations will have a range of staff; young new entrants, clerical, management, experts, etc. This will require different communication methods to be employed.

Table 8.4 offers a range of communication methods available to an organisation to communicate internally.

Table 8.4   Internal communication methods

Method	Description
Intranet	The intranet is a system for distributing information electronically through its internal network.
	Staff can access a broad range of information that can be tailored to specific groups. For example, shop floor staff may be restricted to product information and HR facilities.
	Large organisations can have a number of intranets each serving the need of a particular division.
	Information should be kept up-to-date; otherwise reliability will be questioned by staff.
	Typically the intranet will be the first screen staff will see when they open the PC in the morning.
Email	An impersonal but quick way to communicate with all staff. Fast and cost effective, it can be used to update staff on new developments and urgent changes. It can provide information or be action orientated when the member of staff must take some action having received the mail. The sender of the mail can check if the message has been read.
	However, staff typically get many emails every day and instructions can be 'missed'.
	Staff can clarify aspects of the message if it is not understood.
Seminars	Seminars bring together small groups of people generally for recurring meetings.
	A seminar will focus on one specific area of the business or market and is run by an 'expert' in the particular field.
Briefings	A briefing can be presented in writing or orally. Typically a briefing is given when procedure change or significant organisational change is planned.
Newsletters	Historically newsletters were distributed in paper format. Increasingly, newsletters are now circulated electronically. However, in some organisations, staff do not have access to the web and paper still remains the channel of choice. However, research shows that a high proportion of staff with electronic access still print newsletters off to read at a more convenient time or location.
Mobile	Increasingly mobile phones are being used as a communication for non-voice communication. Mobile phones now have access to the internet and staff can read emails, access the intranet and generally communicate internally through electronic means.

ACTIVITY 8.3

Identify the main internal communications methods used by the organisation where you work, or where you have worked previously. Consider the pros and cons of each.

12 External communications audiences

Each organisation needs to identify who its key stakeholders (discussed in an earlier chapter) are through a process of stakeholder mapping. Then having identified them, it needs to decide who the target audiences are, ie who are the recipients of any communication originated by the organisation.

Potential audiences can be categorised into three groups:

- **Consumers**: the purchasers of the product
- **Channel members**: wholesalers and other members of the distribution channel
- **Stakeholders**: broader interest groups with an interest in the organisation and its activities

The Chartered Institute of Marketing

The role of communications with the external stakeholders is to maintain relationships through on-going dialogue and through multiple points of contact. However, it is not always immediately obvious who the key stakeholders are, and therefore like other stakeholder groups, a mapping exercise needs to be undertaken to establish the key groups.

Below is a broad list of possible external stakeholders that an organisation may want to communicate with. It is generic, so different groups may have a greater relevance than others to the organisation.

12.1 The media

The media is a key stakeholder for most organisations as it can support the organisation in its communication efforts, or conversely it can adopt a negative stance, thereby making the organisation's communication tasks more difficult.

12.2 Trade unions

Trade unions can influence internal practices, which affect the organisation's competitiveness in the market. Organisations may want to introduce efficiencies that may lead to a reduction in employees, these in turn may be rejected by the union.

Equally, unions are a strong source of lobbying different sectors and may be linked with other stakeholders.

12.3 Pressure groups

Pressure groups drive public opinion and shape organisation policy. They can support organisational change, or reject it. While it is often the larger groups (eg Greenpeace, Amnesty International, and Liberty) who have a high media profile, pressure groups operate at all levels campaigning for change. They are often an invaluable source of knowledge to be tapped into.

12.4 Government, regulatory bodies and membership groups

The government affects an organisation in many different ways, from the way the annual accounts are submitted to the amount of tax paid on profits. Often the location of an organisation can be determined by the government as a result of additional grants being made available.

Larger organisations are often regulated or monitored by industry bodies, such as ASA, FSA, or Ofwat. This can influence prices charged now and in the future, determine appropriate codes of conduct for conducting business and offer customers some protection against poor or inferior practices.

Membership groups often work together to improve the public's perception of the industry, or provide consistency of approach when dealing with customers.

12.5 Society

A huge and diverse group which expects to be treated in a certain way, ie that any products offered by an organisation will be fit for purpose, ie will work in a safe manner.

It also impacts on the design of products by buying, or not buying products. For example, society generally wants to be healthier, so organisations need to respond with less sugary drinks and less fat and salt in products.

Primark

Primark is a major retailer and has a reputation for selling reasonable quality clothes at low prices. Despite its focus on costs Primark has gone to great lengths to communicate its environmental and sustainability credentials with stakeholders.

Primark's CSR policy is clear:

'We aim to make our employees, suppliers and local and wider communities part of our success by working with them in every way we can. This means that:

- Employees have equal opportunities based on merit
- Suppliers are treated fairly
- Local communities are respected and supported by Primark
- The company takes its environmental responsibilities seriously'.

(Primark, 2011)

Primark takes every opportunity to display this commitment to CSR through numerous marketing communications, but notably through its advertisements, in-store merchandising and PR.

▶ **Exam tip**

It is imperative that students understand marketing communications strategy and the marketing planning process. As part of the analysis of the case material students should identify the marketing communications strategy(ies) adopted. They should undertake a detailed situation/context analysis of the organisation featured in the case and this should be clearly recorded in the student's pre-prepared analysis.

Students are frequently (but not always) asked to develop a communications plan, a key element of which is to decide on the most appropriate marketing communications strategy(ies). When responding to any questions in the examination, students must ensure that their answers are focused on addressing the issues raised in the case material. Answers must relate to the case material and should not simply be 'generic'. Such answers will not achieve sufficient marks to pass.

- Marketing communications relates to the promotion element of the marketing mix.

- DRIP is often used to describe the role of marketing communications (differentiate, remind, inform and persuade).

- Marketing communications objectives relate to marketing objectives.

- Situation/context analysis is an important part of the communications planning process.

- To develop an effective marketing communications plan it is essential that the marketer has a clear idea of who is the target audience.

- Marketing communications objectives must conform to the usual SMART criteria for objectives.

- There are three marketing communications strategies – push, pull and profile.

- Marketing communications activities can play a key role in building relationships with customers.

- Many campaigns require careful planning and co-ordination as they involve several different elements of the communications mix, which are being executed simultaneously (integrated marketing communications).

- The loyalty ladder shows the sequence in which consumers move from prospects to, ultimately, partners.

- Internal marketing is important to build a sense of marketing orientation within the organisation.

- Internal communications are vital to keep staff informed, engaged and motivated, and aware of new policies and procedures.

FURTHER READING

The Michael Porter's five forces model is useful to identify the dynamic forces within any supply market and provides an effective framework when identifying and analysing competition. If you are unfamiliar with this model here is the original article which explains the rationale behind it and how it can be applied:

Porter, M.E. (1979) How competitive forces shape strategy. *Harvard Business Review*, 57(2), pp137-145.

REFERENCES

Christopher, M. *et al* (2008) *Relationship marketing: creating stakeholder value*. Oxford, Butterworth-Heinemann.

Doyle, P. (2000) *Value-based marketing*. Chichester, John Wiley & Sons Ltd.

Fill, C. (2002) Marketing communications: contexts, strategies and applications. 3rd edition. London, FT Prentice-Hall.

Fill, C. (2006) *Marketing communications: engagement, strategies and practice.* 4th edition. Harlow, FT Prentice Hall.

Hooley, G. *et al* (2008) *Marketing strategy and competitive positioning.* 3rd edition. Harlow, FT Prentice Hall.

Peck, H. *et al* (1999) *Relationship marketing*. Oxford, Butterworth-Heinemann.

Pickton, D. and Broderick, A. (2005) *Integrated marketing communications*. 2nd edition. Harlow, Pearson Education Limited.

Porter, M.E. (1985) *Competitive advantage*. New York, The Free Press.

Primark (2011) Corporate Social Responsibility. Primark, http://www.primark.co.uk/about us/csr [Accessed on 21 January 2012].

QUICK QUIZ

1   What is the role of marketing communications?

2   What is the hierarchy of objectives within an organisation (from a marketing communications perspective)?

3   What tools can be used to help the marketer conduct the situation/context analysis element of the communications plan?

4   Objectives must be SMART – what does SMART stand for?

5   Describe three areas of possible marketing communications objectives.

6   What are the three marketing communications strategies?

7   The loyalty ladder suggests there are six levels of consumer – what are they?

8   What is the aim of internal marketing?

9   List three reasons why internal communications are important.

10   What are the main methods of internal communications?.

ACTIVITY DEBRIEFS

Activity 8.1

The answer to this activity is very much dependent on the marketing communications chosen. For each, you should then consider how it achieves each of the DRIP elements, ie:

- Differentiate – to make a product or brand appear to be different to that of a competitor.
- Remind – to reassure the target audience as to the benefits of making a purchase.
- Inform – to provide new information to a target audience, for example about a new product.
- Persuade – to encourage a target audience towards an action or to change an opinion.

Activity 8.2

You will find that there are many examples of pull and profile marketing communications strategy. Activities supporting the pull strategy are aimed at encouraging the consumer to increase demand for products. Typical examples include advertising, sales promotions, eg BOGOF (buy one get one free) and in store merchandising. Profile activities are focused more on creating general brand awareness, eg sponsorships and PR. Push activities are more difficult to identify as here the manufacturer targets intermediaries within the channel.

Activity 8.3

There are numerous internal communications methods, including:

- Intranet
- Email
- Seminars
- Team briefings
- Newsletters
- Tele/video-conferencing
- Meetings
- Conferences
- DVD/video
- Mobile alerts

QUICK QUIZ ANSWERS

1. The role of marketing communications is often described as DRIP – to differentiate, remind, inform and persuade.

2. Organisation mission statement, corporate objectives, functional objectives (including marketing), marketing communications objectives.

3. PESTEL, SWOT and Porter's five forces. These are just examples, there are other tools too which can be use to analyse an organisation's marketing environment.

4. SMART – specific, measurable, achievable, realistic and time bound.

5. Typical marketing communications objectives might focus on:

   - Changing perception
   - Creating/building awareness
   - Achieving positioning (or re-positioning)
   - Influencing the target audience
   - Generating sales (volumes and/or revenues)
   - Improving customer retention
   - Improving customer satisfaction
   - Supporting the launch of a new product

6. Push, pull and profile.

7. Prospect, purchaser, client, supporter, advocate and partner

8. Internal marketing is concerned with promoting a marketing orientation within the organisation.

9. Internal communications are important for a number of reasons:

   - Staff need to be kept informed about plans, objectives and other developments.
   - Customer-facing staff must be kept informed about new products and relevant policy changes.
   - Clear communication is important for motivation and morale.
   - Support staff engagement
   - Encourage information sharing and cross-functional collaboration
   - Promote customer/marketing orientation

10   There are many internal communications methods, including:

- Intranet
- Email
- Team briefings
- Tele/video-conferencing
- Meetings
- Mobile alerts

CHAPTER 9

Marketing communications activities and measurement

Introduction

In this chapter a range of promotional tools will be introduced and evaluated. While each will be considered in turn, it is important to recognise that it is the 'mixing' of the promotional tools which will generate competitive advantage for an organisation both internally and externally. However, any marketing spend must be measured to ensure that not only is value for money being received, but the objectives set are being met.

The structure and contents of a communications plan are explored and the importance of communications in securing new customers is highlighted.

Communication plans, as we will see, are derived from the marketing plan and therefore, the more robust the marketing plan, the more effective the communications plan is likely to be.

This chapter considers the role of planning and execution in different organisational contexts and sectors.

Topic list

The communications mix   (1)

Advertising   (2)

Personal selling   (3)

Exhibitions   (4)

Sales promotion   (5)

Public relations (PR)   (6)

Sponsorship   (7)

Direct marketing   (8)

Online/social media   (9)

Ambush marketing   (10)

Integrated marketing communications mix   (11)

Copywriting   (12)

Marketing communications models   (13)

Evaluating the effectiveness of marketing communications   (14)

3.3	Critically evaluate a range of communications mixes and recommend appropriate creative, innovative, sustainable and co-ordinated approaches to communications activities and creating the optimal mix for internal and external marketing activities
	▪ Advertising, including writing and checking copy
	▪ Personal selling
	▪ Direct marketing
	▪ Online media
	▪ Media tools and media message
	▪ Sales promotions
	▪ PR, exhibitions and sponsorships
	▪ Online forums; blogs; social networks
3.7	Recommend appropriate methods for measuring marketing communications activities and successful delivery of the marketing communications strategy
	▪ Setting marketing communications objectives
	▪ Measuring the effectiveness of marketing communications activities
	▪ Benchmarking communication effectiveness against other organisations, sectors, countries and competitors
	▪ The role of market research, locally and internationally

1 The communications mix

There are many communications tools available to marketers and Figure 9.1 offers a broad range of examples. Collectively, these tools represent the communications mix. Marketing communications activities are often referred to as above- below- or through-the-line.

Figure 9.1 Marketing communication tools

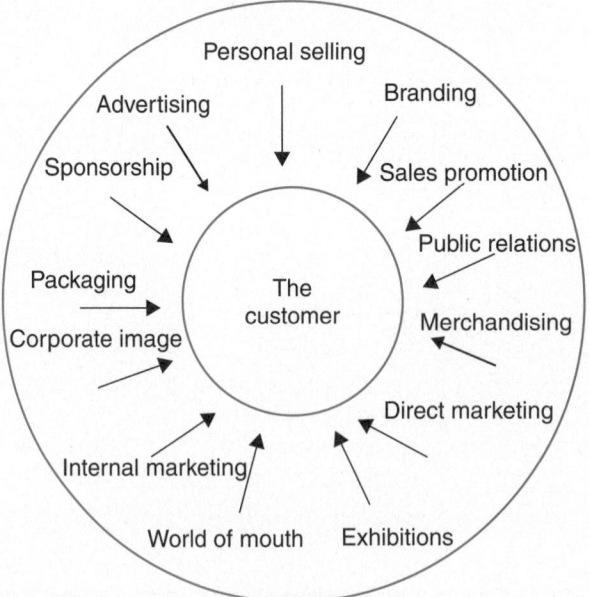

The Chartered Institute of Marketing

1.1 Above-the-line

Above-the-line activity relates to paid-for promotional activities carried out through mass media such as press, magazines, radio, outdoor, cinemas, banners and search engines. Historically the term related to the payment of agency commission.

1.2 Through-the-line

This refers to activity that involves above- and below-the-line communications where one form of advertising points the consumer to another form of advertising, thereby crossing the line. This can include direct marketing, direct mail catalogues, telemarketing and interactive communications including the internet.

The focus has moved from mass to more personalised communications which means relationships can start to be built.

1.3 Below-the-line

Below-the-line includes sales promotion, public relations and personal selling.

There has been a shift from an intervention-based approach (aimed at getting the attention of a customer who initially may not be interested in the product on offer) towards a permission-based approach (communicating mainly with the audience who may already have expressed an interest in the product on offer). As Fill (2006) suggests permission marketing sows the seeds for a relationship which emanates from the audience and not the owner of the brand.

Advertising is better for creating awareness and personal selling is more effective at promoting action and purchase behaviour.

The increasing use of public relations and in particular publicity, is a reflection of the high levels of credibility that this medium holds.

1.4 The communications mix

> ▶ **Key term**
>
> **Communications mix:** a key component of any marketing communications plan. The communications mix comprises a range of tools through which the organisation will attempt to achieve its communications objectives. The most commonly utilised tools are advertising, personal selling, sales promotions, public relations, sponsorships, direct marketing and online.

In summary the main marketing communications tools are:

- **Advertising:** mass media is often used to create awareness or encourage trialling of a product.
- **Personal selling:** common in retail or business-to-business market. Expensive, but often needed when complex products are involved.
- **Sales promotion:** used to encourage trial or increase usage – tactical and flexible.
- **Public relations (including sponsorship):** PR is not paid for, but often requires agency involvement, which can be expensive.
- **Direct marketing:** Increasingly popular tool that can deliver personalised messages.
- **Online:** Has rapidly increased in popularity due to the take-up of use of the Internet and the growth of social networking.

2 Advertising

Yeshin (2006, p1) defines advertising as 'paid-for, non-personal communication from an identified organisation, body, or individual designed to communicate information and to influence customer behaviour'.

The range of advertising channels is huge and if an organisation operates internationally the choice is daunting. However, some potential channels may be restricted because of the nature of the product and the country of operation (or advertising).

The role of advertising is:

- Awareness building
- Engagement with the purchaser or potential purchaser
- Positioning or repositioning brands

Advertising has the ability to reach a large target audience quickly, but this comes at a high cost.

Each day individuals are exposed to hundreds of advertising messages and only a very small percentage of those adverts will make an impact, as we tend to 'filter out' those that do not have any significance.

Marketers need to make decisions not only about which tool(s) to use, but to select the 'right' media in order to achieve organisational objectives effectively. The major advertising media available in the UK, are:

- Cinema
- Internet
- Magazines
- Newspapers
- Outdoor media
- Radio
- TV

2.1 Cinema

Cinema advertising remains popular, with numbers of cinema-goers holding up despite predictions from many sources that these numbers would decline considerably due to alternatives available to consumers. Today the cinema remains popular with families and couples and, as a result, is a highly effective advertising medium. Table 9.1 evaluates the advantages and disadvantages of cinema advertising.

Table 9.1   Advantages and disadvantages of cinema advertising

Advantages	Disadvantages
▪ High audio and visual impact	▪ High cost
▪ Captive audience, so high degree of control, audience not able to 'skim' or 'flick over'	▪ Can be low exposure, ie low capacity in some screens
▪ Segmentation possible by area or region	▪ Measurement hard to evaluate
▪ Good medium for the 'younger' market	▪ Timings depend on local cinema

2.2 Internet/online

Today, it goes without saying, that the internet has grown in popularity as a general communication channel, a channel for the distribution of products and services and as an advertising medium. Customers are increasingly happy to make a purchase on the internet, having evolved from using it as an information source, with the purchase being made through a more established channel.

The Chartered
Institute of Marketing

For marketers the internet offers a choice of web advertising through the presence of an organisation's own site, the use of portals, pop-ups or banner advertising. However, technology has developed rapidly, and continues to do so. Not only is the internet commonplace today but more recent innovations such as Facebook, Twitter and 'blogging' are in everyday use, both between consumers and for B2B and B2C marketing purposes.

Concepts that were initially confined to discrete market segments are now being extended. Not only are blogs, online forums and social networks used to share information between parties who are known to each other they are now commonly used by organisations looking to reach a wider (global) audience.

Table 9.2 evaluates the advantages and disadvantages of internet advertising.

Table 9.2   Advantages and disadvantages of internet advertising

Advantages	Disadvantages
▪ Relatively inexpensive to set up	▪ Some issues about intrusion
▪ Speed of setup can be fast	▪ Still developing medium and not yet mainstream, but growing rapidly
▪ Global reach	▪ Often easy to delete the message without viewing
▪ Creative and interactive options available	▪ Not regulated as yet
▪ Messages can be downloaded for later consumption	
▪ Speed of getting message to consumer very fast	

2.3 Magazines

Stokes and Lomax (2008) estimate that around 14% of the UK press advertising is accounted for by the spend in magazines. Generally magazines offer a cost-effective way of reaching the target audience. However, costs do vary depending on the title and circulation of the magazine.

Table 9.3 evaluates the advantages and disadvantages of magazine advertising.

Table 9.3   Advantages and disadvantages of magazine advertising

Advantages	Disadvantages
▪ Wide range of specialist titles allowing for effective segmentation	▪ Can be long lead in times especially with specialist and trade journals
▪ Can be read frequently, ie more than once	▪ Can be expensive compared with other media
▪ Readership often greater than circulation (waiting rooms, hotels, etc)	▪ Often involves high quality (expensive) production
▪ Long life cycle	

2.4 Newspapers

The internet is having an impact on newspaper sales, as readers are increasingly keen to read the news as it happens, or be part of the news making process through the use of online blogs. Sales have similarly been affected by the availability of free newspapers.

The impact is less dramatic on local newspapers, where they still maintain a strong following and some titles are seeing an increase in sales.

Table 9.4 evaluates the advantages and disadvantages of newspaper advertising.

Table 9.4   Advantages and disadvantages of newspaper advertising

Advantages	Disadvantages
Regional newspapers	
<ul><li>High local readership, often multiple reads</li><li>Low cost production</li><li>Focused on the local area, so will have specialist sections</li></ul>	<ul><li>Generally weekly</li><li>Often not seen as objective</li></ul>
National daily newspapers	
<ul><li>High levels of readership, so mass market</li><li>Short lead in times for media is very responsive to timescales</li><li>Range of newspaper titles, so segmentation can be effective</li><li>Wide choice of advertising options, eg main newspaper (and choice of positioning and size), or specialist section</li></ul>	<ul><li>High number of competing adverts, so 'stand out' harder to achieve</li><li>Limited life span</li><li>Generally need a campaign rather than a 'one-off' advert</li><li>Production costs can be high</li></ul>

2.5 Outdoor media

Outdoor media covers a range of media from adverts in bus stops and washrooms through to billboards and hoardings. Increasingly technology, with the introduction of digital screens, is transforming outdoor media allowing for new campaigns and creative treatments. Table 9.5 evaluates the advantages and disadvantages of outdoor media advertising.

Table 9.5   Advantages and disadvantages of outdoor media

Advantages	Disadvantages
<ul><li>Repeat exposure, generally we go to work the same way, or shop in the same area</li><li>Low cost</li><li>Supportive of other media, ie reinforces messages</li><li>Flexible duration of campaign</li></ul>	<ul><li>Opportunity to see poster can be quite short if passing in car, train or bus</li><li>Random viewing by people</li></ul>

It must be recognised that digital technology will mean advertisers can target their messages by audience, location, or a specific time during the day, and they will be able to change the creative executions at different locations.

The growth of outdoor advertising has been supported by the huge growth in the numbers of hours we spend outside the home and a large increase in the investment and upgrading of key sites.

2.6 Radio

Advertisers have a choice of regional and national radio and there are a growing number of internet stations who allow for segmentation in a variety of ways. Examples are specialists, young children, pensioners, young parents, through to people on their way home through the rush hour traffic.

Table 9.6 evaluates the advantages and disadvantages of radio advertising.

Table 9.6   Advantages and disadvantages of radio advertising

Advantages	Disadvantages
■ Cheap (cost per listener)	■ Radio can be in the 'background' so not actively listened to
■ Can have large coverage	■ Generally ads only last a few seconds, so need repeating
■ Can link in with sponsorship	■ Creativity currently restricted because of the media, but DAB radio increasing opportunities
■ Can be targeted	
■ Portable, ie variety of listening locations, eg car, home	

2.7 Television

Most of us are familiar with TV as a form of advertising, which is typically used by major brands, although smaller companies can use it regionally. It is the most expensive form of media and while it reaches a broad audience it is now competing with online advertising.

Table 9.7 evaluates the advantages and disadvantages of television advertising.

Table 9.7   Advantages and disadvantages of television advertising

Advantages	Disadvantages
■ High impact	■ High cost
■ Mass audiences, so wide coverage quickly	■ Can channel-hop and avoid the ads
■ High degree of creativity available	■ High risk, if ads poorly constructed in terms of message and tone
■ Strong sound and visual qualities	■ Can have long production times
■ Evaluation mechanisms well developed	

THE REAL WORLD

TV and online advertising

'Research from Thinkbox and the Internet Advertising Bureau (IAB) has shown that using TV and online together in advertising campaigns is significantly more effective for advertisers than using either in isolation. Their combined use produces major benefits for advertisers, including dramatically increased positive brand perception amongst consumers – some 50% higher – as well as significantly greater likelihood of purchase.

Key findings from the study include:

■ Using TV and online together results in 47% more positivity about a brand than using either in isolation

■ The likelihood of buying or using a product increases by more than 50% when TV and online are used together

■ 48% of the sample group watched broadcast TV while online, most days

■ Two thirds of this group have watched TV via online providers, primarily as a way to catch-up with broadcast TV and mainly from TV broadcasters' websites

■ Both TV and the internet are used for entertainment (TV, 80%; online 56%) and both have a significant influence on driving purchase (75% and 52%)

■ The findings reinforce the need to ensure creative synergy between TV and online advertising and identify best practice for better effectiveness, which requires more than simply putting together TV ads.'

(Thinkbox, 2012)

3 Personal selling

Personal selling is generally used in the retail or business-to-business environments or where the product is complex or the profit margins are high as personal selling is expensive. However, sales teams now tend to be focused on particular products and range.

Personal selling also allows the opportunity to ask questions (ie dyadic communication). The message itself can be tailored to the needs of the potential purchaser, giving a more individual approach.

Individuals by their very nature are each different, and therefore it can be difficult for an organisation to ensure all staff are performing consistently and consequently there may be variability in the quality of the approach adopted by each individual member of staff.

There doesn't need to be a face-to-face meeting, personal selling can be conducted on the telephone and this can reduce the cost to the organisation.

Stokes and Lomax (2008) identify six different types of selling situations:

- **Delivery selling**: the 'delivery' person also has a selling role. The intention is to penetrate the existing customer base at the point of delivering a product.

- **Retail selling**: selling to customers who come into the premises to make a purchase. Often referred to as 'sales advisers', they provide assistance and advice to help the customer make the purchase.

- **Trade selling**: products are sold into the distribution channel, eg wholesalers. The role also ensures the point-of-sale (POS) material displayed are in keeping with the brand.

- **New business selling**: selling to new customers, ie people or organisations who are not yet customers.

- **Experiential selling**: encouraging purchase through trial or testing

- **Technical selling**: complex products often require a high degree of interaction, so 'technical' assistance is needed, eg purchasing a pension policy.

Reid *et al* (2002) identified three sales behaviours: getting, giving and using information.

- **Getting information**: face-to-face contact can be useful in collecting information about customers, the market and competitors. Often a member of the sales team will be responsible for compiling competition activity reports.

- **Giving information**: providing customers and stakeholders with key or critical information concerning the organisation's reputation in the market, new product information, or updating them on competitor products, sales or innovations.

- **Using information**: collecting information in order to solve a customer's problem.

As organisations are increasingly keen to build relationships with customers rather than simply having a transactional relationship, the role of personal selling can be important in the creation and maintenance of relationships.

Sales people undertake a variety of other roles which have variously been defined as:

- **Prospecting for new clients**: it's important to have a stream of new clients coming through, so the sales team will be continually looking to build leads and generate sales.

- **Communicating**: keeping stakeholders informed about the organisation: development of new products, competitor comparisons, product and brand positioning.

- **Information gathering**: collecting key information about the market, competitors and new initiatives.

- **Servicing**: ongoing client maintenance through the provision of technical information. Problem-solving, suggesting new products, so that the client knows they can rely on the organisation.

- **Allocating**: managing resources and deploying them as appropriate.

- **Shaping**: building and maintaining the relationship with the client.

The exact nature of the role carried out by the sales team will vary from industry to industry and will also vary with the size of the organisation. In larger organisations the sales team may simply be responsible for 'sales' in the narrowest sense of the word, ie closing the sale. Others, sometimes known as relationship managers, will assume responsibility for building the relationship and potentially developing it into a Key Account.

THE REAL WORLD

It is perhaps logical, especially with the advent of technology, to consider that the days of the direct sales force are numbered. Certainly, many organisations have moved to sales models which are more focused around customer self-service, retaining the personal selling approach for more complex products and for dealing with higher net worth customers. Personal selling is more common in B2B environments because of the frequent complexity of products being sold.

However, for some companies, personal selling is still the main method of reaching customers. One such company is Avon, the cosmetic company, which has been selling its products directly to customers for over a hundred years. Much of its success has been built on a firm foundation of relationship building. For many Avon customers, the 'Avon representative' is a family member, friend or neighbour, which clearly builds trust in the relationship.

---

4 Exhibitions

Exhibitions are a popular form of field marketing, both in the UK and overseas, which is increasing in popularity and the opening of new centres in London and Manchester for example reflect this. Exhibitions are used predominantly in the B2B market and give organisations the opportunity to meet new contacts, distributors and customers and see what the competition is offering. Exhibitions are good for raising profile and image, however, having attended an exhibition, there is an implied assumption this will be on an ongoing rather than one-off basis. While exhibitions can be expensive, many are highly targeted offerings. There are also some large B2C exhibitions (eg franchise exhibition, car show, motor show, flower show, ideal home show, etc).

---

5 Sales promotion

The following description of sales promotion is based on the Institute of Promotional Marketing's definition:

'Sales promotion is a range of tactical marketing techniques, designed within a strategic marketing framework, in order to add value to a product to achieve a specific marketing or sales objective(s)'.

The tactical nature of sales promotion means that it can be implemented, as quickly as circumstances require. If sales are sufficiently below the level expected, a sales initiative can be as instigated and it will be of sufficient duration that sales start to move quickly to the expected levels at which time it can be terminated. It is a flexible and fast way to respond to the business environment.

Sales promotions can also be used to increase demand at times when traditionally sales will be low; equally it can be used to support the launch of a new product into the market.

It is not just the consumer who is the target for sales promotion. Organisations will also use it within the distribution channel.

A wholesaler may be encouraged to stock a new product, or increase sales of a range of existing products in return for an increased profit margin or some other form of offer, such as 'sale or return'.

The remuneration paid to a sales team can be increased to encourage the sale of certain products; payment levels would return to normal levels when the objectives have been reached.

While sales promotion has many advantages if used correctly, organisations need to be aware that any price reductions, particularly if considered large, may devalue the product in the mind of the consumer.

6 Public relations (PR)

> ▶ **Key term**
>
> **Public relations (PR):** media coverage about the organisation and/or its products which is not paid for by the organisation and therefore cannot be controlled.

According to the Chartered Institute of Public Relations (CIPR), 'public relations is about reputation – the result of what you do, what you say and what others say about you'.

Public relations (PR) is the discipline that looks after reputation of a company and/or product, with the aim of earning understanding and support and influencing opinion and behaviour. It is the planned and sustained effort to establish and maintain goodwill and mutual understanding between an organisation and its publics.

The role of PR covers two aspects: marketing PR and corporate PR.

Marketing PR supports and manages an organisation's products by supporting the other elements of the marketing mix. It is usually planned and derived from the marketing plan with clear objectives, strategy and measurement. Messages will be tailored to the need of each audience.

Corporate PR tends to be long-term relationship building, clearly positioning the organisation and its values with the wider market. Again, usually planned, with specific measurements agreed. However, it also covers unplanned activities and crises. It ensures:

- Key messages are agreed
- People talking to the media are consistent with the message
- Information is given in a timely manner
- The tone is appropriate for the situation

The range of PR activities includes:

- Media relations
- Marketing (of products, services and issues)
- Copy/writing
- Press office
- Online PR
- Internal PR, journals and briefings
- Sponsorship
- Event and conference management
- Research
- Evaluation
- Corporate identity
- Publications

PR helps an organisation to manage its relationships with key stakeholders, raise awareness of the brand and the organisation's activities.

While it is often suggested that PR is free, this is far from the truth. It can be very expensive to employ a PR agency and attend exhibitions and events.

A criticism often levied at PR is the lack of control an organisation has over the final message that gets published or broadcast. At the other end of the spectrum is the concept of 'spin' where the message is clearly positioned with the audience.

The role of PR is growing and organisations are increasingly recognising the importance of PR and its different forms:

- **Press agency**: a form of one-way communication where the organisation informs or tells the various publics what it wants them to hear (spin).

- **Public information**: providing information that the public needs to know. Usually provided in an objective manner.

- **Two-way asymmetric**: arguments based on research (independent) are made to encourage the public to change their attitude or beliefs.

- **Two-way symmetric**: PR serves to build mutual understanding between the organisation and its publics.

Publics are a group of people or organisations that an organisation needs to communicate with in order to convey its key messages. Publics can be grouped into five categories (Brassington and Pettitt, 2006):

- **Commercial**: Where there is a trading relationship with, or in competition with, other organisations between the parties and synergy and understanding needs to be built, so that a positive and encouraging image can be portrayed for the industry group or market. This group can include, competitors, suppliers as well as customers.

- **Internal**: Often organisations are good at external PR, but they forget to keep staff informed of what is happening, which can be demotivating, but equally can negatively impact on external messages. This group can include staff, management and trade unions.

- **Authority**: Publics which have 'power' because of either their legal, statutory, or voluntary position to influence the organisation. This group can include government, pressure groups, buying or membership groups.

- **Media**: The media is a particularly influential group of publics which can be supportive, or adversarial. The public takes notice of this group and messages need to be carefully managed. This group can include TV, press, radio and increasingly the internet.

- **Financial**: Organisations also need to keep this group of publics informed. Larger organisations that may be listed on the UK Stock Exchange while having a legal duty to provide certain information need to manage expectations with the group both positively and negatively. This group can include the organisation's bankers, accountants, financial advisers and shareholders.

ACTIVITY 9.1

Follow media reports (press, TV, radio and online) closely for a few days and identify the number of references made to different organisations. Consider the impact of these reports on those organisations, ie is the impact positive or negative for the organisation?

7 Sponsorship

According to BDS consultancy, one of Europe's leading sponsorship consultancies, sponsorship can be defined as:

> 'A business relationship between a provider of funds, resources or services and an individual, event or organisation which offers in return rights and association that may be used for commercial advantage in return for the sponsorship investment'.

Reasons for sponsoring an organisation, event or sport include:

- Increased awareness for the brand
- Enhancing brand/corporate image
- Brand association with some popular activity
- Innovative product showcasing
- Product launches, raising the organisation's profile
- Providing clear differentiation from the competition

Sponsorship takes place in sport, television, radio and the arts. It is also used in cause-related marketing. Sport continues to dominate the UK sponsorship market, attracting more than half of all sponsorship expenditure in the first ten years of the new millennium. Major events, such as the Olympic Games attract many hundreds of millions of pounds in sponsorship revenues for the organisers, given the event's appeal to a global audience.

8 Direct marketing

> ▶ **Key term**
>
> **Direct marketing:** marketing communications, using various media, which interact directly with the consumer, generally providing a 'call for action' from the customer, eg to order a product or to telephone for further information.

The American Direct Marketing Association (DMA) defines direct marketing as:

> 'An interactive process of addressable communication that uses one or more advertising media to effect, at any location, a measurable sale, lead, retail purchase, or charitable donation, with this activity analysed on a database for the development of ongoing mutually beneficial relationships between marketers and customer, prospects, or donor'.

Direct marketing includes:

- **Direct mail**: Personalised mail to an identified addressee, used in both the B2C and B2B markets. Can be highly targeted based on the previous behaviour of the individual. Relies heavily on an accurate database being maintained. The UK is one of Europe's heaviest users of direct mail.

- **Direct response advertising**: This form of direct mail can include freepost or free phone response mechanisms, the internet and DRTV (direct response advertising in television).

- **Telemarketing**: Increasingly used as the cost of telephony reduces and technology becomes more sophisticated. A direct approach is made by telephone to existing or potential customers (outbound telephony), or where a customer is encouraged to telephone the organisation (inbound telephony).

- **Online**: Has developed rapidly as a direct marketing tool.

- **Mobile**: Has also developed rapidly although has rather limited capability due to restrictions on length of SMS messages.

- **Mail order**: A traditional form of direct marketing to certain sections of the economy, where products were purchased by viewing a catalogue which was distributed direct to the consumer or via third parties (sales agents). While organisations still use catalogues these are usually linked with some other channel such as the internet. Organisations are increasingly moving to online catalogues

- **Teleshopping**: Includes a broad range of activities such as the internet through virtual stores, or shopping via the internet or telephone in response to television adverts, or home shopping channels which have developed with satellite and cable TV channels.

9 Online/social media

The use of social media is now commonplace in marketing communications. Its aim is the same as any other form of marketing communications in that the organisation is seeking to differentiate, remind, inform and persuade (DRIP) consumers, through the use of communication channels which have become more recently available due to technology.

To the organisation, the use of such media brings many benefits compared to other marketing communications methods. It can be highly targeted, it can be relatively cheap, but above all messages can be spread rapidly on a global scale. Another significant attraction has been the growth in adoption of the devices which connect consumers to the internet, with many individuals today, seemingly, continually interacting with others through mobile devices, PCs and laptops.

9.1 Social networking sites

Social networking is commonplace today, with many millions of people regularly using Facebook, LinkedIn, Twitter, blogs and YouTube. Once used for 'keeping in touch' with friends and family, social networking has become major business and, as a result, is widely used by organisations for marketing purposes.

9.2 Viral marketing

> ▶ **Key term**
>
> **Viral marketing:** a marketing communications activity which is specifically created to encourage the initial recipient to pass it on, generally electronically, to friends and family.

Viral marketing is a relatively recent phenomenon in marketing communications. It is dependent on the organisation creating a message, picture or video clip which encourages the initial recipient(s) to pass it on to other people that they know. As a result, it is the recipients themselves who actually spread to the organisation's marketing communication for it.

Often, for example, the organisation might commission a low budget amusing advertisement and posts it on YouTube. The link is then emailed to a number of recipients who, assuming the YouTube clip is sufficiently amusing and/or thought-provoking, will then forward it on to family and friends. The most successful viral marketing campaigns have spread rapidly across the globe, providing significant coverage for the organisation at very low cost.

THE REAL WORLD

One of the most famous viral marketing campaigns was run by Evian (natural water company) with the suggestion 'Let's observe the effects of Evian on your body'. The 'Evian Roller Babies International Version' featured a 60 second video of babies performing stunts on roller skates (obviously this was not real but looked very much as if it was!). It certainly met the criteria for an effective viral advertisement as the YouTube link spread rapidly with the clip soon registering more than 50 million 'plays'.

At the time of going to print the advertisement was still on YouTube, but we cannot guarantee it will still be available and that it has not been changed in any way.

9.3 Guerrilla marketing

▶ **Key term**

Guerrilla marketing: tactical marketing communications activities which are typically low budget and delivered on a local scale. Such activities are frequently unconventional in nature and designed to have an element of surprise in order to make the activity/brand more memorable.

This is another relatively recent addition to the marketing communications 'toolkit'. Typical characteristics of guerrilla campaigns are that they are low cost and executed on a local, rather than a national, scale. They are also often unconventional and, therefore, have the appeal of an element of surprise and memorability to the consumer. By their nature, similar to 'guerrilla warfare' (from which the term has come), these campaigns have an element of 'agility' in that they are relatively quick to develop and 'surprise' to stand out in the mind of the consumer.

There are many examples including redecorating telephone kiosks, using people pretending to be statues, placing cars or other large items in the middle of shopping centres. The key with these campaigns often is that they focus on something out of the ordinary.

10 Ambush marketing

▶ **Key term**

Ambush marketing: effectively 'piggybacking' unofficially on another organisation's sponsorship of an event.

Ambush marketing is a relatively recent concept and is commonly associated with major events, eg music concerts and sports events. Here the organisation makes a positive decision to leverage association with the event but not through conventional channels, ie it is not part of the official group of sponsors.

One of the most famous examples was during the 2010 football World Cup Finals in South Africa at which the official beer sponsor was Budweiser (a brand owned by Anheuser-Busch). A Dutch beer company hired 36 female models who were dressed in bright short orange dresses and who were advertising that company's beer to attend the match as spectators which drew considerable attention from the world's media. As a result the beer attracted much free publicity, much to the annoyance of the event organisers and, of course, of Budweiser.

11 Integrated marketing communications mix

Having looked at the different promotional tools individually, generally they will be used together (integrated) so that the key messages can be communicated in a consistent way. Each promotional tool and choice of media should be used to support each other and reinforce the key messages. If this does not happen then the customer is likely to become confused as a result of the mixed messages and less likely to make a purchase.

Table 9.8 summarises the various promotional tools assessed against the criteria of communications, cost and control.

Table 9.8 Various promotional tools assessed against the criteria of communications, cost and control

	Advertising	Sales promotion	Public relations	Personal selling	Direct marketing
Ability to deliver a personal message	Low	Low	Low	High	High
Ability to reach a large audience	High	Medium	Medium	Low	Medium
Level of interaction	Low	Low	Low	High	High

The Chartered Institute of Marketing

	Advertising	Sales promotion	Public relations	Personal selling	Direct marketing
Credibility given by target audience	Low	Medium	High	Medium	Medium
Absolute costs	High	Medium	Low	High	Medium
Cost per contact	Low	Medium	Low	Low	High
Wastage	High	Medium	High	High	Low
Size of investment	High	Medium	Low	High	Medium
Ability to target particular audiences	Medium	High	Low	Medium	High
Management's ability to adapt quickly as circumstances change	Medium	High	Low	Medium	High

ACTIVITY 9.2

Identify three examples of organisations which are conducting an integrated campaign. To do this you will need to pay attention to the various marketing communications mix tools which will involve, for example, observing TV and outdoor advertisements, reading newspapers and magazines, listening to commercial radio and paying attention to online communications.

12 Copywriting

Copywriting is the creative process of writing text for advertisements or publicity material. Copywriters are the people who write the text in accordance with a brief they have been given to work to, in order to ensure the messages are delivered to the intended audience. Copywriters work in-house, for large to medium-sized organisations or for a range of agencies including PR, direct marketing and consultancies.

Copywriting is used in all the main forms of advertising–outdoor media, direct mail and digital media including the internet – and needs to engage the interest of the audience so that they feel positive towards the product and go to purchase it. Copywriters need to understand who the target audience is, what their level of understanding is and what you want them to take away from your advertisement. Bowdery (2008) writes 'do you understand the customers you're trying to influence and could you pick them out in a crowd? More importantly, could they pick your ad out in a similarly crowded marketplace?'

When developing the copy it is important not to cause offence and this is especially important when the message is being used outside the country of origination and alternative concepts are needed. Where the creative concept is used overseas, complex word and local idioms must be avoided. Websites need to be carefully worded to ensure consistency and clarity of message.

Copy should be creative but clear, jargon-free and have the right tone of voice for the audience. Finally the message should be grammatically correct with no typographical errors.

13 Marketing communications models

A number of different models have evolved to help marketers develop communications which are more relevant to the target audience. The two most commonly used models are dealt with below.

13.1 AIDA

> **▶ Key term**
>
> **AIDA:** a marketing communications tool focusing on the sequence of reactions from the consumer as a result of an effective campaign (attention, interest, desire and action). This helps the marketer to develop marketing communications activities to influence the consumer to progress through the stages.

This model suggests that the communication(s) should lead the target audience sequentially through:

- Awareness
- Interest
- Desire
- Action

Marketing communications activities should focus on the above, with different elements of the communications mix used at each of the stages. Marketers should, therefore, focus on developing communications which have a clear message that will create awareness and stimulate interest. Further information (or stimulants) can then be used to encourage desire, with a 'call to action' resulting in a change of opinion or closure of a sale. There will not always be a specific 'call to action' from communications activities. The action may be an increase in awareness or brand recognition. In sales campaigns the 'call to action' may be a prompt for the customer to call a telephone number or to click on a website.

13.2 DAGMAR

> **▶ Key term**
>
> **DAGMAR:** a marketing communications tool which assumes that consumers go through a number of stages before making a decision to purchase (unawareness, awareness, comprehension, conviction and action). This helps the marketer to develop marketing communications activities to influence the consumer to progress through the stages.

The DAGMAR (Defining Advertising Goals for Measured Advertising Results) model is similar to AIDA. This model is based on the premise that buyers will go through a number of stages pre-purchase decision. The stages are:

- Unawareness: this stage is pre-communications activities.

- Awareness: this stage is necessary for the target audience to understand the message from the marketing organisation.

- Comprehension: at this stage the buyer must understand the message, ie just awareness is not sufficient.

- Conviction: at this stage the buyer must progress beyond simply comprehending the message they must be convinced of its meaning.

- Action: the communication must guide the buyer through to a 'call for action'.

14 Evaluating the effectiveness of marketing communications

'Half the money I spend on advertising is wasted; the trouble is I don't know which half.' This statement, which has been attributed to John Wanamaker (US department store owner), is frequently quoted to highlight the challenges of evaluating the success of communications activities. It is also often used by Chief Executives in amazement at size of budget requests made by Marketing Directors!

The Chartered Institute of Marketing

14.1 Why measure?

All sizeable organisational expenditure should be justified. ROI is important and resources are limited, especially in the current economic climate and given the pressure faced by financial services organisations. Billions of dollars are spent each year on marketing and organisations are keen to ensure that they achieve an acceptable level of payback.

So, must all marketing activities be measured? The answer is simple – only where the cost of measurement is justified. But certainly most activities can and should be measured. If nothing else, it is useful for the marketing function to 'prove' its value. Otherwise it is easy for the marketing function to be perceived as a 'cost', while sales is accredited with the revenues.

14.2 How to measure the effectiveness of marketing communications activities

The effectiveness of activities will be determined by tracking the benefits gained and comparing against the outlay. To be realistic, the latter should include consideration of the financial costs (development and execution) and resourcing costs.

There are a number of ways to measure the effectiveness of marketing communications activities. These are detailed below.

14.2.1 Advertising

Where the direct response advertising is used, ie where there is a clear call to action, the action is trackable, for example number of calls received. Where the advertising is for general awareness, building measurement is more difficult and expensive. In this case market research can be used to gather data from the target audience on recall and recognition. It is also possible to carry out research to gather views and opinions on brand values etc which will help the organisation to determine and monitor positioning. Advertising used to support specific products can also be measured by the performance of the product, ie have more sales been generated during the advertising campaign?

14.2.2 Personal selling

Typically personal selling is associated with sales and other personal targets. Sales teams nowadays commonly have targets for sales volumes and revenues, product and customer profitability, new business acquisition, customer retention, customer satisfaction (especially for relationship management staff).

14.2.3 Sponsorship

Sponsorship focuses on awareness and brand recognition and so, realistically, can only effectively be measured by market research. Organisations will also track sales activities during specific sponsorships, eg during the RBS Six Nations rugby tournament, although simultaneous to the sponsorship the organisation will also execute many other campaigns so it is difficult to accredit all successes with the sponsorship alone. Sponsorships may change public opinion, eg through sponsoring local or charity events. The public's reaction to these activities can be monitored through market research.

14.2.4 Sales promotions

These are specifically connected to sales activities and are very often trackable, eg where there is 'an offer code'. During the period of offers, eg 'interest-free', sales activity will be monitored closely.

14.2.5 Direct marketing

Traditionally direct marketing has been one of the easiest types of communication to measure. Often campaign or bar codes are used so responses can be tracked and directly attributed to the activity. Specific sales targets can be attributed to campaigns (eg calls, leads and sales generated). Where a marketing agency is used it is not uncommon for remuneration to be based on the success of the campaign. As mentioned above, direct marketing can also be used for general brand awareness building, in which case measurement would be by market research and/or monitoring the buying behaviour of the target audience.

14.2.6 Public relations (PR)

The traditional method of placing a value on PR is to use AVE (the advertising value equivalent). Here the organisation, very often through use of a specialist PR agency, will track its media coverage and will then determine how much an equivalent volume of coverage would have cost through use of advertising. Large organisations can generate considerable volumes of PR, including 'mentions' in the press (local, national and trade specific), radio and TV. The main issues with PR measurement are that not all PR is positive PR and this too should be tracked and taken into consideration.

14.2.7 Online

As with direct marketing, any form of direct response online activity is easily trackable. Similarly, the effectiveness of the organisation's website(s) can be tracked in terms of the 'hit' and 'click-through' activity generated. Online advertising can be measured through market research. Where online communications are used for sales and specific product activities measurement is straightforward and can easily be tracked, measuring the numbers of responses and those which ultimately lead to a sale.

> ▶ **Exam tip**

There have been a number of questions in examinations to date which require students to 'develop communications plan'. A framework for a communications plan was provided in the previous chapter, but it is worth looking again at what 'develop a communications plan' means. To answer this type of question you are required to actually write a plan, which should include the following sections:

1. Situation/context analysis
2. Set communications objectives
3. Target market profile
4. Marketing communications strategy (push/pull/profile)
5. Segmentation, targeting and positioning
6. Develop the communications message
7. Develop an integrated communications mix
8. Schedule media
9. Set promotional budget
10. Allocate resources
11. Execute and monitor
12. Evaluate effectiveness

A key element of such a plan is the communications mix which must be tailored to suit the needs of the target market to deliver the defined communications strategy and objectives.

The main reasons why students fail this type of question can be easily summarised:

1. Some do not know how to construct a communications plan
2. Some write a marketing plan and not a communications plan
3. Some merely write an essay about 'how to write a plan' or 'what are the typical contents of a communications plan'
4. Some plans do not relate sufficiently to the company featured within the case

Remember also to apply your pre-prepared analysis fully in the answer. This does not mean simply referring to it. The analysis must be used to support and reinforce points made. Any reference to it must be clearly related to the question. For example, merely stating 'See my PESTEL analysis, Figure 1.1, which states there is a recession' is insufficient. The statement may be true, but it needs to be made clear how the recession will impact the communications strategy, objectives, activities etc.

ACTIVITY 9.3

Consider how organisations might attempt to measure the effectiveness of the marketing communications tools that you witnessed in Activity 9.2.

The Chartered Institute of Marketing

CHAPTER ROUNDUP

- The communications mix comprises a number of different tools.

- The communications mix (part of the 'promotion' element of the marketing mix) must be tailored to the needs of the intended target audience.

- Advertising is a popular form of communication but can be expensive, eg TV.

- Personal selling is less common today due to other methods of communication being available.

- Personal selling is still popular in B2B marketing and where the products/services being sold are complex.

- Public relations (PR) is a form of marketing communication, which while 'free' cannot be controlled by the organisation.

- Exhibitions are a popular form of field marketing in both B2B and B2B sectors.

- Sales promotions are an important component within the marketer's tactical toolkit.

- Direct marketing is popular and can be highly targeted, and is therefore often viewed as a cost-effective form of marketing communication.

- There are new and emerging communications methods due to technology.

- Facebook, Twitter, blogging and YouTube all now play a key role in marketing communications.

- Copywriting is the creative process of writing text (copy) for advertisements and other publicity materials.

- AIDA and DAGMAR are useful marketing communications tools.

- Measuring the effectiveness of marketing communications activities is a key part of the planning process.

FURTHER READING

For further information on AIDA read the following paper:

Barnham, C. (2008) Instantiation. *International Journal of Market Research*, 50(2), pp203-220.

This article, while quite old now, provides some useful background on DAGMAR:

Marschner, D.C. (1971), DAGMAR revisited: eight years later. *Journal of Advertising Research*, 11(2), pp27-33.

REFERENCES

Avon (2012) http://www.avon.com [Accessed on 25 January 2012]

CIPR (2012) http://www.cipr.co.uk [Accessed on 25 January 2012]

Bowdery, R. (2008) *Copywriting*. Switzerland, AVA Publishing SA.

Brassington, F. and Pettitt, S. (2006) *Principles of marketing*. Harlow, FT Prentice Hall.

BDS Sponsorship (2012) http://www.sponsorship.co.uk [Accessed on 25 January 2012]

The Direct Marketing Association (2012) http://www.the-dma.org/index.php [Accessed on 25 January 2012]

Fill, C. (2006) *Marketing communications: engagement, strategies and practice.* 4th edition. Oxford, FT Prentice Hall.

The Institute of Promotional Marketing (2012) http://www.theipm.org.uk [Accessed on 25 January 2012]

Reid, A. *et al* (2002) The impact of purchase situation on sales-person communication behaviours in business markets. *Industrial Marketing Management*, 31(3).

Stokes, D. and Lomax, W. (2008) *Marketing: A brief introduction*. London, Thomson.

Thinkbox (2012) TV and online: better together. Thinkbox, http://www.thinkbox.tv/server/show/nav.1019. [Accessed on 25 January 2012]

Yeshin, T. (2006) *Advertising*. London, Thomson.

QUICK QUIZ

1   What are the main elements of the marketing communications mix?

2   What is 'above-the-line' activity?

3   What is the main difference between PR and advertising?

4   What types of products and services are typically only sold via a direct sales force?

5   What are the main types of direct marketing?

6   What is viral marketing?

7   What is ambush marketing?

8   What is guerrilla marketing?

9   What is AIDA?

10   How is the value of PR determined?

ACTIVITY DEBRIEFS

Activity 9.1

It is hoped that you have found several examples of both positive and negative PR. It is worth remembering that PR can have a significantly positive or a hugely damaging impact on the organisation. In some cases, negative press comments can adversely affect an organisation's share price. Maintaining good relations with the media, if possible, is a key role for large organisations. There is a frequently used saying that 'There's no such thing as bad publicity', although many organisations through, bitter experience, would argue with this. Gerald Ratner, who used to own the UK jewellery retail chain 'Ratners' famously criticised his own shops' products. His comments were widely reported in the media and as a consequence the business failed.

Activity 9.2

While many companies execute one-off campaigns it is not at all uncommon for organisations to, say, conduct press and TV advertising simultaneously in order to achieve maxim impact. In addition, organisations which are sponsoring major events, if televised, will often also run TV advertisements during the breaks.

The Chartered
Institute of Marketing

Activity 9.3

The various methods used to measure the effectiveness of marketing activities are set out at the end of the chapter. Measurement is important because too often, in the past, marketers have been unable to 'prove' the value of their marketing efforts. A key consideration, however, as to whether or not to attempt to determine the effectiveness of marketing communications activities, is how much the campaign has cost versus the cost of measurement. For example, if it will cost £25,000 to carry out market research in order to determine the success of a £50,000 campaign it would be argued that the cost of the research would not warrant the research being carried out.

QUICK QUIZ ANSWERS

1   Advertising, personal selling, sales promotion, PR, sponsorships, direct marketing and online.

2   'Above-the-line' is paid for mass media communication.

3   Advertising has to be paid for and is therefore controllable. However, PR is not paid for and is therefore out of the organisation's control.

4   Typically, direct sales forces are used to sell more complex products and services. Direct sales forces are more common in B2B marketing.

5   Direct mail, direct response advertising, telemarketing, online, mobile, mail order, teleshopping.

6   Viral marketing requires a highly creative, amusing or shocking campaign that will encourage people to forward it onto their family and friend.

7   Ambush marketing is where an organisation which is not an official sponsor of an event, say, takes advantage and in some way is able to promote its own brand at the event.

8   Guerrilla marketing generally involves low cost campaigns which can be executed quickly on a local scale.

9   AIDA is a marketing communications tool and stands for Awareness, Interest, Desire, Action.

10   PR is measured by AVE (advertising value equivalent).

CHAPTER 10

Agencies and managing agency relationships

Introduction

We have seen that there is a vast choice of promotional tools available to the marketer and when combined with various media, it is clear that effective marketing not only relies on a sound planning process, but sound execution strategies. Consider the various stakeholders and relationship networks that an organisation develops and the overall picture becomes complicated requiring an expert solution.

Large organisations may choose to undertake many promotional activities internally rather than employ external agencies, but increasingly much of the communication activity is given to an external agency. However, this in itself brings some choices in agency selection. What type of agency is needed, how will it be selected, and which will best suit my needs?

Topic list

Communications agencies	1
Agency selection considerations	2
Agency pitch	3
Agency selection process	4
Agency remuneration	5
Agency structure	6
Managing agencies	7

3.5	Critically evaluate and select the most appropriate marketing communications agency for the utilisation of marketing communications capability against agreed criteria
	▪ The role and value of agencies in marketing communications
	▪ The inclusion of innovative and effective means of communication
	▪ How agencies are structured
	▪ Criteria and process for selecting an agency
	▪ Fees and fee structures
3.6	Recommend and justify an approach to managing agency relationships including reporting, monitoring and measuring performance
	▪ Managing agencies locally and internationally
	▪ Conducting regular reviews against clearly defined service level agreements
	▪ Key information in managing agency relationships
	▪ Establishing objectives and measuring agency performance

1 Communications agencies

An organisation has a range of agency types to choose from. Here we focus on creative agencies, of which there are four main types: full service agency, media independents, a la carte and new media.

1.1 Full service agency

▶ **Key term**

Full service agency: an agency which deals with all aspects of the communications process, including planning, design, production and execution.

As the name may suggest this type of agency offers the complete range of products and services which a client may need to advertise its products: research, strategic planning, creative, media planning and buying planning.

Where the agency does not have all the skills in-house, it will sub-contract some of the work to other agencies.

1.2 Media independents

Media independents provide specialist media services such as planning, buying and evaluation. The agency will suggest the media, the size of the advertisement and location, and they provide a report on the effectiveness of the campaign.

It should be noted that media dependents will be part of a full service agency, while media independents will be separate organisations that are free to set their own direction.

1.3 A la carte

A client may choose to select a number of agencies to carry out its communication activities. Each will be selected for its particular area of expertise such as strategic planning, media buying or creative. While this may offer the perceived advantage of specialism, it does mean that the client must take responsibility for managing and co-ordinating the various agencies and their activities.

1.4 New media

This area has grown over the past few years and will continue to grow as technology continues to change the way organisations communicate with stakeholders.

Online brands, mobile communications, email and viral marketing are all growing areas which require a specialist approach. Equally the integration of on- and off-line marketing will require a greater blend of skills.

> **ACTIVITY 10.1**
>
> Consider the reasons why an organisation might decide to use an agency rather than develop a campaign themselves in-house.

> **THE REAL WORLD**
>
> Not all organisations use agencies. Some larger organisations have their own creative and production teams. Provided there is sufficient through-put of work this approach can be cost-effective. However, some might argue that the in-house team might lack the creative flair and freedom of using an external agency.

2 Agency selection considerations

The appointment of an agency is an important and formal process which is time-intensive. When a larger organisation changes its agency or its approach, it often generates substantial activity in the trade press. On occasions where the incumbent agency is not selected, challenges will be made, so an audit demonstrating a fair and open process is needed.

Selection starts with research. The following process assumes the organisation is undertaking the selection process on its own. However, a search of the internet will reveal that there are organisations that will assist a client in the selection, ie act as a consultant.

From the list available a number of agencies should be long-listed with a view to reducing the number of agencies to a more manageable number of around six agencies.

Shortlist criteria:

1   Area of expertise held by the agencies
2   Quality of existing clients (need to consider any competitive issues)
3   Reputation of principals and experience of staff
4   Agency fees and methods of charging and payment
5   In-house resources
6   Geographical cover, ie any international contacts

It is usual to visit the agency premises to see the working conditions and have the opportunity to meet staff who may not be involved in the pitch (see below).

It may be at this stage that some agencies are eliminated and not invited to pitch. Those agencies invited to pitch will be given a brief by the client and a set amount of time to prepare it.

3 Agency pitch

All agencies should be assessed according to a set of consistent criteria. Table 10.1 offers a range of criteria which could be used.

Table 10.1   Agency criteria

Criteria	Explanation
Credentials	Experience of industry sector
	Positive client feedback
	Track record of success
Creative techniques	Evidence of creativity and innovation in current clients' work
Staff	How many staff will be dedicated to the account?
	Experience of staff
	Have they worked on similar sized accounts?
	How long has the team been together?
The agency	Is it well resourced?
	What is the nature of the agency and will it need to outsource any activities?
	What are its objectives?
	How does it measure outcome?
	What SLAs will be available?
	What is its size?
	Location
Specialism	What are the areas that the agency specialises in?
Price	Is the pricing structure clear and reasonable?
Legal	What mechanisms are in place to ensure compliance with voluntary codes of practice and regulatory requirements?
Pitch	Did the pitch meet the requirements of the brief?

Some criteria will be subjective: team working will be an important part of the relationship, and the staff from both the client and agency will need to be able to work effectively with each other for an agreed period of time, which could be up to five years. Short-listed agencies should be invited by the client to present a pitch for the business. The pitch should be measured against predetermined criteria and the business will be awarded to the agency which scores the highest overall.

ACTIVITY 10.2

Develop your own criteria that could be used to select one of a number of short-listed agencies who have delivered a pitch to you. Identify which of the criteria might be more important than others ('weightings' can be used for this purpose).

The Chartered Institute of Marketing

4 Agency selection process

Typically, the process will involve a number of separate stages, commonly including the following.

- Clear articulation of requirements/objectives
- Develop evaluation criteria
- Identify a 'pool' of potential agencies
- Initial visit/meeting
- Ascertain credentials, eg examples of recent/relevant work, CVs, testimonials etc
- Create shortlist
- Prepare brief and issue to shortlisted agencies. Brief should specify, for example:
    - Explanation of product/channel
    - Features/benefits
    - Objectives (be specific)
    - Target audience
    - Timetable
    - Budget
    - Proposed remuneration approach
- Arrange presentations (the pitch)
- Attend presentation
- Analyse and 'score' each pitch against the criteria
- Select winner
- Agree contract details
- Inform unsuccessful agencies

THE REAL WORLD

The process used to hire an agency will depend very much on the value and nature of the campaign. Sometimes organisations put their entire creative business out to tender, either to reduce expenditure or just to reinvigorate the brand by working with a different agency which will bring with it different ideas. For large organisations such an opportunity to win a pitch for the entire business would represent a major coup for the successful agency and, as a result, competition between agencies is often fierce.

---

5 Agency remuneration

There are three main ways in which an agency can be rewarded for its efforts on behalf of its client. These are listed in Table 10.2. In some cases a combination of methods might be used.

Table 10.2   Agency remuneration methods

Reward method	Explanation
Commission	Traditionally agencies were paid a commission in exchange for using a particular publication. Commission was paid at rate of 15%. However, different agencies received different levels and clients increasingly became concerned about agency objectivity when planning media schedules.
	Consequently the fee payment method became more popular and the concept of payment by results gained popularity.
Fees	Whatever media is chosen, payment is by a set fee for a particular activity.
	Monthly fees irrespective of the work put through the agency will be paid, known as a retainer. In addition to the retainer a fixed price will be agreed for each component of a campaign. For example, a client may agree a fixed monthly fee in addition to a menu of prices for specific activity.
Payment by results	While popular overseas, it is used selectively in the UK. Depending on the success of the campaign different payment terms will be triggered. While many would argue the merits of the approach, an agency can argue that success is hard to define and in any event elements of the campaign may be outside its control.

6 Agency structure

The senior management team will consist of the Chief Executive Officer (CEO), and Directors (see Figure 10.1).

Figure 10.1   Agency structure

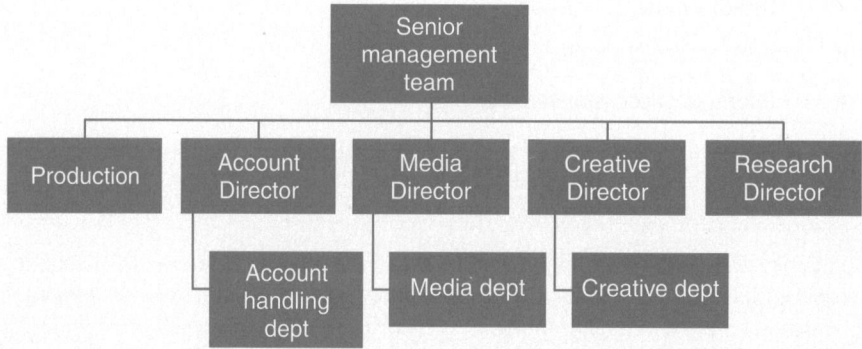

The Account Director is responsible for the management of specific accounts and will have a team of Account Executives who will provide day to day support on the account dealing with routine tasks.

The production team is responsible for progress, known as managing the traffic, and also for the advertisements.

6.1 Accounts team

▶ **Key term**

Accounts team: a key role within an agency. The team comprises individuals, generally headed by the Account Director, who are responsible for managing specific client relationships.

Usually the Account Director will take responsibility for the management of an account or group of accounts depending on the complexity of the relationship. The Account Director will manage the relationship to ensure it is running smoothly and will also ensure its profitability.

Reporting to the Account Director will be an Account Manager or Executive who will manage the relationship on a day-to-day basis, meeting or speaking with the client to take additional commissions or manage progress on

The Chartered
Institute of Marketing

existing work. Where the client is large, then the Account Manager will also liaise with other Account Managers who will be working on other parts of the account in order to have a clear picture of the client's needs. Typically, for the largest clients, Account Directors will be directly involved and will liaise with a Board Account Director, who might also be involved in client management.

6.2 Planning

The Account Planner is a senior role within the agency who works as part of the team and is responsible for planning the advertising.

Yeshin (2006) identifies five key roles for the Account Planner:

1   **Defining the task:** The planner is responsible for bringing together key information from within the agency and commissioning research if necessary in order to clearly define the task.

2   **Preparing the creative brief:** The planner will develop the creative brief which informs the creative process.

3   **Creative development:** The planner will input into all stages of the creative development and be the 'custodian' of the client's brand values.

4   **Presenting to the client:** The planner will join the account handlers and present the advertising concepts to the client and answer questions regarding the rationale for the approach taken.

5   **Tracking performance:** Once the campaign is launched the planner will monitor consumer reaction and feedback to the campaign.

6.3 Creative team

> ▶ **Key term**
>
> **Creative team:** individuals within an agency who are responsible for developing the messages, imagery and soundtracks used in communications.

It is the creative team that is responsible for developing the messages, imagery and soundtrack used in the campaign. It is usual for a copywriter to work with the Art Director to develop the creative concept. This team will interpret the creative brief and turn it into advertising, or some other form of communication.

6.4 The media department

Here the team is responsible, in conjunction with the production team, for ensuring the right material is passed to the right media at the right time. They will also take responsibility for constructing the media schedule so that the campaign objectives are achieved through the placement of advertisements in media that will reach the target audience in an effective and cost efficient way.

The range of available media is vast and the increasing use of 'new media' means that the media team needs to consist of a number of specialists in the different media.

6.5 Production

The production team is responsible for ensuring the quality of the material in terms of ensuring it is in the right format and the final appearance – font, colour, photography – all matches the brief. The traffic team is responsible for scheduling the work across the agency and ensuring that each stage of the creative process is delivered in accordance with the schedule agreed with the client.

The competitive world of marketing communications agencies

Around the world, there are many agencies of different sizes each attempting to convince clients that they offer unique specialist skills and knowledge. The agency world is fiercely competitive and the 'accounts' of major organisations are preciously guarded once gained and, often, aggressively courted by those agencies which are keen to grow. The 'capture' of a new blue chip client account is seen as a major coup in the agency world and can lead to other significant business being gained.

Increasingly, therefore, account management teams are under pressure to retain key clients and will attempt to do this in a number of ways, including:

- Ensuring that agency staff are knowledgeable and empathetic to client needs.

- Proactively managing relationships.

- Continually generating ideas for new business / income opportunities (for the client).

- Ensuring there is a strong focus on adding tangible value for the client (ie income and profit).

7 Managing agencies

All agency relationships are different reflecting not only the structure of the agency, but the culture of the companies involved in the relationship (Yeshin, 2006).

It is not unusual for an agency to stay with a client for many years; equally relationships can change quickly. Agencies must share or understand the values of the client they are working for and they must act as if they have just been appointed ie not become complacent, as this will reduce their effectiveness in a highly competitive industry. As we shall see below, the consequences of changing agencies should not be underestimated. Often when a new agency is appointed there may already be some existing relationship which can be developed, however, when an entirely new agency is appointed there is a steep learning curve to be addressed, which can slow the launch of new campaigns into the market. There are other implications, for example, the media may be worried that an organisation sacking an agency may be a sign of other worries, such as a slide in market share and respond badly. Equally the sacking could be seen as good news, ie the organisation has identified a problem and put a solution in place.

Clearly for the outgoing agency the news is generally seen as negative. However, *Campaign* (2004) suggests that clients change agencies because the agency has lost interest in the client, or is not allocating the amount of time felt warranted. In a small number of situations, organisations stated that they changed agencies as a matter of course.

Beltramini and Pitta (1991) suggest four benefits of effective relationships with agencies:

1   Agencies must have a genuine interest in meeting the needs of the client in order to demonstrate a commitment to maintaining a productive relationship. The agency must always respond to any concerns raised by the clients and it needs to be recognised that relationships can take time to build. Therefore care should be exercised by the client when considering changing agencies.

2   The relationship between the parties often requires sensitive information to be shared and consequently the agency views privileged information which offers an insight in to the nature of the client which may not be ever seen by the customer. The agency should invest time in understanding the client, its DMU and its structure.

The Chartered Institute of Marketing

3   Close relationships need to be maintained between the key players in the agency and the client at both the strategic and operational levels.

4   There needs to be two-way communication between the parties and the agency needs to ensure a constant flow of ideas.

Where there is an international dimension, then the agency relationship will be determined by the strategies adopted for the various markets.

Where the communication is centralised, ie all aspects of the marketing communications process is managed from one central point, a high degree of control will be exercised across the entire process. In the situation where the decisions are taken at local level, ie decentralisation, more autonomy is given to the local staff. Finally some organisations choose a compromise between the two extremes and adopt a combination of both approaches. An increasing trend is to group geographical areas together that have similarities eg Europe or Asia.

Within the agency structure there is an account handling team and the make-up of this tries to mirror the structure of the client organisation.

Having gone through the process of selecting the agency and recognising that the relationship with the client could extend over many years, it is essential to put in place procedures to ensure the relationship runs smoothly. Often a service level agreement is initiated which specifies the minimum standards which the agency can be expected to deliver to.

Part of the selection process is to establish that the teams could work with each other. Equally important is for the client's business objectives to be clear.

A marketing communications plan will guide the relationship and set out any budgetary or financial issues that need to be addressed.

The client needs to ensure the agency has sufficient information prior to launching a campaign. Often informal discussions will take place prior to the agency being formally given a communications brief (see Figure 10.2).

Communication brief	
Objectives	• What objectives have been set for the campaign and how will they be measured, ie sales conversion of leads into prospects? • What behavioural or attitudinal measures will be used and over what timescale? • How does the activity support the overall brand promise? • Does the campaign form part of a wider campaign and if so how does it fit in?
Target audience	• Who is the audience?
Product	• Description, positioning and features • Any conditions for application? • Key competitors • Why should people buy this product? • USPs
Creative and media considerations	• Research undertaken on current creative work?
Logistical considerations	• Any media constraints?
Budget	• Exactly what does the budget cover?

Creative brief
Campaign requirement One off, or number of adverts
The target audience Demographics, lifestyle, product usage/attitudes
What is the advertising intended to achieve?
The single-minded proposition
Rationale for the proposition
Mandatory inclusions Eg stockists, logos, telephone/email contact
Desired brand image Friendly, professional, modern, etc

A communications agency is appointed because it is felt that it can produce better results than conducting the work in-house and it also makes better use of resources.

However, agencies must be monitored to ensure they are providing the client an acceptable level of value.

Before any campaign is launched into the market, it must undergo testing to ensure its messages are effective and understood by the audience. However, it is also import to fully evaluate campaigns that have taken place, not only for the client organisation but including their competitors.

Fill (2006) suggests that competitor strategies should be monitored for style and level of spend in addition to strategic credibility and corporate image. The objective is to improve on the quality and effectiveness of the current communications campaigns.

Pre-campaign research will suggest any changes which may be necessary prior to the campaign launch. However, post-campaign research will establish whether or not the perceived messages were understood by the audience. It is suggested that both internal and external campaigns are addressed.

Campaigns will have performance targets, or key deliverables set, which can be expressed in a variety of ways. Performance will be monitored on a regular basis as appropriate for the effective management of the business. An internet search engine may monitor 'hits' hourly, whereas a university may monitor student recruitment on a quarterly basis.

Achievement of the financial performance is usually relatively easy to measure as the actual performance collected through internal data is generally available.

Many organisations have developed a communications audit based around the work of Ind (1992). Here perceptions are evaluated across different media and across different divisions of the organisation in order to ensure consistency.

However, the criteria for measuring advertising effectiveness must be derived from the objects set at the outset of the campaign.

ACTIVITY 10.3

Observe, for example from the press or TV, three different campaigns and consider how the 'payment by results' method of remuneration might have been applied to the agency.

8 Conducting agency reviews and the information used in managing agency relationships

Conducting performance reviews is a key part of relationship management and this is no different for marketers when managing relationships with their chosen agencies. Performance standards must be clearly stated, agreed and accepted by both parties at the outset. Any Service Level Agreements (SLAs) must be agreed, in addition to agreeing how performance will be measured and the process for monitoring.

Reviews will generally be conducted at two levels. Firstly, the client and agency will need to meet regularly to conduct operational level reviews. These will typically include:

- A review of work in progress
- A review of live campaigns and their performance.

In addition, the client and agency will meet less frequently, possibly annually, to conduct a strategic review. This will typically include:

- A review of future plans
- A review of changes in the market
- A review of the competitive landscape
- Sharing ideas for future initiatives, eg income generation, cost efficiencies, new business acquisition.

In order to conduct meaningful reviews, management information is vital. This must be relevant and up to date. Typical information might include:

- Spend to date
- Spend against budgets
- Performance against targets / SLAs
- Numbers of campaigns
- Sales / leads generated from campaigns
- Press coverage achieved
- Complaints received about activities
- Hits / click-throughs on websites
- Recognition / recall rates (from advertising).

The key to effective performance management is that targets and measures must be appropriate and understood at the outset. Information plays a crucial role as it will underpin the performance review meetings between the client and agency.

▶ **Exam tip**

In the September 2010 examination (Graduate Recruitment Bureau case study) Task Two required candidates to assess the likely rationale for using an external marketing communications agency and to outline the process for appointing the best agency.

In the first part of the Task 'assess' means that answers should have been presented in detail and with points made fully supported. Some candidates simply produced a brief list of bullet points, with just one or two sentences for each reason given. These answers lacked sufficient detail to reach a pass standard.

In the second part, the question only required 'an outline' of the process, so a brief description of each of the stages (as outlined in Section 4 above) was sufficient, ie just two or three sentences on each. Even though the question stated 'outline' some answers comprised just a list of points with just one sentence for each stage. These too fell short of a pass standard.

Another important element is that answers must relate strongly to the case material. Some answers were far too generic, with a number making no reference to GRB at all. So, for example, a key factor leading to the decision to use an external agency was that GRB is a relatively small business and so leveraging the knowledge and skills of experts would bring great value to the business.

- Because communications are important the choice of external agency is of critical importance to the organisation.

- There are different types of agency so consideration must be given to the organisation's precise requirements and objectives before commencing the selection process.

- Selecting the best agency will take time and must be properly managed and resourced.

- Appropriate criteria for selection must be determined.

- The most important criteria can be given higher weightings than those which are less important.

- Agency selection should follow a structured process.

- There are different methods of agency remuneration.

- Payment by results is an effective way of motivating agencies.

- Larger agencies have clear organisational structures comprising teams which have different skill sets.

- Relationship and performance management of agencies are key to ensure that they remain focused on delivering outstanding value for the organisation.

- Measures should include subjective and objective elements and can comprise both financial and non-financial targets.

- SLAs often form an important part of the relationship between the client and the agency.

FURTHER READING

This paper sets out an approach for selecting the most appropriate agency:

Faisal, M.N. and Khan, B.M. (2008) Selecting an advertising agency: a multi-criteria decision-making approach. *Vision* 12(4), pp13-22.

REFERENCES

Anon (2004) Why accounts move. *Campaign*, February.

Banham, M. (2011) ZenithOptimedia lands £50m RBS retail media account. Campaignlive, http://campaignlive.co.uk [Accessed on 3 February 2012]

Beltramini, R.F. and Pitta, D.A. (1991) Underlying dimensions and communication strategies of the advertising agency-client relationship. *International Journal of Advertising* Vol 10(2).

Fill, C. (2006) *Marketing communications: engagement, strategies and practice*. 4th edition. Oxford, FT Prentice Hall.

Ind, N. (1992) *The corporate image: strategies for effective identity programme*. Revised edition. London, Kogan Page.

Yeshin, T. (2006) *Advertising*. London, Thomson.

1   What is a full service agency?

2   What is a media independent?

3   What are typical criteria that might be used to select the best agency?

4   What is a pitch?

5   When choosing a new agency, what considerations should be made about the agency itself?

6   What are the three main types of remuneration for agencies?

7   Which part of the agency is responsible for managing client relationships?

8   Which part of the agency is responsible for actually coming up with the messaging, imagery and soundtrack used in a campaign?

9   What might be typical financial targets set for an agency?

10   What non-financial targets might be set for an agency?

ACTIVITY DEBRIEFS

Activity 10.1

Generally organisations use an external agency because of the following:

- Access to expertise/professionalism
- Specialist skills
- Sector knowledge, expertise and experience
- Independence
- Impartiality/objective view
- Innovation
- Market awareness

Activity 10.2

The criteria will depend on the type of the campaign and the organisation, amongst other things. Typical criteria might include:

- Experience of the agency in the market/sector
- Staff skills
- Creative ability
- Interpretation of the brief
- Price quoted

Remuneration terms, eg not all agencies may be happy with payment by results terms.

Activity 10.3

The answer will very much depend on the campaign. Where there is a specific 'call to action' this may form part of the payment terms, eg how many leads generated or products sold. Otherwise payment might be dependent of changing perception, recall and/or recognition.

1   An agency which offers the complete range of services from research and planning through to creative development and execution.

2   A media independent provides specialist media services such as planning and buying.

3   There are many criteria that could be used including agency credentials, creative techniques/ability, staff, the agency itself, price, remuneration terms, the pitch.

4   The pitch is delivered by a short-listed agency, against a brief, and is one of the last stages of the agency selection process.

5   How many staff work there and what are their skills; what sectors does it work in; what is its reputation; is it big enough or is it too big for us; where is it located.

6   Commission, fees and payment by results.

7   The accounts teams

8   The creative team

9   Typical financial targets might include return on investment (ROI), product profitability achieved, sales leads/volumes generated and customer profitability achieved.

10   Typical non-financial targets might include customer satisfaction, customer complaints, warranty claims, customer loyalty.

The Chartered Institute of Marketing

Section 3:

Senior Examiner's comments

Having completed Section 3 students should have a detailed knowledge of:

- The development of marketing communications strategy and objectives

- The contents and structure of a marketing communications plan

- The elements of the promotional mix and its application in different markets and organisational contexts

- Measuring the performance of marketing communications activities

- The role, management and performance measurement of agencies in marketing communications

Communication (both internal and external) is a key aspect of marketing and this is reflected by the higher weighting of this area of the syllabus (30%). To succeed, students must be able to apply the aspects of the syllabus in different organisational contexts and markets. In particular, students must be able to develop appropriate communications strategies, objectives, plans and activities that will contribute towards the achievement of organisational objectives, for example, income and profit growth; customer retention; new business acquisition; and enhanced customer satisfaction.

The market is full of examples of communications strategy 'in action'. Students are urged to supplement their study by observing and analysing what is happening in the media around them, and further afield. There are many examples daily of how organisations are successfully executing integrated communications activities, which provide excellent case studies for evaluation.

A further key aspect is measurement. Communications activities, generally, represent the highest amount of marketing expenditure for organisations. So, measurement plays a key role in 'proving' the value of marketing to the business overall.

Section 4:

Managing and achieving customers' service expectations through the marketing mix

This final section of the syllabus addresses how organisations, across a range of sectors and operating in different markets (including domestic and international), develop the marketing mix in order to meet customer service expectations.

A thorough knowledge of the extended marketing mix components is paramount. You will then be expected to use this knowledge and apply it to different scenarios and to demonstrate, through application, a detailed appreciation of what constitutes 'service' to various types of customers.

The syllabus examines a range of tools and techniques in delivering high quality service to customers, from customer service planning, to managing key account customers and the use of SLAs (service level agreements) with customers.

The key role of customer and product information, its management, storage and retrieval, is also examined. You will be required to understand how organisations undertake these activities, and the risks and issues they face where they are not managed effectively.

CHAPTER 11

Customer service and customer care

Introduction

This chapter begins with a review of the characteristics of services and how the marketing mix is used to overcome the issues and challenges faced by services marketers. The chapter goes on to address what actually constitutes service quality to customers and discusses the application of SERVQUAL, a useful model for assessing the dimensions of service quality. The chapter concludes by focusing on customer care.

Topic list

What are services? 1

The marketing mix for services 2

Issues for service providers 3

What constitutes service quality? 4

Service and customer loyalty 5

Creating competitive advantage 6

Economic effects of customer loyalty 7

Managing and improving service quality 8

The customer service programme 9

Benefits of customer acquisition and retention 10

Monitoring quality of service 11

4.1	Develop clear objectives relating to the provision of service to customers
	■ The importance of service
	■ Identifying the needs and behaviours of customers
	■ What constitutes 'service' to customers?
	■ The role of service in building customer loyalty and competitive advantage
	■ Organisational and financial benefits of customer acquisition and retention
	■ Determining customer service requirements
	■ The role of key account management in developing customer service excellence
4.2	Develop a customer service plan and customer care programme, designed to support customer service requirements, including innovative communications; relationship management and development; support; and operations/process management
	■ Identifying and evaluating key components of the plan/programme
	■ Identifying, analysing and managing key issues
	■ Use of resources
	■ Effective implementation
	■ Measuring and monitoring performance
	■ Role of communications in delivering customer service
	■ Importance of operations and processes in delivering customer service
4.3	Assess the value, importance and financial implications of providing service level agreements to customers
	■ Role of service level agreements with customers
	■ Typical service level agreements
	■ The costs of delivering against service level agreements
	■ Benefits to the organisation of establishing service level agreements with customers

1 What are services?

Services are referred to as being 'intangible' and consist of industries such as banking, insurance, government, education, professional services and tourism. Services embrace the not-for-profit sectors and can be intended to satisfy both business and personal customer needs.

Unsurprisingly, there are many definitions of a 'service'. Philip Kotler has provided one of the most commonly referenced definitions (1991, p455):

'A service is any act or performance that one party can offer to another that is essentially intangible and does not result in the ownership of anything.'

Services can be split into:

■ Business services
■ Consumer services

Figure 11.1, adapted from Brassington and Pettitt (2006), demonstrates the difficulty of classifying some services, although it is clearer at the extremes.

The Chartered
Institute of Marketing

Figure 11.1   Trying to classify services (Adapted from Brassington, 2006)

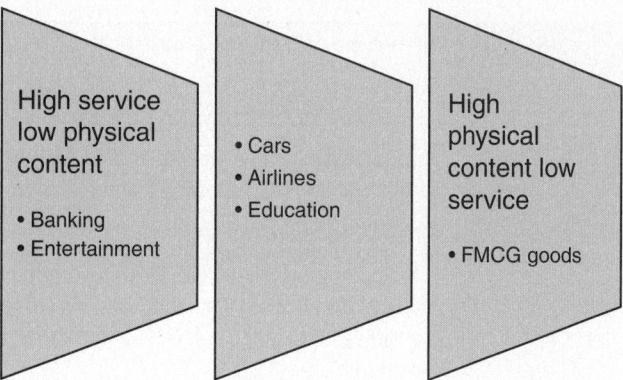

2 The marketing mix for services

> ▸ **Key term**
>
> The **extended marketing mix:** comprises all seven elements of the marketing mix, ie product, price, place, promotion, people, process and physical evidence.

The concept of the marketing mix (Borden, 1964) consists of four elements which when combined together create an offering for the customer. The mix known as the 4Ps (product, price, place, promotion) is not sufficient for the service sector and three additional Ps was proposed by Booms and Bitner (1981),were now generally referred to as the 7Ps. The additional Ps are:

- **People:** take part in the production and delivery of the service and, as we will see later, may interact directly with the customer or be part of the support team

- **Processes:** the operational process that moves the customer from making the order through to taking delivery

- **Physical evidence:** the tangibility given to the product, so for example decor or brochures or the business infrastructure

Each of the additional Ps is discussed in more detail in Table 11.1.

Table 11.1   The extra three Ps

People	Services typically require people to deliver them, often having just created them. Consequently for many customers 'people' represent the brand and where a relationship builds, it becomes difficult for a competitor to take the business away from that organisation. Clearly where there is no rapport, it is much easier for the customer to take the business to a competitor, or for the competitor to capture the business.
Processes	Processes refer to the actual delivery as well as the support in the provision of the service. In a university a new lecturer will be given guidance on how to deliver a lecture, while support teams will be providing timetables to the students and registering them for a particular module and collecting the fees, or reminding students to pay.
Physical evidence	This relates to the tangible aspects of the services. So in the example above, the lecturer will provide the students with a set of class notes. The tutor room or lecture theatre also acts as physical evidence along with the quality of the decoration.

Table 11.2 shows a plan to overcome service encounter issues using the marketing mix.

Product	What is the collection of benefits that the product offers?
	Organisations offering services will still break the product into ranges. A chain of leisure centres may choose to market each one as a separate product.
	Bank accounts can be grouped into savings and current accounts and further segmented within this grouping into classic and premium current accounts.
	Airlines offer economy, premium economy, business and first class seats on some aircraft.
Price	What does our price represent? Are we premium priced to reflect the high quality of the product? Do we price differently for different products? Of course the nature of services makes the setting of price quite difficult and different approaches are used and even the pricing models are changing.
	Typically travel companies reduce the price of holidays the closer the dates of availability become.
	Estate agents charge a commission for selling a property and often solicitors will charge a standard fee for a particular activity.
Place	Where is the product to be delivered? Physical evidence is closely related to place and should reflect on the quality of service.
	The consumption of services can take place in hundreds of different places from the dentist's chair to high in the sky. This can limit consumption, ie there are only a certain number of flights per day.
	The internet is also changing the place of consumption.
Promotion	The promotional activity must reflect the positioning the product occupies in the consumer's mind based on reputation, quality and reliability.
	Also it must be able to communicate the benefits of the service.
People	Staff must be trained in the organisation's products and values. Where possible staff should be empowered to ensure customers are fully satisfied.
Processes	Processes need to be developed so that the variability in service can be reduced.
Physical evidence	This can relate to the decoration, the staff uniforms, the style of the menus, each reflecting the brand of the organisation.

3 Issues for service providers

It can be more challenging for customers to differentiate between service providers in the same industry because they all appear to be similar. Equally it can be difficult for an organisation to manage and measure the quality of the service provided as much will depend on the customers' expectations of the service.

Marketing services presents the marketing function with some additional challenges compared with the non-service sector, particularly around the four key characteristics of services which are

- **Intangibility/lack of ownership:** Services cannot be touched, seen, tasted, heard or smelled before being purchased, nor can they be owned. Similarly once the service has been consumed it cannot be experienced again in the same manner.

- **Inseparability:** Services cannot be stored and sold later and they cannot be separated from the provider.

The Chartered
Institute of Marketing

- **Perishability:** As services are effectively produced and consumed at the same time they cannot be stored, so a better management of demand is necessary.

- **Heterogeneity:** The quality of the service is dependent on the person providing it, therefore it will vary.

Examples of each of these categories are:

- **Intangibility/lack of ownership:** Create tangibility by providing some physical evidence, eg brochures, premises, certificates or membership.

- **Inseparability:** Develop standardised processes to maintain quality, eg pre-packed foreign currency, new systems and staff training.

- **Perishability:** Introduce better 'demand management' systems, eg low-cost airlines where flights are cheaper the further in advance seats are booked.

- **Heterogeneity:** Similar to 'inseparability', ie standardised processes for producing the service, eg in a coffee bar to ensure the same tasting coffee each time it is produced.

The challenge is for an organisation to be able to overcome the service characteristics and develop marketing approaches (Meek and Meek, 2001) which:

- Promote the advantages of non-ownership
- Make available a tangible symbol or representation of ownership
- Increase the chances or opportunities of ownership

To help deal with these challenges the marketer must utilise all the 7Ps of the marketing mix, for example as suggested in Table 11.2.

THE REAL WORLD

The marketing mix for an airport

This is what the marketing mix might look like for an airport:

- **Product:** Good service, convenient location, easy car parking and rail links, wide range of destinations and airlines.

- **Place:** Central location five miles outside the city centre, with check-in available at key railways. Bookings can be made by use of the internet and telephone.

- **Price:** Competitively priced airlines, gateway for budget airlines with wide range of consumer goods offered at below high street prices.

- **Promotion:** Online, magazines and newspaper advertising. Sponsorship of travel programs. Direct marketing to travellers. Loyalty card for frequent flyers.

- **Physical evidence:** The appearance of the building and the range of high quality retail shops, the cleanliness and functionality of the building.

- **Process:** Large number of check-in desks, closely located to the security area and boarding gates no more than ten minutes from the shops. An effective online service

- **People:** Highly trained and helpful staff who know the importance of good service and want to exceed your expectations.

Think of a service that you have experienced recently (for example a hair cut or a meal at a restaurant) and identify how the supplier has used the extended marketing mix to deliver the service to you.

---

4 What constitutes service quality?

> **Key term**
>
> **Triangle of quality perception (Grönroos):** Grönroos identified three key elements which will influence the customer's perception of service quality, ie technical, functional and customer expectations.

The delivery of high quality service is one of the most important and difficult tasks that any service organisation faces (Dibb *et al*, 2005); after all, customer service is an abstract concept.

Service quality is judged by the customers, not the organisation and can be defined as customers' perception of how well a service meets or exceeds their expectations.

Grönroos (1984) argues that the quality of service, which is a series of processes, is whatever the customer perceives it to be. However, customers often see service as a broad concept and an organisation must understand the basis on which customers judge service.

There are separate elements which collectively determine service quality experience (Grönroos, 1984):

- **Technical:** Eg waiting times such as the amount of time a customer is kept waiting on the telephone, or in a queue, or having their query dealt with. Another example is the decor in the bedroom of a hotel room.

- **Functional:** How is the measurable aspect of the service delivered? For example, was the customer advised that there would be ten-minute wait, or that the decision on a customer's loan application will take seven days?

- **Expectations:** Here the customer has their own expectation about the level of service, so the relevant factor is has the actual service lived up to their expectations?

Customers will have an expectation about the service provided, and collectively the elements of technical quality, functional quality and customer expectation are known as the triangle of quality perception.

Clearly, for an organisation to be successful the challenge is to get the balance right because customers evaluate the service received across a number of dimensions particularly in respect of their expectations and often they experience 'gaps' in their expectations. This would suggest that there is no point in providing a service to customers that is not valued. A methodology needs to be implemented so that service quality aspects which are important to customers can be understood and processes put in place not only to meet, but exceed (delight) customer expectations.

THE REAL WORLD

Service quality means different things to different types of customers. For services organisations, therefore, the perception of its service quality will have a direct impact on its positioning. For example, in the hotel business, while all customers will expect at least a standard of cleanliness and the availability of facilities the differences on offer between providers is significant. In the UK, a 'budget hotel' can often provide a room for the night, even in a major city, for less than £50, while '5 star' hotels in the same location will justify overnight rates of maybe four or even five times as much.

5 Service and customer loyalty

Service has a key role to play in building loyalty as well as generating financial benefits for an organisation through customer acquisition and retention. However, it should be noted that customer satisfaction and loyalty are not the same thing (Piercy, 2001).

Satisfaction is an attitude (how a customer feels about a company's product), while loyalty is behaviour (do they buy from us more than once?).

However, a 'zone of indifference' is often noted. The zone of indifference is where customer satisfaction ranges from satisfied to just satisfied. It is suggested there are two important conclusions to be drawn:

- The quality of the service provided must be outside the zone of indifference, ie it must at least make them 'very satisfied' if they are to be expected to make subsequent purchases.

- Customers must be clearly identified as to their satisfaction levels in order for the organisation to develop the appropriate actions to build enduring relationships.

It is suggested an organisation needs to offer more than a good service and acceptable value if it is to create loyalty with customers. Piercy (2001, p29) cites the defection rate among BA 'satisfied customers' as 13%: exactly the same as dissatisfied complaining customers.

Another important reason for building customer satisfaction is the fact that only very satisfied customers will be prepared to undertake word-of-mouth support for the organisation, which is one of the more credible communications channels when encouraging purchase. Conversely those people who have encountered poor service will be negative and act as 'terrorists', keeping people away from the product. It is an often-cited fact that each customer who has received poor service will tell at least five of their friends or colleagues. Equally, it is significantly more expensive to recruit new customers than retain existing ones.

6 Creating competitive advantage

It has been stated previously that organisations will use service to create a point of differentiation from the competition, because good service is hard to easily replicate.

Dibb *et al* (2005) suggest that a competitive advantage is 'something desired by the customer that only one company can offer'.

It is much harder to develop a competitive advantage in services, but nevertheless, just like in any industry, any competitive advantage gained must be sustainable. Otherwise any advantage gained will be lost along with the costs of the initial investment.

Key factors in developing a competitive advantage are shown in Table 11.3.

Table 11.3   Key factors in developing a competitive advantage (based on Dibb *et al*, 2005)

Key factors	Comment
Key sectors	What market sector(s) does the organisation need to develop?
Products	What product(s) need to be offered to the sectors identified? This should be based on market research.
Competitors	What advantages (perceived or otherwise) does the competition offer and what are their strengths?
Service gaps	Where are the service gaps between what the customer expects and what is delivered?
Sustainability	How can the advantage be maintained in the future?

7 Economic effects of customer loyalty

The key benefits to be derived by an organisation when improving customer loyalty include:

- **Premium pricing:** existing customers tend to be content to pay a higher price than new customers. This can be attributed to a mutual understanding between organisation and customer.

- **Cost savings:** as seen above, once an organisation and customer understand each other, the need for expensive advertising to build that part of the relationship (brand awareness) is no longer needed and more product specific (targeted) advertising can be undertaken instead.

- **Income growth:** as the relationship builds (ladder of loyalty), it would be expected that the customer would place additional and ongoing business with the organisation with the additional income they produce.

- **Costs of acquisition:** it is generally regarded five times more expensive to recruit a customer than it is to retain one, so the less need there is to recruit new customers the greater the savings. Equally, it can take a couple of years to recoup the costs of acquisition.

8 Managing and improving service quality

> ▶ **Key term**
>
> **SERVQUAL (Parasuraman et al):** a model designed to measure and manage service quality, featuring five service dimensions, ie reliability, assurance, tangibles, empathy and responsiveness (also known as RATER).

Parasuraman *et al* (1985) developed a service quality model (SERVQUAL) that is used to identify the key components used in the evaluation of a service. They also developed a model of customer service gaps relating to the management perception of service quality and the tasks associated with delivering the service to the customer.

Figure 11.2 shows that customers measure the five dimensions of quality against a number of other influences which leads to an outcome on the level of service provided.

Figure 11.2   Factors in perceived service quality

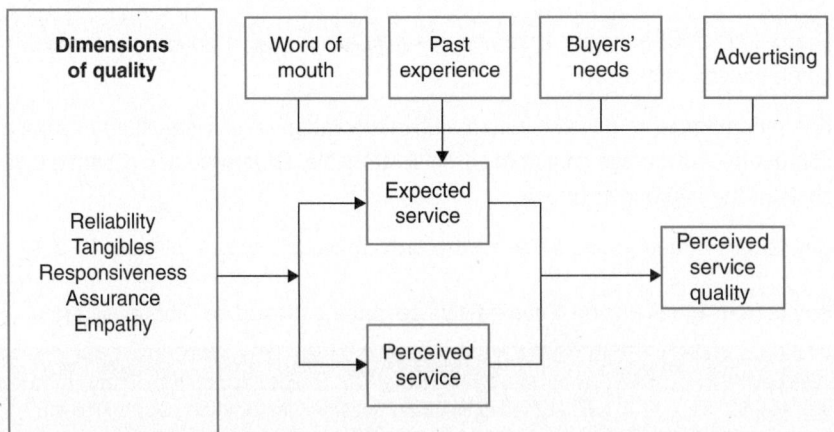

A customer may be influenced by talking to a friend or colleague who has influenced the purchase (positively or negatively). It may well be that the customer has previously experienced the service (may be through contacting an overseas call centre). Equally they may be experiencing the service based on an evaluation of their needs or responded to an advertisement. All of these influences when measured against the five dimensions of quality (see below) will establish the perceived level of service (seen from the perspective of the customer).

8.1 Dimensions of customer service

The components or dimensions of customer service are:

- Responsiveness
- Assurance
- Tangibles
- Empathy
- Reliability

Sometimes the components are referred to by the mnemonic RATER. Table 11.4 shows the components in relation to the additional three elements of the marketing mix.

Table 11.4   SERVQUAL applied to the additional 3Ps in the marketing mix

Marketing mix	SERVQUAL components
Process	▪ Reliability, the ability to perform the service, accurately, dependably consistently and in accordance with the instructions given.
People	▪ Responsiveness, ability to offer a timely service that meets customer expectations. When there is a problem does the organisation respond quickly? ▪ Empathy, focus on the individual needs of the customer. ▪ Assurance, the ability to convey trust and confidence.
Physical evidence	▪ Tangibles, look and feel of offices, cars, appearance of staff and marketing collateral.

Given that customers often view different service providers in the same industry as being the same (for example, banks), organisations are looking to differentiate themselves through the quality of their service offering. This requires a concerted effort to ensure customer needs are not just met, but exceeded (customer delight). However, the differentiation needs to be sustained, otherwise the organisation simply enjoys a short-term advantage which is quickly lost along with the investment in securing that advantage.

Organisations must establish exactly what the customer wants. But having established exactly what the customer wants an organisation must also have a clearly established service quality culture that all staff should follow.

Internal marketing is a key ingredient in improving the service encounter. There is evidence to suggest (Dibb et al, 2005) that there is a strong relationship between satisfied employees, marketing orientation and organisational performance.

Success is built on communications, the ability to be responsive to changing needs and a unified sense of purpose between employees.

The key steps include:

- Creating internal awareness
- Understanding of corporate aims
- Identification of internal customer and supplier
- Communication of expectations to internal suppliers
- Internal suppliers making modification to their activities to reflect customer views
- A measure of internal service quality

But having established exactly what the customer wants, an organisation must have a clearly-established service quality culture which all staff should follow.

Using the SERVQUAL dimensions of service quality (RATER) consider how a bank delivers service quality to its customers via its online banking service.

8.2 Service gaps

▶ **Key term**

Service quality 'gaps': a useful tool to analyse deficiencies (ie gaps) in the delivery of service to customers.

According to Zeithaml and Bitner (2003) in the gaps model of service (Figure 11.3), quality builds from the customer and organisational tasks are constructed around what is needed to close the customer gap, ie the gap between what customers expect and what they receive. The central focus of the gaps model is the customer gap – the difference between customer expectation and perception.

Figure 11.3   The gaps model of service (Zeithaml and Bitner, 2003)

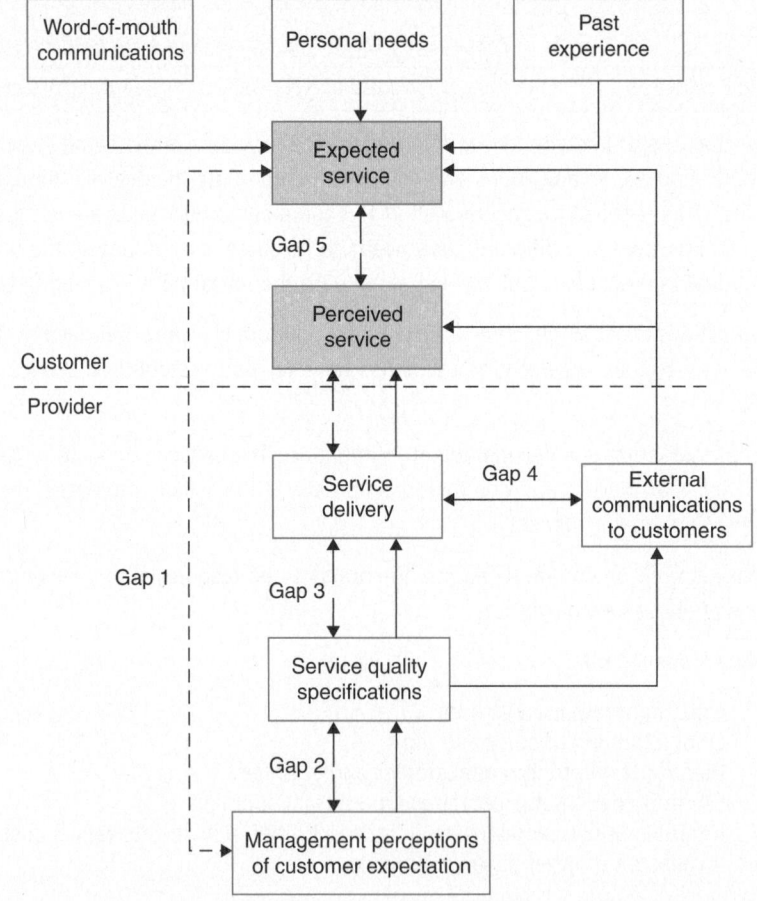

8.2.1. Gap 1

This gap means that management perceives the quality expectations inaccurately, or, looked at another way, there is a difference between the customer expectations of the level of service to be received and the management's understanding of that expectation.

Lack of research, ineffective feedback and management being too far removed from customers can contribute to this gap.

Empowering employees when things go wrong can often close the gap.

8.2.2 Gap 2

A recurring theme in service companies is the difficulty experienced in translating customer's expectations into service quality specifications (Zeithaml and Bitner, 2003). This gap refers to the difference between company understanding of customer expectations and the translation into customer-driven designs and standards.

8.2.3 Gap 3

This gap exists because the actual service delivery, before or after the event, has failed to meet the set standards. It can be the case that even when company guidelines exist for performing services well, employees may still fail to deliver satisfactory services. This may result from a flawed HR system, or processes.

It is important that all employees understand the standards, otherwise efficient and quality service provision may be impacted upon.

Gap 2 and Gap 3 together represent the employee gap which is a significantly important issue for the proposed organisation.

8.2.4 Gap 4

This gap refers to the differences between service delivery and the service provider's external communication, ie the levels of service are not correctly communicated or understood by the customer.

8.2.5 Gap 5

The service falls short of what the customer hoped for.

Do note though, it is not always possible to remove the gaps completely.

ACTIVITY 11.3

Consider how the 'gaps' model might be applied to an organisation of your choice.

---

9 The customer service programme

Having identified gaps in the level of service an organisation can take steps to address the issues. So, for example, we could try to close the gaps in the ways shown in Table 11.5.

Table 11.5   Ways of closing gaps

Gap 1	Hold regular team meetings and management briefings to ensure they are customer focused. Research in the form of customer satisfaction surveys could be undertaken to establish customer expectations and ways to exceed or delight the customers.
Gap 2	Better interaction between management and staff to establish realistic targets for staff to aspire to.
Gap 3	All customer-facing staff need to be clear on what their roles are, and what targets they are expected to achieve. Clearly internal marketing has a key role to play. It is important that staff feel valued and want to work effectively.
Gap 4	Service delivery standards need to be maintained and stronger targets set, but customers must be clear on what they can expect.
Gap 5	Clearly, if people have an expectation of what they expect, then the organisation needs to ensure the highest levels of customer service are achieved and a customer-centric approach is adopted.

Closing the gaps is, in many ways, a reactive approach. A more proactive approach is to develop a relationship marketing plan that can be based around the six markets model (discussed in earlier units) which in summary would cover:

- **Supplier markets:** building relationships with suppliers to ensure the chain is maximised and the overall quality of the customer service experience has reached its potential, and where things need to be improved there is a supplier relationship development process.

- **Recruitment:** the importance of recruiting staff with the right skills cannot be underestimated and robust procedures must be in place not only to ensure the 'right' employees are selected, but they stay with the company for a reasonable amount of time.

- **Internal markets:** companies need to create internal awareness for the corporate aims, objectives and mission, as well as determine the expectations of the internal customer. This may also cover training, systems and processes as well as change management.

- **Influence markets:** the company may need to change its perception with the media and key stakeholders.

- **Referral markets:** often new business comes through third parties, who will simply stop introducing business if it is felt that sub-optimal service is being given.

10 Benefits of customer acquisition and retention

Most academics would agree that it costs much more to recruit a new customer than retain an existing one. It is therefore surprising that organisations still spend a disproportionate amount of time and money on the recruitment of new customers without sufficiently considering the needs of existing customers. The general feeling is that it is five times more expensive to recruit a new customer than it is to retain an existing one. Consequently the use of the marketing budget needs to be challenged where the focus is simply on new customer recruitment. Naturally some organisations are still looking for a transactional relationship, ie are only interested in the immediate purchase, rather than the overall relationship.

Improving the acquisition process is concerned with the following aspects (Christopher *et al* (2002)):

- Acquiring customers at a lower cost
- Acquiring more customers for the same cost (or lower)
- Acquiring more attractive customers
- Acquiring more customers using new channels

However, this data needs to be collected at the segment level.

As the costs, size and potential of each segment will differ, an organisation will want to reduce the cost of recruitment while maximising revenue. Electronic channels will be an important part of the overall channel mix, and organisations, while not being able to force customers to interact through any one channel, will want to

The Chartered Institute of Marketing

encourage customers through the most cost-effective by offering (in some cases) incentives such as an 'internet only rate'.

However, an important point to note is that while recruitment is the lifeblood of an organisation, only profitable customers generate income. Therefore those customers who are recruited in the knowledge that they are unlikely to be profitable should be discarded.

10.1 Customer retention

Having invested in recruiting the customers to the organisation, they need to be kept! Reichheld, a professor at Harvard University, is the acknowledged expert on customer retention and his research has indicated that even a small increase in customer retention levels has a dramatic effect on profitability.

Reichheld and Sasser (1990) offer the following reasons why retention levels improve profitability:

- Customer acquisition is expensive and can take many years to recover and then generate profits.

- As customers become more satisfied and confident in their relationships with an organisation they are more likely to direct additional business.

- As the relationship develops, mutual understanding and collaboration increases which can generate efficiencies and lower operating costs. Organisations are often willing to share services to reduce costs down further.

- Satisfied customers often refer other customers to the organisation that can reduce the costs of acquisition. In some markets customer advocacy is particularly important.

- Loyal customers tend to be less price-sensitive and less likely to 'shop around' when considering a new purchase.

10.2 Improving profitability levels

Given the benefits which have been identified as a result of better customer retention, the process adopted by an organisation should be formalised and structured and not just left to chance.

The following outlines a three step process to improving customer retention (based on Christopher *et al*, 2002):

1   **Measure customer retention:** The customer base needs to be analysed to identify the retention rates. This will need to be evaluated for each customer segment, the product(s) purchased and a timeline established so that trends or events can be analysed. Having identified the retention levels, it is then possible to identify future trends and identify profit levels.

2   **Key service issues:** It is now necessary to understand exactly why customers stop doing business with the organisation. Large organisations will often undertake syndicated research to understand defection. Customers are not always totally honest and the questionnaires designed to understand may not be robust enough to extract the true reasons for defection. It may be the case that the organisation is a secondary supplier and a change in policy has resulted in supplier rationalisation and consequently unless the organisation becomes the main supplier it is likely that the business will be lost.

3   **Corrective action:** Having identified trends, and obtained some ideas why customers are defecting to the competition, the final stage in the process is to put plans in place to prevent customers from leaving, or give them a reason to stay. The actions needed will depend on the reasons given for defection.

11 Monitoring quality of service

Monitoring the quality of the service provided is difficult because of the subjective nature of the assessment. There is considerable debate about the most effective measures of monitoring performance. The following pathway is based on Christopher *et al* (2002), built on the premise that monitoring the quality of service

provided is based on the organisation undertaking regular tracking studies and identifying not only current service issues but those issues which are on the horizon.

A six stage procedure is suggested:

1   **Customer service tracking studies:** The needs of customers must be clearly identified and monitored over time, so that changes can be detected at an early opportunity and action taken if necessary to address. Customers do not always know what they want from a relationship with an organisation and therefore a two-way dialogue needs to be established which enables suggestions about future improvements to be exchanged.

2   **Quality maintenance index:** The physical service environment needs to be monitored through the use of a checklist. Key areas to be measured can include lighting, decorations, accessibility, parking and cleanliness. In the virtual environment such as the internet, it is the website which becomes the physical environment and should similarly be audited.

3   **Mystery shopper:** A researcher poses as a customer and measures the service received against an agreed list of criteria which could include helpfulness of staff, length of time kept waiting, decor of the premises, stock of leaflets, etc.

4   **Staff climate monitor:** This measure looks at the customer service issue from the perspective of the member of staff and asks them where they think the gaps or issues may lie.

5   **Risk point analysis:** Analysis can identify those points in the delivery of the relationship that can cause particular problems and ensure careful monitoring.

6   **Service standards review:** Having collected all the key information, it now needs to be analysed and new service standards can be implemented in order to better match the organisation with the needs of the customer.

Moller (1988) suggested '12 golden rules' to help organisations to aid the delivery of quality service:

1   Set personal and organisational quality goals. In this way staff know what they are expected to deliver and similarly the expectations of the organisation are clearly stated.

2   Establish personal accountability. It needs to be clearly documented where responsibility for actions lies.

3   Regular checks must be made. As we have seen above, customers must be asked for their views on the level of service provided.

4   Regard the next link in the chain as your customer.

5   Avoid error: Standardised systems cut down on errors, but human error needs to be eliminated wherever possible.

6   Effective performance of tasks. Tasks need to be performed as effectively as possible within the current organisational capability.

7   Resource utilisation: Resources must be used as effectively as possible.

8   Commitment: Both the organisation and staff need to be committed to the delivery of quality service.

9   Finish: Activities started must be completed.

10   Stress: Procedures and practices need to be developed to eliminate or manage the effects of stress.

11   Ethics: Be ethical.

12   Quality: Demand quality.

Waitrose

'Waitrose is number one supermarket says Which? – Waitrose tops Which? annual supermarket survey'

15 December 2011

In the Which? annual supermarket customer satisfaction survey Waitrose has come out in first place for the third consecutive year. Waitrose has established a strong reputation for customer service and quality and so its dominant position, for customer satisfaction, is perhaps no surprise. There has been a shift, in terms of other retailers, with Aldi and Lidl both moving ahead of Marks and Spencer for the first time. Perhaps this move reflects the tightening economic conditions which are encouraging many consumers to prioritise value for money over quality at any price. The survey results show Waitrose as the clear leader, scoring 83% for satisfied customers, with Aldi at 72% and Lidl at 68%.

Whilst service and quality are clearly important in the retail market, the results have perhaps sent a clear message to supermarkets that pricing too is a key consideration for consumers when they are evaluating the overall offering available.

▶ **Exam tip**

In the September 2011 examination (Waitrose case study) Task Three required students to:

'Evaluate, from a marketing perspective, how Waitrose has achieved its status as the UK's favourite supermarket for customer satisfaction.'

Successful students approached this question in one of two ways, both of which were valid. Some students structured their answer around RATER, ie responsiveness, assurance, tangibles, empathy and reliability, and explained, for each, the approach adopted by Waitrose. The alternative approach was to identify how the company had applied the extended marketing mix (7Ps) in the context of customer service/satisfaction.

A common failing on this question was to simply 'list' the points. Brief bullet lists do not constitute evaluation, as required in the question, and so these answers fell short of the required standard to achieve a pass.

CHAPTER ROUNDUP

- Customer service and customer care are vital to the organisation and play a key role in customer retention, satisfaction and loyalty.

- There are specific characteristics of services which create particular challenges for services marketers.

- The extended marketing mix comprises seven elements and has been created to help marketers to address the characteristics of services.

- Service quality is subjective and can therefore be difficult to determine.

- As customers are different they might all have varying ideas of what would constitute 'good service'.

- Developing customer loyalty brings many benefits to the organisation.

- SERVQUAL is an important model in service quality.

- The dimensions of service quality can be remembered by RATER – reliability, assurance, tangibles, empathy and responsiveness

- Grönroos developed the triangle of quality perception.

- The 'gaps' model is useful to assess potential deficiencies in customer service.

- The ongoing monitoring of service quality is important in order to identify changes in performance levels as they arise.

FURTHER READING

If you are unfamiliar with SERVQUAL two papers provide further reading on the model. The first is the executive summary and the second is the full paper.

Parasuraman, A., *et al* (1988) SERVQUAL: a multiple-item scale for measuring consumer perceptions of service quality. *Journal of Retailing*, 64(1), pp5-6.

Parasuraman, A., *et al* (1988) SERVQUAL: a multiple-item scale for measuring consumer perceptions of service quality. *Journal of Retailing*, 64(1), pp12-40.

REFERENCES

Anon (2011) Waitrose is number one supermarket . Which?, http://www.which.co.uk/news/2011/12/waitrose-is-number-one-supermarket-says-which-273468/ [Accessed on 4 February 2012].

Booms, B.H. and Bitner, M.J. (1981) Marketing strategies and organisation structures for service firms. *In*: Donnelly, J. and George, W.R. (eds) *Marketing of Services*. American Marketing Association, Chicago.

Borden, N. (1964) The concept of the marketing mix. *Journal of Advertising Research,* June, 23(2), pp2–7.

Brassington, F. and Pettitt, S. (2006) *Principles of marketing*. Harlow, FT Prentice Hall.

Christopher, M. *et al* (2002) *Relationship marketing creating stakeholder value*. Harlow, Butterworth-Heinemann.

Dibb, S. *et al* (2005) *Marketing: concepts and strategies*. 5th European edition. Boston, Houghton Mifflin.

Grönroos, A. (1984) *Strategic marketing management in the service sector*. London, Chartwell-Brace.

Kotler, P. (1991). *Marketing management: analysis, planning, implementation and control*. 7th edition. New Jersey, Prentice-Hall.

Meek, H. and Meek, R. (2001) *Marketing management*. Canterbury, Financial World Publishing.

Moller, C. (1988) *Personal quality.* Copenhagen, Time Manager International.

Parasuraman, A. et al (1985) A conceptual model of service quality and its implications for future research. *Journal of Marketing*, 49(fall), pp41–50.

Piercy, N. (2001) *Market led strategic change*. Oxford, Butterworth-Heinemann.

Reichheld, F.F. and Sasser, W.E. (1990) Zero defections: quality comes to services. *Harvard Business Review*, Sept–Oct.

Zeithaml, V.A. and Bitner, M.J. (2003) *Services marketing: integrated customer focus across the firm*. 3rd edition. Maidenhead, McGraw-Hill.

QUICK QUIZ

1   What is the difference between a product and service?

2   The extended marketing mix for services comprise seven elements – what are they?

3   What are the characteristics of services, which make them different to goods?

4   Describe Grönroos' triangle of quality perception.

5   Why is customer loyalty important to an organisation?

6   What are the dimensions of service quality, as comprised within SERVQUAL.

7   Explain the gaps model of service.

8   Why can it often be difficult to monitor the quality of service provided to customers?

9   What is 'mystery shopping'?

10   How might a staff climate monitor help to improve standards of customer service?

ACTIVITY DEBRIEFS

Activity 11.1

The answer will depend on the service chosen. For example, for a meal at a restaurant it might include:

- Product: choice and quality of food on the menu
- Price: pricing quoted; special offers
- Place: the restaurant itself; perhaps offering take-away meals and/or home delivery
- Promotion: flyers delivered to local houses; advertising in local media
- People: friendliness and approachability of staff
- Process: efficiency of booking system; booking by telephone and maybe online
- Physical evidence: décor and ambience of the restaurant; dress and appearance of staff

Activity 11.2

Here is a suggested answer.

- Responsiveness: speed of technology used; prompt follow-up of requests
- Assurance: secure site; confidence in the brand; security of deposits placed
- Tangibles: 'look and feel' of the site; perception of the brand
- Empathy: use of language which customers can relate to; brand value
- Reliability: accessibility of the site; ease of navigation; delivering any requested follow-up on time

Activity 11.3

The answer to this activity will depend on the organisation chosen. There are five 'gaps' which should be considered, ie

- Gap 1: consumer expectations and management perceptions of those expectations
- Gap 2: management perceptions of consumer expectations and the organisation's quality specifications
- Gap 3: service quality specifications and actual service delivery
- Gap 4: actual service delivery and external communications about the service
- Gap 5: the difference between the perceived service and the expected service

QUICK QUIZ ANSWERS

1   Products are tangible whereas services are intangible.

2   Product, price, place, promotion, people, process and physical evidence.

3   Intangibility/lack of ownership, inseparability, perishability, heterogeneity.

4   Technical, functional and expectation.

5   Customer loyalty brings many organisational benefits, including increased sales, cross-selling and up-selling. Customer retention forms the foundation for market share growth, as loyal customers sometimes provide referral business and 'word of mouth' communications.

6   The dimensions are RATER – reliability, assurance, tangibles, empathy and responsiveness.

7   The gaps model (which outlines five potential gaps) indicates where the key areas exist for 'gaps' to arise between the actual service experience of customers and the intended service standard (and customer expectations of service). The theory is that the organisation should identify services areas which are deficient and take corrective action.

8   Quality of service is highly subjective and customers have different expectations and needs in terms of service quality.

9   Mystery shopping is commonly used to measure and monitor service quality. With the technique a researcher pretends to be a customer and experiences service as if they were an actual customer. They can then gather information on the customer service experience and provide feedback to the organisation.

10   With a staff climate monitor staff members consider the service provided to customers and consider where any gaps or issues arise.

CHAPTER 12

Managing key account customers

Introduction

Key Account Management (KAM) is often referred to in different contexts; it is used when referring to global, national, or major corporate accounts, however as we will see below, the management of strategically important accounts overseas requires a modified approach. Often KAM is associated with an organisation's 'biggest' or 'best' customer. It has at its heart the concept that not all customers are equal and has been used in various industries such as advertising and banking for many years. It is a very important area for businesses as managing relationships in the wrong way will lead to high levels of attrition and will, therefore, adversely impact on revenues and profitability.

Topic list

What is key account management?	1
Classifying customers	2
KAM management	3
KAM cycle	4
The role of communication in KAM	5
The role of people in KAM	6
Role of the marketing mix in key account management	7
Managing overseas accounts	8

4.1	Develop clear objectives relating to the provision of service to customers
	■ The importance of service
	■ Identifying the needs and behaviours of customers
	■ What constitutes 'service' to customers?
	■ The role of service in building customer loyalty and competitive advantage
	■ Organisational and financial benefits of customer acquisition and retention
	■ Determining customer service requirements
	■ The role of key account management in developing customer service excellence
4.2	Develop a customer service plan and customer care programme, designed to support customer service requirements, including innovative communications; relationship management and development; support; and operations/process management
	■ Identifying and evaluating key components of the plan/programme
	■ Identifying, analysing and managing key issues
	■ Use of resources
	■ Effective implementation
	■ Measuring and monitoring performance
	■ Role of communications in delivering customer service
	■ Importance of operations and processes in delivering customer service
4.4	Determine the most feasible and viable approaches for managing key account customers for different organisational contexts
	■ Criteria for and identification of key account customers
	■ Different approaches for managing key account customers
	■ Role of communications
	■ The role of people in key account management and service provision
	■ Key accounts in different organisational contexts and sectors

1 What is key account management?

> ▶ **Key term**
>
> **Key account management (KAM):** the relationship management of customers which are strategically important to the business.

Millman and Wilson (1995, p9) define a key account as 'a customer identified by a selling company to be of strategic importance'. McDonald *et al* (1997, p737) describe key account management as 'a natural development of customer focus and relationship marketing in business-to-business markets'. Key account customers can still apply in a B2C context.

KAM is sometimes referred to as an extension of sales management, however Cheverton (2008, p23) provides an alternative view: 'the customer is an investment made by the supplier in its own future. Key account management is about managing those investments, which is something rather different to selling. Put simply, key account management is about managing the future'.

KAM is the process adopted by an organisation in order to provide effective management to strategically important customers which contributes directly to the organisation's business objectives. KAM seeks to achieve mutual gain between the organisations, in other words it is about building relationships with certain customers. Gone is the time when suppliers were managed at a distance, now suppliers are managed with openness and

relationships built at different levels within the organisations. The concept of KAM ensures that 'key' accounts are provided with an enhanced level of service in relation to the value they offer the organisation.

While profit is usually the ultimate driver, key accounts can be selected for a number of reasons including technical expertise, image, ie the prestige of having a specific supplier as one of your clients, geographic proximity, or market expertise (however, this list is not exhaustive).

Equally the often-cited Pareto's Law, otherwise known as the 80/20 rule, helps us. This suggests that 80% of an organisation's income is delivered by 20% of its customers. While the actual percentages will vary across industry sectors and organisations, the rule generally holds true. The implications are clear; organisations must identify and focus on those customers delivering the income.

Hooley *et al* (2008) suggest KAM has becoming increasingly widespread as a result of:

- Increasing levels of competition in many markets with the consequence of higher selling costs for suppliers

- Increased customer concentration as a result of mergers and acquisitions

- Growing customer emphasis on centralised strategic purchasing

- Active strategies of supplier-base reduction by larger buyers to reduce purchasing costs

1.1 Criteria for selecting accounts

It is well recognised that it is much more expensive to recruit new customers than to retain existing ones, so the criteria for selecting a key account has to be clear. It is of course the case that there are both 'hard' and 'soft' measures to be established when selecting key accounts.

Below are some suggestions as a basis for selecting key accounts.

- Profitability: current and historic trends.

- Potential: what is the rate of growth and in the future?

- Annual turnover: does it meet the threshold now?

- Brand association: does the brand convey financial or non financial benefits?

- Relationship: will the status of being a key account lead to additional business or block out the competition?

The selection criteria must recognise characteristics other than size and therefore it follows that key accounts are not just the 'largest' accounts. Having a sound basis for selection is important. Often key accounts are those which offer the greatest future potential for revenue and profit generation.

It is often the case that having established the criteria for KAM status, not all accounts can be managed in this way because of a lack of internal resources, and decisions need to be made as to the ranking given to the non-KAM accounts. Inevitability some will be 'demoted' to lower tier accounts as their potential is poor.

ACTIVITY 12.1

Using an organisation with which you are familiar, consider who the key account customers are and develop criteria that might have been used when selecting key accounts.

2 Classifying customers

It is important to select those customers who would benefit from a KAM approach. The whole purpose of KAM is to build relationships with key customers and by implication this means being highly selective in the approach adopted. Cheverton (2008) developed a matrix that helps an organisation in an objective manner, seen in Figure 12.1.

Figure 12.1   Key account matrix

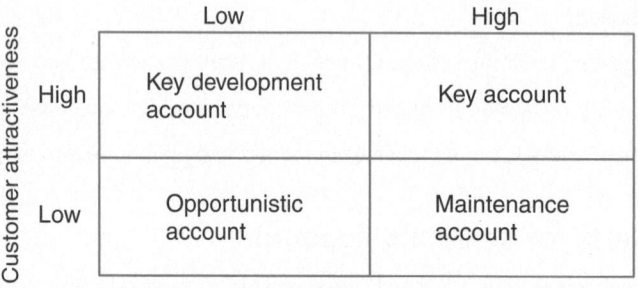

There are two dimensions to be considered: **customer attractiveness** (what makes the customer or potential customer appealing to the organisation?) and **relative strength** (how attractive is the organisation to the customer relative to the competition?).

The matrix in Figure 12.1 (Cheverton, 2008) shows four categories: key account, maintenance account, opportunistic account and key development account.

2.1 Key account

These are the accounts you have identified as the ones to build a strategic relationship with. They are highly attractive and you have significant strengths compared to the competition, ie the attraction is mutual.

2.2 Key development account

Here the account is very attractive to you, but you are not the best performer in comparison with the competition. There is work to be done in developing your strengths and making you more attractive. Depending on the number of accounts within this category, selective investment may be needed.

2.3 Maintenance account

You have a high relative strength, but the account is not seen as particularly attractive. Here if you do not want to 'drop' the account, it must be managed effectively so that scarce resources are not wasted. The relationship could be conducted on the telephone rather than face-to-face, or visits could be untaken on a less frequent basis.

2.4 Opportunistic account

Here you have a low relative strength and the customer is relatively unattractive to you. No resources are invested, but both parties will be happy to deal with each other on an ad hoc/transactional basis.

ACTIVITY 12.2

Using the classification matrix consider how an organisation might manage relationships with customers in each of the four quadrants.

3 KAM management

It has been identified that KAM is concerned with long-term relationships and this can come about through gaining access to new markets, better ways of working, or through technological development. Fundamental to a long-term relationship, and hence success, is the way KAM is managed. We will see shortly the importance of people in the KAM process, but there has to be a strategic match between the needs of the supplier and the customer, otherwise frustration will develop early in the relationship. Risks to the relationship will occur when the customer demands more from the relationship and of course the other way around, when the supplier is not willing or able to provide the supplier with the relationship originally expected.

KAM relies on clear management responsibility for relationship. A structure for managing the relationship needs to be put in place and Fill (2006) identified three possible organisational approaches to KAM which are summarised in Table 12.1.

Table 12.1   Three possible organisational approaches to KAM (based on Fill, 2006)

Approach	Summary
Assigning sales executives	This approach is warranted in smaller organisations and is very much 'hands-on'. There is a clear point of contact, roles and responsibilities are clear and there are the added benefits of flexibility and responsiveness. However, objectivity should still be maintained in this approach. Fill (2006) alerts us to the fact that this type of relationship can offer key accounts a disproportionate level of attention.
Creating a key account division	Creating a separate division can require significant structural changes, but it has the advantage of integrating the key support functions necessary in KAM. This approach is not without additional costs as many functions will be duplicated.
Creating a key account sales force	Here the decision is made to build a dedicated KAM team who can be trained to 'higher' levels so they will offer an enhanced level of service to key accounts through a solid understanding not only of the key accounts but the markets they operate in. This approach is not without its problems as once again there is duplication of work (see above).

4 KAM cycle

Having identified the criteria the organisations need to satisfy, the key accounts have to be identified and a relationship built. Various commentators have developed models to reflect the various relationships and Table 12.2 is based on Millman and Wilson (1995).

Table 12.2   KAM cycle (based on Millman and Wilson, 1995)

Pre-KAM	At this stage there is no relationship and the task is to identify accounts that meet the selection criteria and have the potential to become key accounts. An important consideration here is to establish that the various parties could work with each other.
Early KAM	The relationship has started, but it is still transactional and there is an element of testing each other out. Communication channels will be formal.
Mid KAM	The relationship has now developed, the organisations are starting to understand each other and work proactively together.
Partnership KAM	The organisations recognise the importance of the other and first choice supplier status is achieved.
Synergistic KAM	Both organisations see themselves as one organisation where they create synergistic value in the marketplace.
Uncoupling KAM	At this stage and for a variety of reasons, the relationship is being terminated and procedures are put in place to 'wind down' the relationship.

All the various stages are of equal importance, however, knowing at which stage a particular relationship is will determine the resources that need to be applied, or anticipated.

The transition from one stage to another differs in time and McDonald (2000) suggests the speed of transition depends on how quickly a sufficient level of trust is built. Therefore an organisation will typically have its key account portfolio at a range of stages in the cycle.

You will recall specific criteria was outlined to establish the suitability for KAM, now a profile for each key account needs to be established so that the potential to move to the next stage can be established and clear objectives and strategies set. Some accounts will 'stick' and will need to be managed accordingly, for others the growth potential may be reduced and close account monitoring will be necessary.

It needs to be recognised that in some situations the KAM relationship may need to be terminated or 'uncoupled' and procedures should be put in place for the smooth termination of the relationship.

5 The role of communication in KAM

KAM is concerned with building and retaining long-term relationships. People are at the heart of the relationship and this requires a 'push', communication strategy where communication is focused on the key account.

The various different KAM stages will require different communication approaches recognising the developing nature of the relationship which should be regular, high quality and personalised.

KAM will ensure that an on-going dialogue is maintained which continually seeks to build value in the relationship. While regular communication is essential it must be co-ordinated so that planned and consistent messages are delivered to multiple levels across the organisations which are supportive and motivational.

Ideally the on-going dialogue supports the different KAM stages and builds trust which is essential to the success of the relationship.

 The Chartered Institute of Marketing

In determining the most appropriate communications mix, the needs and characteristics of key accounts need to be determined which will then enable messages to be developed to reflect the purpose of the relationship and build constructive and long-term relationships.

6 The role of people in KAM

Within the KAM approach, the role of the Key Account Manager is to develop the relationship in line with the objectives set. While there is a strong sales element to the role, it is much wider and covers:

- **Problem solving:** Difficulties will be a feature of the relationship and the KAM manager must use a range of skills to ensure problems are identified and resolved quickly. Strong negotiating and implementation skills are needed along with business and project management. Creative problem-solving skills are essential.

- **Relationship building:** Strong inter-personal skills are needed to build key contacts and then nurture them both professionally and socially.

- **Communicating:** Sharing key information in an open and timely manner is vital to success. Often confidential information is shared to build the relationship. Trust and mutual respect having been built through personal contact. Marketing and strategic thinking skills are helpful in seeing the 'big picture' rather than focusing on the often unnecessary detail

- **Personal selling:** Negotiation, handling objections, and training to support the need for managers to achieve sales targets which may ultimately drive motivation and reward. Product and technical knowledge is important to the customer as they will need reassurance that they are making the right decisions.

THE REAL WORLD

A common feature of key account management is the importance of the role of the Account Manager. Relationship management is a vital element of managing key accounts. The Account Manager must possess a wide range of skills, in particular 'inter-personal' skills, eg negotiating, building relationships, dealing with conflict and influencing. The Account Manager not only deals directly with the customer but is also a key internal interface. Therefore stakeholder management is also an important feature of the Account Manager's role.

The Account Manager is really the 'jam' in the sandwich where the role is to balance the needs of both parties to achieve mutual benefit. But the role and skills of the Account Manager change with the various stages in the KAM cycle.

For example at pre-KAM the role will be to identify potential accounts and screen them. The associated skills will be communication and product or technical knowledge. As the account enters the synergistic stage, the skills needed will tend to be more along the lines of business management and the role is more concerned with coordination.

While the Account Manager role may appear daunting, there are several tools and frameworks that can help them in their role, for example:

- PESTEL analysis
- Porter's five forces analysis
- SWOT analysis
- Porter's value chain analysis

Cranfield School of Management has undertaken considerable research in the area of KAM and some of the findings are listed below.

- KAM is a long-term solution and organisations need to view KAM as an ongoing relationship

- Relationships are vulnerable in the early stages of the relationship

- Not all accounts process through the cycle

- Account teams are more effective than an account management working alone
- Key Account Manager is critical to the relationship and requires skills and training beyond a sales person
- Global Account Management (GAM) has additional complexity and is particularly challenging

7 Role of the marketing mix in key account management

We have already seen, above, the importance of communications and the key role of people in managing key account relationships. However, the whole marketing mix plays a vital role in this important activity.

7.1 Product

Products must remain relevant for key account customers, who will often be involved in helping the organisation to identify opportunities for product enhancements and developing new products. Product capabilities must support the key account's future plans and ambitions.

7.2 Price

A relationship-based approach to pricing might be adopted, taking into account past and future revenue streams from the client. A life-time value approach may be taken, considering the potential income and profit achievable from the client over the longer term. Discounts may be offered in recognition to loyalty and in some cases this may be further recognised through the use of loss leaders.

7.3 Place

Flexible channels of distribution may be used, to meet the needs of the client.

7.4 Promotion

Use of the communications mix will be focused on building long-term relationships. Communications will be highly tailored, relevant to the client and perceived as adding value to the client's business. For some clients, relationships will be managed on a personal one-to-one basis.

7.5 People

The role of people has already been discussed (above). The supplier will provide the key account customer with named points of contacts, perhaps at different organisational levels, eg operational (for day-to-day issues) and strategic (for long-term relationship issues). Staff must be highly trained, credible and have a good understanding of the key account client and the markets it operates in.

7.6 Process

All processes must be efficient and quick. Speed of responsiveness and reliability are vital in dealing with key account customers. Inefficiencies are potential sources of customer dissatisfaction and should be eliminated for key account customers.

7.7 Physical evidence

Offices must look professional as should be the appearance of staff. Consistency of the brand is important, across all channels and media. This is of even greater importance where services are being provided as a

The Chartered
Institute of Marketing

degree of tangibility can be achieved through the effective management of the physical evidence element of the marketing mix.

8 Managing overseas accounts

> **Key term**
>
> **Global account:** Global accounts are large companies that operate in multiple countries, often on two or more continents, and are strategically important to the supplier.

The overseas or international aspect of KAM has been left to the end of the chapter very deliberately. Many text books refer to KAM as being a umbrella phrase for the management of strategic accounts irrespective of location. The syllabus requires you to apply the concept of strategic account management in the UK and overseas, so you need to be clear on the differences which are discussed below.

The nature of competition requires many organisations to operate overseas and this brings about the need to manage key accounts in a similar way to domestic accounts.

However, there are points of difference which need to be explored: first, where key accounts are located in different countries they are known as global accounts and their management referred to as global account management (GAM), and second, there is a defined set of competencies needed to qualify for GAM.

The delivery of GAM requires three competencies (Wilson *et al*, 2000):

- A forum where the customer is involved and collaborates as a part of the overall process
- Clear management of the process especially with respect to the supply of information and communication
- A co-ordinated and globally competent supply chain

ACTIVITY 12.3

Consider the issues and challenges faced by an organisation which has major global account customers.

- Key account management is much more than sales management.

- Key account management enables an organisation to focus on its most important customers.

- Customers are different and can be classified as key accounts, key development accounts, maintenance accounts and opportunistic accounts.

- The organisation should adopt different approaches for each classification of customer.

- Criteria should be considered to form the basis for selecting the right customers to be managed on a KAM basis.

- There is a defined KAM cycle for the evolution of customer relationships.

- Communication is a vital component of KAM.

- The role of people in KAM cannot be over-stated.

- The marketing mix can be adapted to suit different types of customer management.

- Global relationships require additional consideration.

FURTHER READING

While this article was written in 1997 it provides a useful background to Key Account Management.

McDonald, M. *et al* (1997) Key Account Management: theory, practice and challenges. *Journal of Marketing Management*, 13(8), pp737-757.

REFERENCES

Cheverton, P. (2008) *Key Account Management*. 4th edition. London, Kogan Page.

Fill, C. (2006) *Marketing communications: engagement, strategies and practice*. 4th edition. Oxford, FT Prentice Hall.

Hooley, G., *et al* (2008) *Marketing strategy and competitive positioning*. 4th edition. Harlow, FT Prentice Hall.

McDonald, M. (2000) *Marketing management: a relationship marketing perspective*. Basingstoke, Palgrave.

McDonald, M. *et al* (1997) Key Account Management: theory, practice and challenges. *Journal of Marketing Management*, 13(8), pp737-757.

Millman, T. and Wilson, K. (1995) From key account selling to key account management. *Journal of Marketing Practice: Applied marketing science*, 1(1), pp9-21.

Wilson, K. *et al* (2000) *Global Account Management Study Report*. The Sales Research Trust.

1   What do you understand by the term 'key account'?

2   What is the difference between KAM and GAM?

3   Set out the criteria for KAM.

4   What are the four categories of customers?

5   What is the difference between a key account and a key development account?

6   Why should opportunist accounts be retained if possible?

7   What are the three possible organisational approaches to KAM?

8   What are the six stages of the KAM cycle?

9   Why is communication important in KAM?

10 Why are people a key element of the marketing mix in KAM?

ACTIVITY DEBRIEFS

Activity 12.1

The criteria will vary depending on the business. Commonly, criteria include profitability (current and future), income/profit potential, turnover, brand association and relationship.

Activity 12.2

There are potentially many different approaches. Here are some suggestions:

- Key accounts: Activities focus on reinforcing loyalty and retention. One-to-one personal management. Highly tailored communications. Relationship pricing.

- Key development accounts: Focus on influencing the customer in terms of the organisation's competitive positioning. Communication of new products and any awards, eg for customer services. Use of customer testimonials. Possible use of concessionary pricing (introductory offers).

- Maintenance account: A difficult category to manage. Management should be on a low cost basis. Minimal one-to-one personal contact. Use of direct marketing.

- Opportunistic accounts: Minimal effort. These customers offer potential for higher pricing and higher profit margins.

Activity 12.3

There are many issues and challenges, including:

- Costs
- Maintaining consistency
- Adopting a 'single customer view'
- Risks and impact of losing the relationship
- Profit margins are likely to be low
- Labour-intensive to manage
- Cultural issues

1   A customer identified by a selling company to be of strategic importance.

2   With GAM (global account management) the emphasis is on relationships with global customers.

3   The criteria might vary depending on the organisation and its goals – typical criteria include profitability, future potential (income and profit), annual turnover, brand association and relationship aspects.

4   Key account, key development accounts, maintenance accounts and opportunistic accounts.

5   With key accounts there is already a degree of mutual respect. A key development account is attractive to us but we need to reinforce to them how strong we are, relative to our competitors.

6   Opportunist accounts can be useful as they require little management time and effort and often profit margins can be higher on these than on other accounts.

7   Assigning sales executives, creating a key account division and creating a key account sales force.

8   Pre-KAM, early KAM, mid KAM, partnership KAM, synergistic KAM and uncoupling KAM.

9   Communication plays a vital role in building and developing relationships. It also plays a key role in customer retention.

10 Most key accounts are managed on a one-to-one basis, involving an account manager. Relationship building is vital in key account management.

CHAPTER 13

Sales and product information and relationship risks

Introduction

All customers want to feel valued and an important part of any relationship is the ability of an organisation to offer customers something of value, based on previous product purchase or knowledge of the market. However this is only possible if the organisation has detailed knowledge of its customers and the markets in which it operates. All too often organisations launch a new product into the market that simply fails to meet the needs of the customers. Similarly, ineffective marketing campaigns are launched which fail to attract the 'right' customer.

The reader will see that organisations typically collect vast amounts of information on customers, but often it is not integrated with other information so an incomplete customer or market profile is built.

It has been noted in earlier chapters that the intangible aspect of any product makes it harder for the competition to copy that aspect. Similarly an organisation that collects market information in a systematic way can also achieve competitive advantage through the information it has collected. However this advantage can only be realised and sustained if the information is collated and made available to those people in the organisation who, because of their role or position, can make effective use of it. Kotler (2003) suggests that as sellers use more complex marketing approaches and face more competition, they need information on the effectiveness of their marketing tools, along with information to make timely decisions.

No matter how robust and comprehensive the information held on customers, competitors, or markets, relationships can break down in some way and we will look at possible risks and contingency planning to help overcome such problems.

Topic list

Marketing information system (MIS) (1)

Revenue generation (2)

The customer relationship (3)

Overcoming potential problems (4)

Communication (5)

4.5	Assess the role and value to the organisation of sales/product information, including storage, retrieval and communication of information and its role in ensuring that revenue is increased or maintained for key account customers
	▪ Use and value of information and how it will be used
	▪ Managing information
	▪ Storing and accessing information
	▪ Using information to develop marketing activities
	▪ Role of information in revenue generation
4.6	Critically evaluate and assess the customer relationship for possible risks, problems and issues and prepare contingencies for dealing with those risks as they emerge
	▪ Likely risks, problems and issues in managing customer relationships
	▪ Contingency planning
	▪ Role of communications in dealing with problems

1 Marketing information system (MIS)

> **▶ Key term**
>
> **Marketing information system:** a system which stores and disseminates marketing related information within an organisation.

Organisations typically collect huge amounts of information on customers, but often the information is not used because it is not in an accessible format, or it may just be old and no longer valid. This is a waste of resources and money. Organisations, irrespective of size, need to be able to collect useful information, store it and retrieve it in a timely manner so that it can be used to tailor offers to customers, but also measure the effectiveness of marketing activity. This activity should be measured not just against targets the organisation may have set itself as part of the planning process, but so it can be used to benchmark the organisation against the market generally.

Historically organisations may have collected large amounts of data on their customers. However, it was not necessarily in an accessible format, or in some cases, it just wasn't made available to the right people and opportunities to increase sales were missed, or the opportunity to build closer relations with customers lost, hence competitive advantage was lost or reduced.

Now most organisations are investing in a marketing information system (MIS) to improve data management.

An MIS stores and disseminates information within an organisation. In essence an MIS is a framework which allows for information to be collected from a variety of sources, both internal and external to the organisation. This information is then combined with other relevant information to produce a specific range of reports that helps the organisation manage its marketing more effectively.

Large organisations generate vast amounts of information and to be effective the MIS must be specific to the organisation. What data should be collected? How should it be collected? When and who should it be made available to?

Figure 13.1 shows a simple MIS which consists of three parts: external inputs, a central processing unit and outputs. It is the marketing team that should not only drive the structure of the MIS, but they also are the recipients of the information.

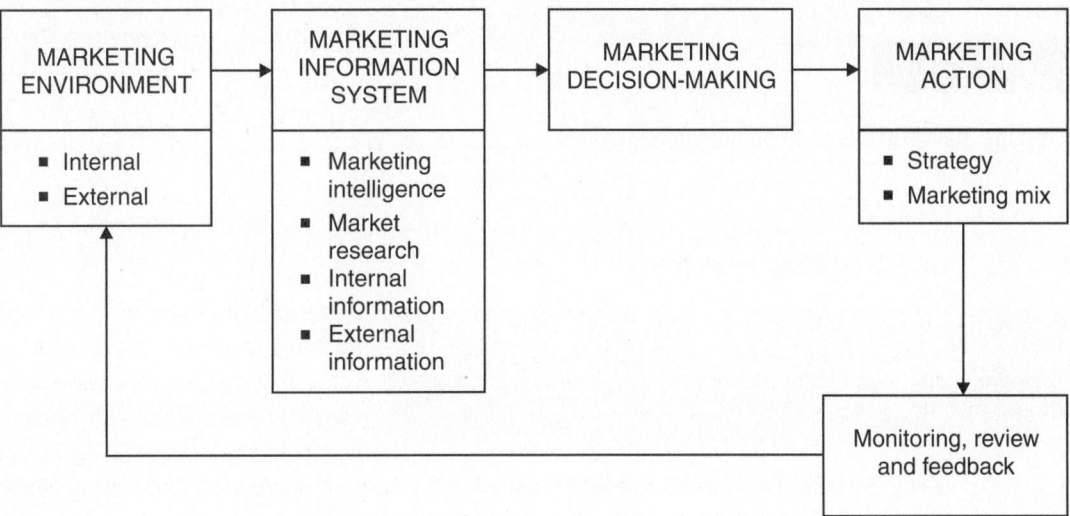

Consider the role of sales and product information when making marketing decisions.

1.1 External inputs

Figure 13.1 shows a range of typical information which could be specified, but it is not exhaustive, and could be supplemented with sales team information on the competition, new products being launched or planned, accounts gained by the competition and any pricing issues.

1.2 Central processing unit

In summary information is collected from a variety of internal sources including:

- Results from market research, either primary or secondary
- Sales data, margins, distribution channels, year-on-year comparisons, average transaction values
- Key customer data covering sales, transactions and purchase frequency
- Customer complaints or suggestions for product improvement
- Marketing campaigns, costs and results

1.2.1 Marketing intelligence

> **Key term**
>
> **Marketing intelligence:** information which is useful to the marketer and which comes from a wide range of sources.

Intelligence will come from a range of sources that the organisation feels are important. This can range from evaluating competitor products, to financial data, external research such as TNS (a global market and business information provider), or where overseas sales could include research from Neilsen Media.

Clearly, some information can be collected freely from the market, but it can be necessary to buy information from research organisations either in the home or overseas markets.

Organisations with large sales teams will use them as the organisation's 'eyes and ears' reporting back key data which forms part of the intelligence gathering process.

Press cuttings, audited accounts, trade bodies or associations and the internet form part of the intelligence gathering process.

ACTIVITY 13.2

What are the main sources of competitor intelligence?

1.2.2 Marketing research

> ▶ **Key term**
>
> **Marketing research:** data/information which is obtained in a structured and proactive manner.

Research, while similar to marketing intelligence, is much more structured and proactive. An organisation will identify gaps in its knowledge and commission a research project which can be completed internally, or by appointing an external agency which may have specialist skills. Often it is not exactly clear what the cause of a problem is and exploratory research will be undertaken prior to a full research study being undertaken.

THE REAL WORLD

For data/information to be gathered, analysed and presented effectively, it is important that organisations adopt a structured approach to undertaking marketing research. This approach incorporates a number of defined stages:

1   Define the problem.
2   Set research objectives.
3   Construct the proposal.
4   Specify the data collection methods.
5   Select the sample.
6   Collect the data.
7   Analyse the results.
8   Present findings.

1.2.3 Internal records

Most organisations are not short on internal records and collect information from a vast range of sources including sales, payment terms, payment period, cash flow, stock levels, and stock turnover, etc.

1.2.4 Information analysis

Separate isolated pieces of information in themselves are not of much value and need to be combined together to offer a comprehensive profile of particular segments, or individuals

1.3 Outputs

Having been analysed and refined, the data is now distributed, or made available to marketing managers in a predetermined format and agreed time.

For most organisations this information is made available to staff electronically and the marketing decision-makers will usually specify the information they need, the format they need it in and the time it is required. The format of the information is usually available as a standard report, but changes can be made by re-specifying the information, or, in the case in larger organisations, by staff having access to the core data and being able to manipulate it themselves.

An MIS will hold large quantities of information, therefore it is essential that the quality of the data is maintained, otherwise it simply becomes a costly exercise with no beneficial output.

Each decision-maker, ie recipient of the information, will need to specify their data requirements, such as:

- **Format/presentation of the information**: defined report in hard or soft copy?

- **Data sources (external)**: is the information from Mintel reports, company/competitor websites, annual report and accounts, industry reports, government data or economic data?

- **Data sources (internal)**: key account(s), purchasing trends/patterns

- **Frequency of reports**: for example, weekly or daily?

Some organisations have moved beyond MIS and now use MDSS (marketing decision support systems) which is software that aids the decision-making process by helping managers anticipate certain outcomes based on the information available. In effect managers can interrogate the database and develop scenarios.

Given the considerable amount of data that will be held in the system it should be quick and easy to access.

Knowing the purchasing patterns of key customers allows for the effective management of them.

If they are making fewer purchases than sales forecasts suggested then knowing what they are buying, and, equally, what they are not buying, will enable a strategy to be formulated to win back sales. It may be the case that your competitors are offering promotions, and given the information you have on the customer, you can develop a counter attack.

Different divisions of an organisation will commission research or collect data from a variety of sources and as we have seen in the CPU above, it must be centralised and automated so that access to the system can be made electronically, and the database interrogated to produce ad hoc or standard reports.

THE REAL WORLD

Marketing information and CRM play an increasingly dominant role in marketing today. They are both vital in direct marketing, where the outcome of activities is so dependent on the accuracy and reliability of customer, and other, data held. 'Data driven marketing' is now commonplace and regarded by many organisations as one of the most cost-effective elements of the communications mix. However, the challenge with data is that quality output is only achievable if the input is of equally high quality.

2 Revenue generation

▶ **Key term**

Customer Relationship Management (CRM): CRM involves the use of a database to store and disseminate important customer information to support the management of customer relationships. CRM systems can be expensive, but when effective can deliver significant value to the organisation.

An MIS will help an organisation to better understand its market, so that when it comes to developing strategy and marketing plans, the organisation can set SMART objectives which will be realistic. Equally, marketing information has no value unless it is used to make informed decisions. Consequently when it is given to marketing managers it becomes an effective tool for guiding decisions which will make the organisation more profitable and build relationships with customers, through more effective targeting of customers based on an understanding of their needs. In fact the MIS is the engine which drives Customer Relationship Management (CRM).

The MIS will guide decisions to establish which segments of the market the organisation should target and potential income generation.

Equally, it helps in decisions about the selection of products and use of channels – particularly in regard to the potential income that may be generated.

While this source of data is largely invaluable it has to be used consistently and effectively and without being intrusive on the customer relationship. The customer wants to see the organisation making tailored offers which meet their needs rather than being treated to a demonstration of just how sophisticated the database is.

---

3 The customer relationship

> ▶ **Key term**
>
> **Partnership relationship life cycle:** the cycle through which partnership relationships (with customers) develop.

While marketing information is necessary for any organisation which wants to compete effectively in the market, the customer journey is not always without problems. While the MIS can identify potential problems there are a number of issues which may impact on the relationship and bring it to an untimely close.

The main issues which may impact on the relationship are:

- **Misconceptions:** there is a misunderstanding between the organisation and the customer, with the customer not receiving what they were expecting. This could range from an incomplete service to a service only partially delivered.

- **Inadequate resources:** caught in the desire to secure a new client or offer a competitive price, the organisation may not be able to resource the relationship as fully as would have been expected. Staff sickness and the lack of cover can lead to service deterioration and dissatisfaction.

- **Inadequate delivery:** it is expensive to train new staff and existing staff may themselves be poorly trained leading to a disappointing service being experienced by the customer. Staff changes on both sides of the relationship can often become a friction point, each deciding to change procedures. Quality of the product may be disappointing in relation to the price and there are too many occasions where performance is below the expected level of standard.

- **Exaggerated promises:** it is often tempting for an organisation to make promises they cannot deliver on, but make the promise in order to secure the business. This can be delivery dates, availability of a specific type of hotel room, or the benefits that the product can offer which often leads to a breach of trust.

Just as products go through a life cycle it can be argued that relationships go through a similar process. The ladder of loyalty offers one view of how a relationship develops and is managed over time. Similarly the partnership relationship life cycle offers a similar perspective and this is summarised in Figure 13.2.

Figure 13.2   Partnership relationship life cycle

Partnership stage	Initiation stage
• Recognition of the importance of the account to the organisation • Multiple relationship contacts at all levels	• Interest generated and targets identified • Matching products to customer needs • Understanding customer needs
Consolidation stage	Development stage
• Focus on building customer loyalty • Innovation and new product development/offering	• Demonstration of organisation's ability to meet customer promises • Building resources to support the relationship

Good customer relationships are about adding value for the benefit of both parties and therefore it is essential that relationships (as we have seen) are monitored at the various stages to ensure corrective action can be initiated when necessary.

 The Chartered Institute of Marketing

If organisations do not have robust internal systems in place to meet the needs of customers then the relationship will be terminated early and the investment costs lost.

Porter's value chain analysis (Porter, 1985) offers an organisation a process which is actually a framework for establishing exactly what the customer uses the product for and then to develop an offer which fits in with the customer's needs. To achieve, the organisation needs to ensure that the activities of each department are aligned and deliver value to customers. There is no benefit in a product that goes through various departments where the cost of adding the value is not compensated by the additional value perceived by the customer.

To understand where potential problems (identified above) can arise, organisations often map out the current or potential processes to identify issues or alternatives that could be used along the customer journey. The fishbone diagram is a diagnostic tool that allows companies to identify and resolve potential problems that may not be immediately obvious.

Identifying potential problems and alternatives is a good way for an organisation to improve its offerings, but also to put contingency plans in place for when things go wrong.

4 Overcoming potential problems

Problems can be overcome by focusing on the needs of staff.

Staff that are motivated and happy in their work are more likely to convey positive images to the customers who in turn will be satisfied and more likely to remain as customers. Organisations can improve the service through:

Training: Service failures can often be attributed to staff who simply do not follow the existing procedures or make mistakes in carrying out a process. Sometimes it is a motivational issue; staff feel under pressure, but do not feel adequately rewarded.

Fishbone analysis could be used to identify all the customer contact functions and seek to improve customer/staff interaction. It could also review the remuneration package to ensure it is appropriate for the level of responsibility involved. Staff need different skills to undertake the various roles within an organisation which simplistically can be broken down into visible and non-visible staff. Visible staff are those who have a direct or indirect involvement with the customer. For example where a member of staff interacts with the customer on the telephone they will need a good telephone manner, but they can dress very casually. On the other hand staff who meet customers face-to-face will not only need a pleasant manner, but will need to dress appropriately.

Where staff are not performing to an acceptable standard, the organisation will need to consider developing an appropriate training course, or sending staff on a course delivered externally.

Productivity: We have looked at the measurement of service in an earlier chapter and the difficulties identified. Where the levels of productivity are perceived to be below that acceptable to the organisation or the industry average, processes should be put in place to address this but the underlying cause needs to be identified.

Technology: Increasingly technology is being used to improve the customer experience. The major supermarkets are introducing self-service tills along with a number of high street stores in an effort to improve the customer experience. If we need a regular prescription from the doctor, we can now collect from the pharmacy without the need to see the doctor.

Customer interaction: Increasingly we are moving to a team-based solution to customer needs rather than an individual one. Banks have 'account teams', doctors have Group Practices; individual shops have migrated to department stores or supermarkets. With a team approach the likelihood of service failure is reduced as another member of staff should be trained and available to deal with the issues. We are also used to customer interactions taking place at lower levels of an organisation as staff become empowered to deal with complaints.

Aligning supply and demand: Supermarkets use sophisticated stock management systems to ensure minimum stock levels are kept to eliminate 'stock outs'. In the past the customer would have simply accepted that there was a likelihood that stock may not always be available.

5 Communication

The role of people is critical to the customer relationship, but communication is also important to the relationship, the challenge is to balance cost and frequency. The relationship between people and effective communication is fundamental to the success of the client relationship. Staff must be well trained, informed and their role valued.

Each stage of the relationship will require a different blend of the communications mix to ensure that every opportunity to maintain and build on the client relationship is taken and maximised in terms of client satisfaction and organisational profitability. This is a key area and the effectiveness of the communications will have a direct impact on the effectiveness of the client relationship and its resilience to future challenges and threats potentially from competitor activity.

A wide variety of communications channels exist, from face-to-face through to use of paid-for media. Each channel should be explored to understand what role it can play in achieving effective communication with the client. A key element of this will be a sustainable communication message and everyone involved in doing business with the client should be aware of what the message is and what his/her role is in communicating that message. The importance of front line customer-facing staff must be understood here and their role in presenting a consistent and meaningful message to the client is critical to the sustainability of long-term profitable relationships with clients.

Organisations must be open to new technologies which many customers prefer to use when doing business with organisations, such as social networking and text messaging which are the preferred communications channels in some important and growing customer segments.

It is important to have key points of accountability for communications throughout the organisation ensuring that there is vertical integration from the senior account manager through to the administrative and support staff. The client relationship will rely heavily on a single, integrated communications message that everyone understands. Conflicting messages do not create confidence in the minds of clients who want to see a single cohesive and integrated organisation in their dealings with it.

The role of information in relation to effective communications is also important. Clients must be able to identify who to contact, how, when and by what means. Any changes must be communicated to clients in a timely and effective way in order to ensure continuity and maximise customer satisfaction.

Effective communication is two-way and within the client relationship there should be every opportunity for the client to communicate with the organisation in order to have a positive view of the relationship. This applies at every level from simple transactional information through to contact about significant issues. Clients must be able to access the organisation in ways and times that are convenient to them and not solely determined by the organisation's needs.

Effective channels of communications can be critical to the relationship with the client particularly in times of crisis when the client needs to be able to obtain instant and easy access to somebody they know and trust in a timely way. This is particularly the case in relation to complex high value services such as banking where clients expect a knowledgeable, informed point of contact who knows them and has sufficient authority and autonomy to act quickly. It is of less importance in simple transactional relationships such as retail purchases where clients, in the main, have lower expectations.

When the client relationship is under threat from competitor activity, the value of effective relationships supported by sound two-way and responsive communication will prove critical in defending relationships

against aggressive competitors. It is much more difficult to steal business from a competitor if the client feels valued, well informed and able to access key people they know and trust.

Many organisations now recognise the importance of communications in developing and maintaining long-term profitable relationships that can lead to referrals for new business from clients who have progressed up the loyalty ladder to become effective advocates. This is recognised in the investment that those organisations are now making in corporate communications which sustain and support relationship management at account level.

THE REAL WORLD

Consumer dissatisfaction with financial services organisations has been widely reported. It is a market in which customer service is important (often a key differentiator) and where there are many providers, 'switching' is not only possible – it is easy. Whilst it is the ultimate aim that all customers remain satisfied, especially key account clients, it is inevitable that on occasions the level of service delivered falls short of the customer's expectation.

So, how have many financial services organisations (FSOs) set about dealing with the issue of overcoming potential problems within customer relationships?

Most FSOs have invested in ongoing customer satisfaction surveys, enabling changes to be carefully monitored. In addition, many FSOs also undertake regular (annual) benchmarking studies to identify how they are performing against their main competitors.

Customer communications has been identified as playing a key role, especially in the notification of charges for services provided. Tailored communications are vital to building customer satisfaction.

Importantly, FSOs have focused on making the right marketing mix decisions, to reinforce the importance of customer service in all they do. All seven elements of the marketing mix play a vital role in managing customer relationships. Products must be carefully managed and remain relevant to customers. Pricing must be transparent and represent value to the customer. Place must be carefully managed to deliver the required standards in accessibility and convenience. Promotion, as already stated, must be tailored and appropriate. People, so often a key element in financial services marketing, must be trained and empathetic. Process, becoming even more important now that so many customer relationships operate on a 'de-personalised' basis (ie online and telephone banking). Physical evidence is also important, given the intangible nature of services.

ACTIVITY 13.3

What are the main areas of potential risks and issues in key account relationships?

▶ **Exam tip**

The aspect of managing customer relationship issues has featured within questions in a number of examination sittings to date. The key to answering the question is to identify the precise focus from the question, eg 'Analyse the role of marketing communications in dealing with customer relationships for XYZ organisation'. Here the emphasis, clearly, is on the communications aspect of the mix only. Students should focus, therefore, on the communications mix elements and for each, that they have identified, they should analyse its use in relationship management. However, the answer needs to go beyond this and must be answered within the context of the organisation featured within the case material.

- Detailed knowledge of its customers, markets and products is vital, so that the organisation can continue to respond to changes, deliver value to customers and achieve sustainable competitive advantage.

- Organisations typically collect vast amounts of customer, and other, data. For this data to be useful, organisations use a marketing information system (MIS).

- The MIS stores data and disseminates information to people in the organisation for decision-making purposes.

- The MIS contains data from a range of sources, both internal and external.

- The MIS plays a key role in supporting relationship management and generating revenues for the organisation.

- Inevitably there are areas where issues can arise in customer relationships.

- Partnership relationships go through a series of stages in their life cycle.

- Staff play a key role in delivering service and can therefore be a source of potential conflict in customer relationships.

- Communication is critical in building and developing customer relationships.

- Effective application of the communications mix, within the marketing mix, can deliver significant value both to the customer and the organisation.

FURTHER READING

This is an interesting paper which discusses how market research and other information can be used to inform decisions in managing customer relationships.

Valos, M.J. and Bednall, D.H.B. (2010) The alignment of market research with business strategy and CRM. *Journal of Strategic Marketing*. 18(3), pp187-199.

REFERENCES

Anon. (2011). High street banks remain poor for customer satisfaction: Big bank dominance is sign of a failing market . Which?, http://www.which.co.uk/news/2011/09/high-street-banks-remain-poor-for-customer-satisfaction-265356/ [Accessed on 5 February 2012].

Kotler, P. (2003) *Marketing management*. New Jersey, Prentice-Hall.

Porter, M.E. (1985) *Competitive advantage*. New York, The Free Press.

The Chartered Institute of Marketing

1   What is a marketing information system?

2   Why is marketing information important to marketers?

3   What are the main components of a marketing information system?

4   What is marketing intelligence?

5   What is marketing research?

6   What key facts should recipients of information from a MIS specify, to ensure that their needs are met?

7   What are the main issues which might impact on customer relationships?

8   What are the stages in the partnership relationship life cycle?

9   What is the relationship between the organisation's MIS and its CRM system?

10 Outputs from the organisation's MIS should be provided to who?

ACTIVITY DEBRIEFS

Activity 13.1

Sales and product information is vital. It can help in many ways, including:

- Sales volumes versus targets
- Market share statistics
- Trends
- Product performance (profitability)
- Products compared with competitor offerings
- Product gaps

Activity 13.2

There are a range of sources, including:

- Their advertisements
- Visit their retail outlets
- Their customers (through marketing research)
- Their website
- The internet
- Their annual report and accounts

Activity 13.3

There are potentially many areas, including:

- Relationship, including personality clash
- Poor/inappropriate communication
- Pricing too high
- Products lose pace with customer needs
- Customer proposition becomes uncompetitive
- Too slow to respond
- Late deliveries
- Sub-standard goods
- Poor decision-making
- Organisation is not sufficiently innovative
- Mis-match of views of the relationship
- Poor performance
- Onerous terms and conditions

QUICK QUIZ ANSWERS

1. A MIS stores and disseminates information within an organisation.

2. Marketers have to make important decisions. Data and information are key in decision-making and so the MIS plays a vital role to ensure that correct decisions are made.

3. The main components are external inputs, the central processing unit comprising marketing intelligence, marketing research, internal records and information analysis, and outputs.

4. Data and information from a wide range of sources, eg competitor intelligence.

5. A structured and proactive approach to gathering data.

6. The frequency and format they require, and data sources. The reason why they need the information might also be useful.

7. There are many, but in particular misconceptions, inadequate resources, inadequate delivery and exaggerated promises.

8. Partnership stage, initiation stage, consolidation stage and development stage.

9. It is said that the MIS is the engine that drives the organisation's CRM system.

10. Outputs from the organisation's MIS should be provided to anyone in the organisation who is responsible for making marketing decisions.

The Chartered
Institute of Marketing

CHAPTER 14

Analysing the case material and preparing for the examination

Introduction

In this final chapter we shall consider the assessment for Delivering Customer Value through Marketing (DCVTM) and how you can prepare for it. There are three elements. First, we shall consider how to analyse the case material. Second, we shall then look at how you should prepare for the examination. Then, finally, we will consider what you need to do during the examination to enhance your chances of success.

Topic list

The DCVTM assessment   1

What is a case study?   2

The DCVTM case study   3

Why have a case study?   4

Analysing the case study   5

The pre-prepared analysis   6

Preparing for the examination   7

In the examination   8

1 The DCVTM assessment

The assessment for DCVTM) is a three-hour closed-book examination. The paper comprises three Tasks (questions). The first Task is worth 50 marks and the other two Tasks 25 marks each. All three Tasks must be completed. Some Tasks may be broken down into two or more questions. Where this happens the question will state how many marks are available for each part of the Task.

So, all questions are compulsory, ie there is no choice of questions. This, clearly, places a significant emphasis on the importance, to students, of covering every aspect of the syllabus in detail.

In addition, students should note that all questions relate to the case material, which is provided to students ahead of the examination. These two aspects are important and must be duly recognised by students. As a result, all answers must also relate to the case material, ie 'generic' answers (which do not relate sufficiently to the case material) will not pass. The purpose of issuing the case material ahead of the examination is to enable students sufficient time to carry out detailed analysis of the case and so that this analysis can be applied within answers.

2 What is a case study?

According to Thomas (2011, p3) 'A case study is about the particular, rather than the general. You cannot generalise from a case study'. So, the case material will provide students with particular information about a particular company and/or industry. As a consequence, the examiner is expecting students to answer the questions in the context of the case, rather than in the context of the general.

Ellett (2007, p19) provides some further thoughts 'A case is a text that refuses to explain itself. How do you construct a meaning for it?...Start by recognising some contextual factors that help limit and narrow the analysis. Cases are usually studied in a course. A marketing case requires you to think like a marketer'. As a result, irrespective of the content, for DCVTM, students must consider the case from a marketing perspective and answer the questions in a similar light.

Stake (2005, p443) provides a different perspective on the fact that the case study itself does not define a method (of analysis), saying that a 'case study is not a methodological choice but a choice of what is to be studied'. This is an important point and students should note that the choice of analytical tools (used to analyse the case study) is not prescribed and will vary depending on the case content. However, what is to be analysed is prescribed, because this forms the case study content.

3 The DCVTM case study

As has already been mentioned, the case study is available to students ahead of the examination. For information, cases used in the examination to date are shown in Table 14.1.

Table 14.1   Previous case studies

Case study	Examination date
Innocent Drinks	N/A – Specimen
Black & Decker	December 2009
Eskom	March 2010
Daler-Rowney	June 2010
Graduate Recruitment Bureau	September 2010
The Prostate Cancer Charity	December 2010

Case study	Examination date
The Prostate Cancer Charity	March 2011
Waitrose	June 2011
Waitrose	September 2011
MINI	December 2011
MINI	March 2012

Cases can feature any type of organisation from any sector, or will focus on a sector itself. Some key points for students in terms of the case study:

1   The case study provides the context for the answers.

2   All the information the students need to answer the questions will be contained within the case study. So, students are advised not to waste time collecting unnecessary additional data, either about the company or the sector/market generally.

3   On no account should students contact organisations featured in the case. This is strictly forbidden.

4   Students are expected to be aware of general and topical issues which might not be specifically mentioned in the case, eg global economic issues and the impact of the recent global financial crisis.

5   Sometimes, information provided in the case study is an extract only (from more detailed sources). In compiling the case material, therefore, some anomalies may arise. Where the student identifies these they should not contact The Chartered Institute of Marketing, but should instead state clearly, within their answer, any assumptions they have made.

6   The student's version of the case study must not be taken into the examination. The invigilator will issue students with a clean version of the case study at the start of the examination along with the question paper.

4 Why have a case study?

The purpose of the case study is to provide students with the opportunity, in the examination, to demonstrate their ability to analyse and evaluate information, using material provided, from which they can identify key issues and develop solutions. It also provides an opportunity for students to contextualise answers, ie students can show that they are able to apply the theory they have learned through study specifically in the context of the case (and of course also in the context of the questions).

The ability to analyse and evaluate information, based on facts presented, are key marketing skills in the workplace. As a result, this approach is precisely in line with what many marketing managers have to tackle in the work place. They are also key academic skills, together with the ability to apply tools within a given context, which are a feature at this level of qualification. So, students who write answers which do not demonstrate sufficient analysis, evaluation and application can only expect to fail as their answers will not meet the required academic standard for DCVTM.

By distributing the case study ahead of the examination the student is able to devote time for thorough analysis of the material, including the identification of key issues and the evaluation of potential solutions, all before the examination itself. In this way, time in the examination can be 100% focused on answering the questions, which should be supported by reference to the student's pre-prepared analysis.

This latter point is of vital importance, because a common failing, in the examination, is that (many) students simply either do not refer to their pre-prepared analysis or, if they do, it is not 'applied'. Simply making reference to the pre-prepared analysis will not gain marks. The analysis must be used to fully support and reinforce points made (more about this later).

5 Analysing the case study

Analysing the case study is key to success in the examination. Ellett (2007, p19) explains, 'In English, "analysis" has two closely related definitions: to break something up into its constituent parts; and to study the relationships of the parts to the whole. To analyse a case you therefore need ways of identifying and understanding important aspects of a situation and what they mean in relation to the overall situation'.

Analysing the material is much more than just reading the case several times. As Ellett (2007, p20) puts it, 'You should spend more time thinking about the case than reading it'. But what does this mean? Ellett goes on to explain, 'As you start reading it, you ask questions about the content. Then you seek answers in the case itself. As you find partial or full answers, you think about how they relate to each other and to the big picture of the case. You don't make knowledge by reading'.

While there is no definitive process for analysing a case study there is no doubt that reading the case is not only a key start point but it also plays a vital role in analysis and the development of ideas. Ellett (2007, p26) explains that:

> 'The key to the process is active reading. Active reading is interrogative and purposeful. You ask questions about the case and seek answers. Questions give a purpose for reading; they direct and focus study on important aspects of a situation... Active reading is also iterative, meaning you make multiple passes through a case. With each iteration, the purpose of reading changes; you are looking for new information or looking at old information in a new way'.

Far too many students simply read the case study and continue to re-read it without purpose. It is not an issue of continually reading the case so that it becomes familiar, through repetition. Analysis involves thinking about, and interpretation of, the facts.

5.1 Analysing the case – process

At this level of qualification students are expected to develop their own thinking, specifically in the context of the case, with regard to an appropriate methodology for analysing the case. A suggested approach would involve the following (and is set out in Figure 14.1):

1   Assessing the current situation.
2   Problem and opportunity identification.
3   Determining the causes of the problems.
4   Identifying the sources of the opportunities.
5   Ascertaining the impact of the problems.
6   Deciding on the opportunities to exploit.
7   Developing and evaluating solutions.
8   Developing strategies and tactical plans.

Figure 14.1   A process for analysing the case study

A process for analysing the case study

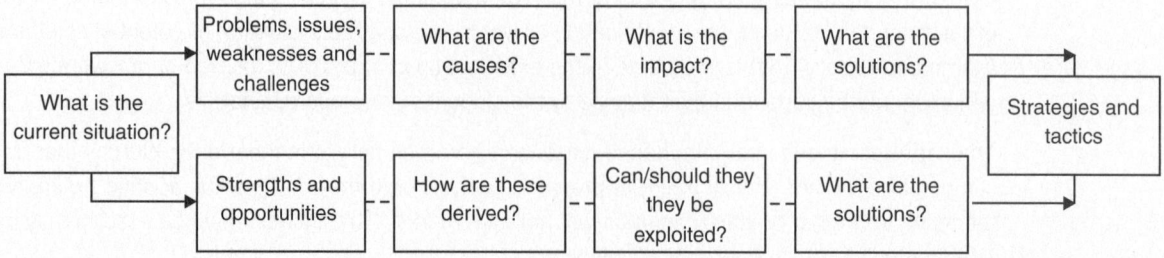

The Chartered
Institute of Marketing

5.1.1 Assessing the current situation

Figure 14.2 suggests a number of aspects of an organisation's current situation which should be assessed. This will depend on the case study content, ie some of these aspects may not be able to be considered. The purpose of this stage is to ensure that students have a thorough grasp of the organisation, its customers and its markets.

Figure 14.2   Assessing the current situation

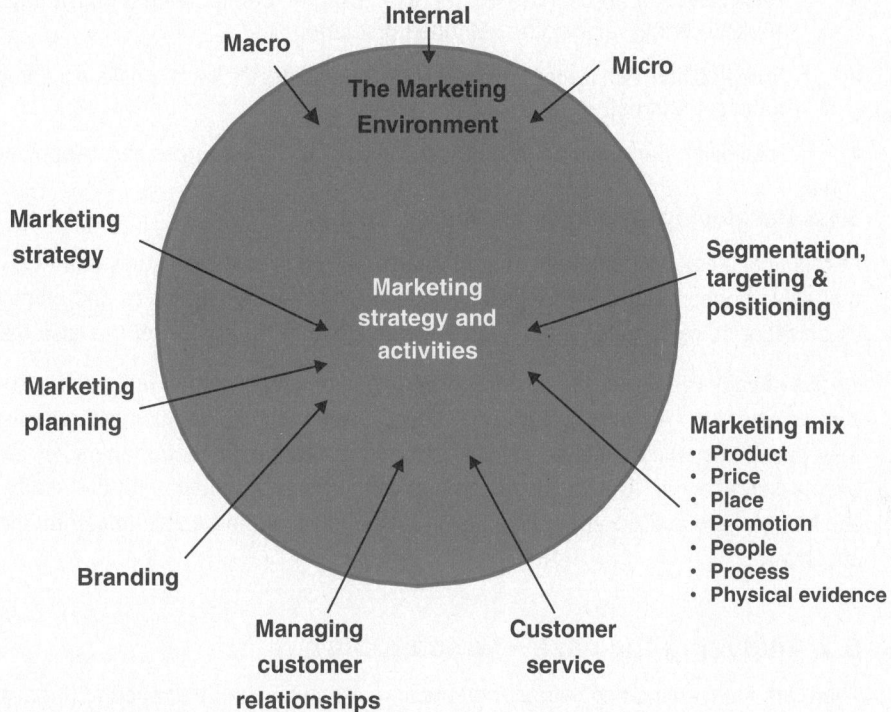

Many students get to this stage in their thinking but fail to progress.

5.1.2 Problem and opportunity identification

Here, students should consider, based on their assessment in 5.1.1, what are the main problems, issues, threats and challenges facing the organisation?

5.1.3 Determining the causes of the problems

Having identified the problems, issues, threats and challenges, students should now consider what is creating these. Perhaps they might be common across the industry. Alternatively, they may be caused by actions undertaken by the organisation itself.

5.1.4 Identifying the sources of the opportunities

Having identified the opportunities, students should consider what is creating these. Does the organisation have a unique advantage in some way? Does it stem from its brand? There could be many opportunities and sources.

5.1.5 Ascertaining the impact of the problems

Not all problems, issues, threats and challenges are significant. Some might exist within the market and simply cannot be managed/avoided by the organisation. Clearly, the focus for the organisation should be on addressing those problem areas where the potential impact is significant.

5.1.6 Deciding on the opportunities to exploit

Not all opportunities can be pursued by the organisation. Here students should focus on the key areas.

5.1.7 Developing and evaluating solutions

Potential solutions, to reduce/eliminate the main problem areas and to exploit the key opportunities, should be developed and fully evaluated. For example:

- Suitability: Is it appropriate for the organisation? Will it create an advantage for the organisation in the market? Will it remedy the identified problem?

- Acceptability: Will it meet the needs of stakeholders? Are the risks acceptable and will it generate sufficient returns?

- Feasibility: Can the organisation deliver it within its resources and capabilities?

5.1.8 Developing strategies and tactical plans

At this final stage, students should be prepared, based on the case study content, with strategies and plans that exploit opportunities and/or tackle problem areas. These strategies and plans should enable the organisation to meet stated goals and be credible within the context of the case material provided.

As has already been said, the key to succeeding is much more than just reading the case and assessing the current situation. As Ellett (2007, p6) states, 'Case method students need two distinct sets of skills. First, they need to be able to analyse the case, to give it meaning in relation to its key issues or questions that have been asked about it. The goal is to come to conclusions congruent with the reality of the case, taking into account its gaps and uncertainties. Second, students have to be able to communicate their thinking effectively.'

5.2 Analysing the case – which tools?

There are many marketing related theoretical tools which can be applied to the case study material. There is no definitive list, because the tools which are relevant will vary depending on the nature of the case study provided. It is difficult to imagine a case study where it is not possible, or where it is unnecessary, to analyse the organisation's macro environment. Therefore, use of PESTEL analysis should also be considered. Students must consider, however, that analysis of the micro environment may also be relevant and perhaps a review of the organisation's competitive/supply market should also be considered (Porter's five forces can be used for this).

Students should also consider:

- Where product information is provided consideration should be given to using the BCG Matrix, GE Matrix and product life cycle.

- Consideration of the organisation's strategy might be relevant, in which case Ansoff's and Porter's generic strategies might help.

- Where stakeholder information is available consideration of these using Mendelow's power/interest matrix might be useful.

- Certainly, analysis of the organisation's current marketing mix is likely to be relevant for every case.

- The service aspects can be analysed using SERVQUAL and the gaps model.

There are many tools which could be of help to students and just some of these are list in table 14.2. It is, however, stressed that this list is not exhaustive, ie there might be others which could be relevant. In addition, the list is by no means compulsory. Indeed not all of the tools might be relevant. However, a common failing is that far too many students use just three or four tools, which at this level is too narrow a range.

Table 14.2   Marketing tools and models

Six markets framework	Financial analysis	Porter's five forces model
Ansoff matrix	Gaps model	Porter's generic strategies
BCG matrix	GE matrix	Pricing policy/strategy
Brand loyalty	Macro environmental analysis	Product levels
Brand onion	Market share analysis	Product life cycle analysis
Cateora's 7Cs	Marketing mix analysis	Segmentation analysis
Channel management analysis	McKinsey 7S framework	SERVQUAL
Communications strategy analysis	Mendelow power/interest matrix (stakeholder mapping)	Shell directional policy matrix
Competitor analysis	Perceptual maps (positioning)	SWOT analysis
Diffusion of innovation	PESTEL analysis	Targeting strategy

6 The pre-prepared analysis

The pre-prepared analysis must represent the student's own work. The analysis must be no more than four sides of A4, no smaller than font size 11. The content of tables, models, diagrams etc must be no smaller than font size 8. It is important that the analysis is legible. The different tools, diagrams, tables etc must be numbered for ease of reference when answering questions.

The analysis must be hole punched and stapled in the top left hand corner. It must state clearly the student's CIM Membership Number and the examination centre name on the top right hand corner of each page (of the analysis). It should **not** include the student's name. At the end of the examination the analysis must be attached to the Answer Book using the treasury tag, which will be provided by the invigilator.

The numbering of tools and models etc (in the student's pre-prepared analysis) is important. When the student refers to their analysis in answers it must be absolutely clear which tool or model is being referred to and precisely which part of the content.

It is vital that the pre-prepared analysis is used with answers. It is surprising how many students produce quite detailed analysis but make no reference to is at all in their answers. It is worth stressing that there are no marks available for the pre-prepared analysis. However, those students who score the highest marks use their pre-prepared analysis to support their answers.

What does this mean? Weaker answers simply refer to the analysis, eg 'See Table 1 in Appendix 2' or repeat what it says. Better answers might state something like 'Global recession – see my analysis Table 1 in Appendix 2. The impact on the organisation's communication strategy will be significant particularly in respect of … which is why greater emphasis should be placed on …'. In this example the student is taking their analysis and applying it precisely in the context of the question (in this case relating to marketing communications).

Finally, the pre-prepared analysis must relate to the case material. Simply writing the tools and models, but not entering relevant content about the case is not allowed. Similarly, the analysis must not contain pre-prepared answers to possible questions. Both of these approaches are tantamount to cheating as this is a closed-book examination. Examiners review the pre-prepared analysis submitted and where either of these approaches are adopted it could result in the student being disqualified.

7 Preparing for the examination

Preparing for the examination is straightforward. Students should adopt a structured approach to study, ensuring that they allow sufficient time for:

- Studying the syllabus in its entirety
- Reading more widely than just the core text (a key feature of study at this level)
- Revising ahead of the examination
- Analysing the case study material

Students should watch out for other support available. For example The Chartered Institute of Marketing occasionally runs Webinars in some subjects, which sometimes are delivered by the Senior Examiner.

A good way of supporting study is for students to notice and consider the marketing activities of organisations in the world around them. Focus on activities which are relevant to the DCVTM syllabus and then question why they are being delivered. What is it that the organisation is trying to achieve? In what ways is it making itself appear different to the competition? How might success be measured?

8 In the examination

The final stage for students will be the examination itself. This is the student's opportunity to demonstrate to the examiner that they are sufficiently competent (for the level of the qualification) to deserve to pass. It is vital therefore that students do themselves justice in the examination. It is a fact that some students let themselves down at the last hurdle by poor examination technique.

Students should focus on the following in the examination:

- Answering all questions fully

- Managing time effectively. Students should spend time on each question which is proportionate to the marks available

- Presenting their answers in a carefully considered format and ensuring that handwriting is legible throughout

- Using the pre-prepared analysis to support and reinforce points. This analysis must be applied in answers and not simply referred to

- Making reference in answers to appropriate marketing tools, models and theory

- Producing answers which are strongly focused on the case material

- Ensuring that answers are complete and comments are always fully supported

- Avoiding irrelevant content

- Answering the precise question set

- Providing evidence within answers of wider reading (note that Harvard referencing is **not** required in the examination)

- Ensuring that the content of answers fully addresses the 'command word' used in the question. Typically, in DCVTM, questions require students to 'analyse', evaluate', 'assess', 'examine' and 'explain'. Therefore, to satisfy these answers must be detailed and points supported

- Using appropriate examples to support the points they are making

- Questions which instruct the student to 'develop a plan' require just that, ie the answer must be presented in a recognised plan format, not as an essay

- Avoid presenting answers as simple, and unsubstantiated, bullet point lists

- Preparation ahead of the examination is crucial.

- It is worth considering why the case study approach has been adopted for DCVTM.

- Success depends on more than just reading the case study material.

- There is no definitive approach to analysing the case material.

- A useful start point when analysing case studies is to consider the (featured) organisation's current situation.

- Students must pose questions to themselves as they read, and re-read, the case study.

- Key issues need to be identified and solutions developed.

- Revision, ahead of the examination is important and time must be factored into the study programme for this.

- There are no marks available for the pre-prepared analysis and so it is vital that it is properly applied in answers to be rewarded.

- In the examination, pay attention to the command word and ensure that the level of detail provided will satisfy the examiner in this respect.

REFERENCES

Ellet, W. (2007) *Case study handbook: how to read, discuss, and write persuasively about cases.* Boston, Harvard Business School.

Stake, R.E. (2005) Qualitative case studies. *In:* Denzin, N.K., Lincoln, Y.S. (eds) (2005) The Sage handbook of qualitative research. 3rd edition. California, Sage.

Thomas, G. (2011) *How to do your case study: a guide for students and researchers.* London, Sage.

Section 4:

Senior Examiner's comments

On completion of Section 4 students should have a detailed understanding of the:

- Meaning of 'service' to different types of customers and in various organisational contexts
- Development and implementation of customer service plans and customer care programmes
- Identification, management and development of 'key account customers'
- Management and use of information in the development of customer relationships
- Determination of service standards and measuring levels of customer satisfaction

Students must be able to apply marketing tools and techniques, especially the marketing mix, in the context of delivering service to customers. To do this effectively, students must understand how customers' service needs can first be ascertained and how these can then be met through the appropriate adaptation of the marketing mix elements and other marketing approaches.

Students also need to be able to make the connection between the execution of an outstanding customer service proposition and the attainment of critical marketing objectives, in particular customer retention, high levels of customer satisfaction and strong customer loyalty. Through these, important benefits will flow, including the achievement of differentiation and competitive advantage as well as the generation of additional revenue growth from cross-sales activities.

Exceeding customers' service expectations is key in the development of long-term customer relationships, which in turn is vital to achieving sustainable future business growth. It is especially important that students understand how organisations identify their 'key account customers' and develop (and execute) plans for their long-term development.

Delivering Customer Value Through Marketing

Index

Above-the-line, 161

Accounts team, **186**
Actual product, **4**
Adaptation, 10
Advertising, **162**
Agency pitch, **184**
Agency remuneration, 185
Agency selection, 183
Agency structure, 186
AIDA, **174**
Ambush marketing, **172**
Analysing the case – process, 248
Analysing the case study, 248
Assessment, 246
Augmented (or extended) product, **4**

Balanced Business Scorecard (BBS), **126**

Below-the-line, 161
Bench mark accreditations, 122
Benchmarking in channel management, 86
Boston (BCG) matrix, 30
Boston Consulting Group (BCG) matrix, **30**
Brand, **38**
Brand equity, **41**
Brand management, **39**
Brand values, **40**
Branding, 38
Branding categories, 39
Branding strategies, 41
Building market share, 53
Building relationships, 142

Case study, 246

Categorising stakeholders, 107
Cateora's 5Cs, **81**
Channel conflict, **109**
Channel innovation, 89
Channel intermediary, **98**
Channel objectives, 73
Channel structure, 78
Classifying customers, 222
Communicating with stakeholders, 111
Communication in KAM, 224
Communications agencies, 182
Communications brief, **188**
Communications in channel management, 83
Communications mix, **161**, 161
Conflict, 109
Consumer channels, 73
Contractual requirements, 119
Copywriting, 173
Core product, **4**
Corporate objectives, 139
Cost based pricing, 54

Creative team, **187**
Customer based pricing, 55
Customer loyalty, 143, 207
Customer Relationship Management (CRM), **237**
Customer retention, 213
Customer value, **26**

Dagmar, **174**

Diffusion of innovation, **13**
Dimensions of customer service, 209
Direct marketing, **170**
Distribution channel, **70**
Distribution strategy, 75
DRIP, **139**

Ethical considerations in channel management, 87

EU public sector bodies, 119
Evaluating channel options, 84
Evaluating the effectiveness of marketing
    communications, 174
Exclusive distribution, **75**
Extended marketing mix, **203**
External communications audiences, 152

Full service agency, **182**

General Electric (GE) matrix, **32**

Global account, **227**
Global branding, 43
Guerrilla marketing, **172**

Idea generation, **7**

Influences on channel strategy, 76
Integrated marketing communications, 142
Intensive distribution, **75**
Internal communication methods, 150
Internal communications, 150
Internal marketing, 149
International standards, **122**
Internet/online, 162

KAM cycle, **224**

Key account management (KAM), **220**
Key account matrix, **222**
Key development account, **222**
Key Performance Indicator (KPI), **125**

Managing agencies, 188

Managing channel relationships, 81
Managing overseas accounts, 227
Managing stakeholders, 104

Marketing communications, **138**
Marketing communications message, 142
Marketing communications objectives, 140
Marketing communications plan, **140**
Marketing communications strategy, **141**
Marketing information system, **234**
Marketing intelligence, **235**
Marketing research, **236**
Mark-up, **54**
Measuring the effectiveness of intermediaries, 124
Mendelow's power/interest matrix, **107**
Monitoring performance, 126
Monitoring quality of service, 213

New and emerging channels, 90
New product development process, 6
NPD, **6**

Overseas distribution considerations, 79

Partnership relationship lifecycle, **238**
Penetration pricing, **54**
Personal selling, **166**
Positioning, **11**
Preparing for the examination, 252
Pre-prepared analysis, 251
Price changes, 58
Price elasticity of demand, **57**
Pricing, 50
Pricing decisions, 51
Pricing for new products, 53
Pricing frameworks, 54
Pricing in international markets, 57
Pricing objectives, 51
Product, 4
Product adoption, 12
Product categories, 6
Product innovation, 14
Product life cycle (PLC), **27**
Product management, **24**
Product management process, 24
Product portfolio management tools, 26

Product positioning, 11
Product standardisation, **10**
Production adaptation, **10**
Professional pricing, 56
Profit margin, **54**
Public relations (PR), **168**

Quantitative, 125

RATER, **209**
Rebranding, **42**
Relationship marketing, 147
Role of the intermediary, 100
Role of the marketing mix in key account management, 226

Sales promotion, 167
Screening, **8**
Selective distribution, **75**
Service characteristics, **205**
Service level agreement (SLA), **120**
Service quality, 206
Service quality 'gaps', **210**
Services, 202
Services pricing, 58
SERVQUAL (Parasuraman et al), **208**
Six markets framework, **104**
Skimming, **53**
Specification, **120**
Sponsorship, 170
Stakeholder, **102**
Stakeholder power, 108

Terms and conditions, **121**
The customer service programme, 211
The Loyalty ladder, **143**
The marketing mix for services, 203
Through-the-line, 161
Triangle of quality perception (Grönroos), **206**
Type of intermediaries, 98

Viral marketing, **171**

The Chartered
Institute of Marketing

The Chartered
Institute of Marketing

The Chartered
Institute of Marketing

Review form

Please help us to ensure that the CIM learning materials we produce remain as accurate and user-friendly as possible. We cannot promise to answer every submission we receive, but we do promise that it will be read and taken into account when we update this Study Text.

Name: _____   Address: _____

_____

_____

1. How have you used this Text?
(Tick one box only)

☐ Self study (book only)

☐ On a course: college_____

☐ Other _____

3. Why did you decide to purchase this Text?
(Tick one box only)

☐ Have used companion Assessment workbook

☐ Have used BPP Texts in the past

☐ Recommendation by friend/colleague

☐ Recommendation by a lecturer at college

☐ Saw advertising in journals

☐ Saw information on BPP website

☐ Other _____

2. During the past six months do you recall seeing/receiving any of the following?
(Tick as many boxes as are relevant)

☐ Our advertisement in *The Marketer*

☐ Our brochure with a letter through the post

☐ Our website www.bpp.com

4. Which (if any) aspects of our advertising do you find useful?
(Tick as many boxes as are relevant)

☐ Prices and publication dates of new editions

☐ Information on product content

☐ Facility to order books off-the-page

☐ None of the above

5. Have you used the companion Assessment Workbook?　　　　Yes ☐　　No ☐

6. Have you used the companion Passcards?　　　　Yes ☐　　No ☐

7. Your ratings, comments and suggestions would be appreciated on the following areas.

	Very useful	Useful	Not useful
Introductory section (How to use this text, study checklist, etc)	☐	☐	☐
Chapter introductions	☐	☐	☐
Syllabus learning outcomes	☐	☐	☐
Activities	☐	☐	☐
The Real World examples	☐	☐	☐
Quick quizzes	☐	☐	☐
Quality of explanations			
Index	☐	☐	☐
Structure and presentation	☐	☐	☐

	Excellent	Good	Adequate	Poor
Overall opinion of this Text	☐	☐	☐	☐

8. Do you intend to continue using BPP CIM products?　　　　☐ Yes　　☐ No

On the reverse of this page is space for you to write your comments about our Study Text. We welcome your feedback.

Please return to: CIM Publishing Manager, BPP Learning Media, FREEPOST, London, W12 8BR.

TELL US WHAT YOU THINK

Please note any further comments and suggestions/errors below. For example, was the text accurate, readable, concise, user-friendly and comprehensive?